Dancing with God

Dancing with God

Everyday Steps to Jewish Spiritual Renewal

Rabbi Wayne Dosick

HarperSanFrancisco
An Imprint of HarperCollins*Publishers*

HarperSanFrancisco and the author, in association with The Basic Foundation, a not-for-profit organization whose primary mission is reforestation, will facilitate the planting of two trees for every one tree used in the manufacture of this book.

A TREE CLAUSE BOOK

HarperCollins Web Site: http://www.harpercollins.com
HarperCollins®, 📖®, HarperSanFrancisco,™ and A TREE CLAUSE BOOK®
are trademarks of HarperCollins Publishers Inc.

FIRST EDITION

Library of Congress Cataloging-in-Publication Data
Dosick, Wayne D.
Dancing with God : everyday steps to Jewish spiritual renewal / Wayne Dosick.
Includes index.
ISBN 0–06–061955–4 (cloth)
ISBN 0–06–061956–2 (pbk.)
1. Spiritual life—Judaism. 2. Jewish meditations. 3. Judaism—United States. I. Title.
BM723.D67 1997
296.7—dc21 96-47349

97 98 99 00 01 ❖ RRDH 10 9 8 7 6 5 4 3 2 1

Again
for

REB ZALMAN
and
REB SHLOMO זצ״ל

bringers of the new light

and for

THE MEMBERS AND FRIENDS
of
THE ELIJAH MINYAN

fellow seekers, all

Contents

אור חדש על ציון תאיר . . .
O God,
we pray:

"Cause a new light to shine
upon us;
and, soon,
may we all
reflect
its splendor."

Acknowledgments

I AM A CLASSICALLY TRAINED, RATIONAL, "SCIENCE of Judaism" rabbi.

In my seminary—and it was much the same in the other American rabbinical seminaries at the time—my classmates and I talked about Jewish history and contemplated the Jewish future, which, we were sure, would be quite dazzling, especially since we would be its leaders and its shapers. We talked about the Jewish sense of social justice that would inspire us to feed the hungry and save the oppressed. We talked about the Zionist dream and our love for the State of Israel.

But we never talked about God.

Except in a theoretical sense in a theology or philosophy course, except in a ritualized liturgical formula, discussion about God—and conversation with God—was not on the agenda of those training or being trained to be the "spiritual leaders" of American Jewry in the last quarter of the twentieth century and beyond.

No one ever asked me what I believed about God or, for that matter, if I believed in God at all. No one ever asked me to articulate my relationship with God. No one ever asked me if I talked to God.

I certainly did not enter the rabbinate because I had heard a "call." I have rabbi-ed for almost two and a half decades now, and I am deeply committed to observing the commandments, reciting the prayers, doing the rituals, celebrating the festivals, living the ethics. The services I conducted and the classes I taught were well known for their joy and their fervor. I was a passionate advocate of everything Jewish. I guided and inspired my congregants to embrace Judaism's traditions and teachings, Jewish life and lifestyle.

But over the years, I came to realize that despite all that seemed right, it "wasn't working" for most Jews, both the ones in my congregations and the ones I met all over the country. And before long, with a knowing born from that most reflective place where we are brutally honest with ourselves, I came to realize that it "wasn't working" for me.

It "wasn't working" because God's presence was slowly but profoundly revealing itself in my heart and my soul. I was coming to know God—not the God whom we meet through law or ritual, but the God we come to know personally and intimately at the deepest place of faith and spirit.

I came to witness and know that, for so many Jews, all the elements of contemporary Judaism that we deem important—and they *are* important—are, ultimately, hollow without God at their center.

So this book is about bringing God back into our lives or, more correctly, bringing our lives back to God—personally, imminently, intimately—by reclaiming and renewing the Jewish spiritual practices that can make us whole and holy. It is about getting beyond personality, ego, and personal proclivity, becoming an open and clear channel, and letting God come through.

I thank God for having brought me to evolving awareness through glimpses of continuing revelation. And I pray that I will be a worthy advocate for God's word and will and spirit.

I thank the *g'dolim,* the great masters and sages of our people: Moshe Rabbenu, our teacher Moses; Eliyahu HaNavi, Elijah the prophet; Rabbi Israel ben Eliezer, the holy Baal Shem Tov; and Rabbi Menachem Mendel of Kotzk, the holy Kotzke Rebbe. Their lives taught that the journey to the promised land of understanding and enlightenment must begin in the quiet seclusion—and the sometimes painful loneliness—of the wilderness.

I thank the teachers and rebbes who opened the world of God's spirit for me with their Torah, their teachings, their stories, their songs, and their faith. I gratefully honor my dear friend Dr. Gary Hartman, who was the first one of us to go on the journey of seeking. I am especially grateful to Arthur Kurzweil and Rabbi Moshe Shur, longtime friends and extraordinary servants of God and Judaism. Each in his own way, while serving as scholar-in-residence at my congregation, made me realize that I was like the ones "who have mouths but do not speak; have eyes but do not see; have ears, but do not hear" (after Psalms 115:5). Gently but powerfully they tugged me from the world of the mind to the world of the spirit. I am profoundly grateful to the two men to whom this book is dedicated, Rabbi Zalman Schachter-Shalomi and Rabbi Shlomo Carlebach ז״ל, whose teachings and songs, vision and courage have brought us to new light.

I am deeply grateful to my parents, Hyman and Roberta Dosick, to my parents-in-law, Clarence and Anna Kaufman, who, while comfortably rooted in tradition, are open and opening; and to my sons, Scott and Seth, who, each in his own unique way, is wrestling with tradition and change, and struggling to find his own place on the continuum.

I extend deepest appreciation to:

- the men and women who have woven a new tapestry of prayers and songs with which to encounter God, especially Danny Siegel, whose poetry so poignantly captures our condition, and Rabbi David Zeller, whose music brings us closer to God.
- Shendl Diamond, whose magnificent Hebrew calligraphy graces these pages; Catherine Ahrens, whose drawings and illustrations illuminate this work; and Betsy Platkin Teutsch, whose *Shiviti* draws us into God's presence.
- Ione Calley, who brought a unique perspective to the reading of the manuscript and whose musical transcriptions will help enhance the quest.

- my dear friends and cherished colleagues, whose wisdom is surpassed only by their spirit, who tempered their critical reading of the manuscript with their deep love for Judaism and for God: Joseph (Yossi) Adler, Rabbi Marc Berkson, Dr. Gary Hartman, Rabbi David Posner, Ed.D., and Dr. Yehuda Shabatay.
- my beloved friend, the Reverend James J. O'Leary S.J., who is the blessed, humble, and most grateful servant of the Holy Spirit.
- my esteemed literary agent, Sandra Dijkstra, who, as always, keeps the faith.
- my distinguished editor, John Loudon, who truly honors the spiritual quest; his most able assistant editor, Karen Levine; Tom Grady; Mimi Kusch; and all the folks at HarperSanFrancisco whose books are filled with learning and light.

My deepest gratitude and admiration to the members and friends of The Elijah Minyan—the "living laboratory" for so many of the ideas and practices in this book—for being on the journey and joining in the quest.

And, most of all, my immeasurable and never-ending thanks and gratitude to Ellen. She is the inspiration and the fulfillment. On her wings, we soar to the greatest heights; in her vision, we see beyond seeing and know beyond knowing; through her spirit, we joyously come to the holy places of God.

Introduction

The State of the Faith

Hear, O Israel

WHEN WAS THE LAST TIME GOD SPOKE TO YOU?

When God wanted to speak to our biblical ancestors, He* simply called out to them.

God spoke directly to Abraham, creating a covenant of faith.

God spoke directly to Isaac, giving protection and blessing.

God spoke directly to Jacob, assuring guidance and safekeeping.

Out of a bush that burned but was not consumed, God spoke directly to Moses, calling him to sacred mission.

From the top of the mountain, God spoke directly to all the Children of Israel, giving them the precious gift of law.

Again, from the top of the mountain, God spoke directly to Moses, bathing him in the light of Divine encounter.

---

*Limitations of English make it impossible for any one word to encompass God's inherent masculine and feminine attributes. Throughout this introduction, with its emphasis on historical Judaism, the masculine pronoun will be used in reference to God, with the understanding that it represents the totality of God's existence. For a discussion and meditation on the masculine and feminine aspects of God, see chapter 2, "In Her Image."

God spoke directly to Joshua, filling him with the spirit of wisdom.

Over and over again, God spoke directly to the prophets, calling them to deliver the Divine word.

To every person who was an open and willing channel, God came directly—in words, in visions, in dreams.

God spoke to our ancient ancestors as a sometimes stern but always loving parent to precious children. The relationship was intimate and deeply personal.

And, except out of humility or fear of inadequacy, the response was always immediate and fervent: "Here I am. Thank You for being with me. Send me on Your mission. I am ready to do Your work."

There were, as there are in every intimate relationship, times of disappointment and frustration, even bitterness and anger. But deep faith in each other and even deeper love for each other always prevailed.

Just knowing these accounts, just being witness to the conversations, the commitment, and the passion between God and our long-ago ancestors, who among us is not a little envious, not a little jealous?

We know what it was like for our ancestors, and we wonder why it is not the same for us.

For who among us hears the word of God these days? Who among us sees God in a vision?

To whom does God speak today? To whom does God appear? For whom does God have a mission? Who among us is called, and who is ready to reply, "Here I am"?

Hear, O God

If we feel bad about not hearing from God, just think how bad God must feel about not hearing from us.

When was the last time you spoke to God?

We contemporary Jews are the children of modernity. We are the great-grandchildren of the Enlightenment and the Emancipation; we were brought up worshiping at the altars of rationalism and science, and we were the willing sacrifices at the intellectual shrines of Harvard and Stanford.

For most of us, the world of the mind has become the highest order and the highest good. The world of God is distant; the world of the spirit is little more than bedtime *bubbe meises,* "old grandmothers' tales," and flights of fancy.

Many of us are unfamiliar with the transcendent world of the spirit.

We hardly know God.

We don't know *about* God; we seem embarrassed to talk *of* God; we seem uncomfortable trying to talk *to* God.

When, in our gladness or our pain, we are somehow moved to speak to God, we barely have the words. When, in our desire or need, we are moved to find God, we don't know where to look.

What Happened?

After World War II, we built and maintained our new suburban synagogues and Jewish communal institutions to reflect our highly rational, intellectual worldview.

Contemporary Judaism became, and remains, more communal and cultural than spiritual, let alone mystical.

We Jews became very successful at creating community, doing acts of social justice, saving oppressed Jewry, supporting the State of Israel, raising money for "good causes," building Jewish institutions, defending against discrimination, and, with a few notable and most lamentable exceptions, fulfilling Judaism's ethical mandates. We are an accepted and respected part of the fabric of America. And we have contributed mightily to the ongoing growth and development of our society in virtually every aspect of human endeavor.

But the one thing Judaism is supposed to do best, it rarely does at all anymore.

Judaism is supposed to help each person find the way to create a personal, intimate relationship with God; a life of cosmic meaning and purpose; a life of soul-satisfaction, true inner happiness, and deep-felt joy and fulfillment.

There are, of course, sincere and serious contemporary Jews of every denomination of modern Jewry who feel a personal closeness to God found through faith, piety, and devotion to study, ritual, and worship.

But for most Jews, Judaism—the way it is practiced and conveyed in contemporary America—has failed to respond to our deepest yearnings and most profound needs.

While Judaism got caught up in modernity's reverence for rational, scientific, intellectual discourse and in the myth that building communal institutions and grand buildings meant the same thing as building Jewish hearts and souls, most Jews began to feel the ache of spiritual emptiness.

When Jews came to Judaism seeking God, most often all we found were sign-up sheets for the Hebrew school carpool and pledge cards for the building fund.

The synagogues, schools, and the community organizations and we the rabbis, teachers, and Jewish leaders failed our Jews. We failed to convey the greatness and the grandeur—indeed, the very existence—of the world of the Jewish spirit.

That is why, despite all of Judaism's outward manifestations of success in America, the vast majority of Jews are "voting with their feet," staying far away from Judaism, from the synagogue, from Jewish life and lifestyle.

The contemporary Judaism we have created does not speak sufficiently to searching Jewish hearts and does not sufficiently nourish hungering Jewish souls; it has become, for too many, stale, hollow, and irrelevant.

We Jews rarely, if ever, hear the word or see the vision of God anymore.

We hear no still small voice calling out to us.

We do not know how to find the voice or even where to search.

So we respond in silence.

The *pintele Yid,* the ever-enduring spark of Judaism, still burns, but the *Yiddishe neshamah,* the Jewish soul, the hearts and souls of individual Jews, are empty and forlorn.

Hungering for the Sacred

YET, THERE IS AN INHERENT HUMAN HUNGER, A continual human yearning, for the sacred, for the spiritual, for the transcendent, for the eternal.

We all want to be in touch with our creation and our Creator; we want answers to the mysteries of existence—to understand and somehow to tame the mighty forces of the universe; to define our place and our purpose in being.

We want to find meaning and value in life; to celebrate joy and triumph; to understand pain, suffering, and evil; and, ultimately, to confront death and the vast unknown.

No less than did our ancient forebears, we contemporary Jews want the explanations, the answers, the assurances that religion brings.

We want all that Judaism is supposed to offer: a spiritual pathway from and to God; intellectually honest and emotionally fulfilling answers to the questions of existence; life made holy by ethical commands that ennoble the human spirit; rituals and observances that give rhythm and purpose to the everyday; a community, linked by history and faith, deeply committed to the common good and to the dignity and sanctity of each human being.

We long for the deepest understanding, the timeless, the holy. We want, as the modern prayer so profoundly puts it, "purpose to our work, meaning to our struggle, direction to our striving." We hunger for God and for the world of the spirit, but, sadly, we rarely find it in institutional Judaism.

And so, many Jews, young and older alike, turn to other places seeking connection to God and the universe, seeking spiritual satisfaction and fulfillment.

Our Jews wind up in the meditation centers, the ashrams, the spiritual retreats, the communes, the self-improvement seminars, the twelve-step programs, the support groups, the yoga classes, the self-help bookshelves, est, Esalen, and the cults.

Three stories—of the thousands that could be recounted—tell the tale.

Not long ago, a sincere and serious young man phoned my call-in radio show to report that he, a Jew, attends Friday evening services every week but feels very little spiritual connection or uplift. His wife, also a Jew, meditates at the Self-Realization Fellowship and feels a great sense of cosmic connection and inner peace.

Recently a young woman told me, almost sheepishly and then with increasing passion and a face filled with light, that only a few months ago, when she was feeling deeply depressed, she went on a seven-day Buddhist retreat of silence where she found self-awareness, spiritual inspiration, and life guidance. She reported that sixty of the one hundred participants and three of the four leaders in this Buddhist retreat were Jews.

In the mid-1990s, a book called *The Jew in the Lotus,* by Rodger Kamenetz, chronicled the journey of several rabbis and Jewish leaders who met with the Dalai Lama to discuss the similarities between two seemingly disparate religious traditions. The book became an instant "cult classic" among Jews who were already integrating and balancing Eastern and Western spiritual traditions in their lives, and among Jews who were just learning that there is more to the Jewish spiritual journey than was ever taught in a suburban synagogue.

The Longest Journey Begins and Ends at the Same Place

WE ALL KNOW PEOPLE — WE ALL ARE PEOPLE — who jog *religiously,* who exercise, sail, cook gourmet meals, perform in community theater, collect stamps, read, or play trumpet *religiously.*

We do things we love, we love the things we do, because doing them makes us feel better, happier, more fulfilled; doing them brings us satisfaction and joy and makes our lives richer and fuller. Without them something important is missing; there is a gap, an emptiness, in our very existence.

If Judaism made us feel more satisfied, more fulfilled, made us happier and better human beings, we would practice it *religiously;* we would embrace it with the same joy, enthusiasm, and intensity that joggers and stamp collectors bring to their passions, for it would touch us at the core of our beings, at that deep place where happiness and fulfillment reside.

Jews! Listen!

Though no one ever told us, though no one ever showed us, everything we want, everything we need, everything we have been searching for, everything that will satisfy our souls, everything that will bring us to God is not far from home. It need not be sought in another place or another culture, another heritage or tradition. It lies in what is familiar, what is comfortable, what is us.

All that we are seeking is right in Judaism.

It is in Judaism's beginnings and its forever, in Judaism's sources and texts, in Judaism's words and prayers, in Judaism's rituals and practices, in Judaism's music and movement, in Judaism's "sounds of silence."

And all that we are seeking is right in us.

It is in our Jewish history and destiny, it is in our vocabulary and language, our poetry, our idiom, our metaphor. It is in our consciousness and in our deepest, hidden places; it is in our source, our roots, our rhythms, our genes, our DNA.

Within Judaism are the sacred pathways for our spiritual journey guiding each one of us to a personal, intimate relationship with God; bathing our souls in God's guidance and love; helping us struggle with and prevail over life's most perplexing questions and mysteries; leading us toward a rich, noble, fulfilling existence; bringing us wholeness and holiness at the very core of our beings.

Judaism's deeply spiritual pathways, which began with God's direct and personal conversations with our long-ago ancestors, are still indelibly carved into the collective Jewish memory and experience. They are the channel into God's presence; they are the guideposts for the transformation of Jewish hearts and souls.

Judaism's rituals and practices, which have become, for so many, empty and sterile rote, can still hold the deep spiritual secrets, the viscerally felt life-cadence rhythms that bring harmony to body and soul, that provide the pathway to the holy, to God.

These pathways have been hidden and sent underground, where they were shrouded in the shadows of Jewish life. But they are there, waiting to be joyously reclaimed and renewed by this generation of Jewish seekers.

Tradition and Change

DURING ITS FIRST TWO THOUSAND YEARS, JUDAISM was characterized by direct revelation enhanced by God-given law. In this period—which we now call Biblical Judaism—each person could hope for and expect personal communication and a personal relationship with God.

Born with Abraham (ca. 1800 B.C.E.) and affirmed by Moses at Sinai, Biblical Judaism continued through the period of the judges, the kings, and the prophets.

During all this time, our ancestors worshiped God by means of animal and agricultural sacrifices brought, eventually, to a centralized altar at the Holy Temple in Jerusalem. There, priests officiated over the sacrifices, hoping that God would be pleased by the "sweet smells" that wafted up to the heavens.

But then the world changed radically.

In quick succession, Jews experienced exile and return, religious reformation, religious repression, political persecution, the birth of a powerful new religion, destruction, and, once again, exile.

Any one of these traumas and challenges—and, surely, all of them together—might have been enough to decimate the Jewish people. When prophecy was silenced, they could have claimed to no longer hear God. When the Temple was destroyed, they could have claimed to no longer be able to worship God. When their land was ripped away from them, they could have claimed to have no place to be with God.

Instead, the Jews rose up to meet the challenges, totally revamped the Judaism they knew, developed a new Judaism, and reconstituted themselves as a new and stronger faith community.

The Holy Temple was replaced by the synagogue, the cultic priest was replaced by the scholar-rabbi, and animal sacrifice was replaced by prayer.

Most significantly, direct Divine revelation—personal prophecy—was replaced by the advent of Oral Law, the extension of Torah Law that was given at Sinai.

The rabbis and sages who introduced the Oral Law contended that God's word and will would no longer be given directly to individuals but would come through this new law, which would be articulated only by the sages themselves. Continuing revelation, they claimed, came through them alone.

This new Judaism came to be called Rabbinic Judaism. It is the Judaism that we have lived and practiced for these past two thousand years.

Born and sustained out of flexibility and adaptability, it was committed to maintaining the core of tradition while at the same time being ever ready to interpret, modify, and change in order to meet new circumstances and challenges.

Transcendent beyond the limitations of time and space, Rabbinic Judaism saved Judaism from possible ruination and oblivion.

Yet Rabbinic Judaism's unwavering commitment to the world of the law stifled and frustrated proponents of the world of the spirit, those who still sought direct revelation from God and direct communication with God.

To be certain that the people would not enter realms where they no longer belonged, the sages tell this story in the Talmud.

Four went into paradise, into the dwelling place of God. They went seeking the deepest meaning of God's word, and so, metaphorically, they entered into the glory of God's heavenly kingdom.

One was so overcome by what he saw that he died; another went mad; the third became an apostate. Only one could look upon God's holy place and delve into the deepest meaning of God's holy word and survive unscathed. And that one was Rabbi Akiba, the greatest scholar of them all.

The message from the sages was clear: unless you are as great and learned a scholar as Rabbi Akiba—and none of you is—then don't even think of entering the realm of personal prophecy, of continuing revelation, of the mystical interpretation of God's word. For if you do, you will cease to believe, you will go mad, or you will die.

✦

Then, just as the primacy of Jewish law was being deeply ingrained into the collective Jewish psyche, another messenger came into the world.

Jesus taught that in the relationship between God and humankind, the world of the law is far less important than the world of the spirit.

Jesus contended that belief, faith, and love, which Judaism assumes and sometimes takes for granted, are really the core of the relationship between God and His children and thus should be the central spiritual quest of humankind.

While Judaism rightly rejected the basic *forms* of Christianity—for they contained theological assertions that we simply could not accept—Judaism also ignored the *substance* that we would have done well to reaffirm: that God and humankind are connected through deep faith and love, that God can truly be a personal God, deeply involved in the life of each human being.

✦

All the while, human consciousness was evolving and growing. The universe was revealing more of its secrets; people were wiser, more attuned. Simple answers that had satisfied desert-dwelling ancestors were no longer enough.

The parameters imposed by the sages constrained the human spirit.

So twice in these ensuing two thousand years of Rabbinic Judaism, movements within Judaism—most notably the Kabbalists, beginning in the thirteenth century, and the Chasidim of the early eighteenth century—have tried to bring Jews back to finding the spiritual, to celebrating faith.

But their attempts were most often smothered and rejected by the rationalists and the legalists.

The world of the spirit was, at best, sent to the far edges of Jewish life and, at worst, was hidden away and practiced by only a few mystics and their followers.

In these last 250 years, since the Enlightenment and the Emancipation, attempts to bring Judaism back to the world of the spirit have been eschewed by the so-called rationalists and intellectuals as but fanciful conjecture, folk fantasy, overworked imagination, or mere superstition.

The Coming New Era

IN THE PAST 250 YEARS, THERE HAVE BEEN MASSIVE and radical changes in the Jewish and in the secular world: the Enlightenment with its emphasis on scientific scholarship; the Emancipation with its territorial and political freedoms; global warfare with its threat of mass destruction; the rise and growth of the highly creative American Jewish community; the devastation wrought by the Holocaust; the rise and growth of political Zionism and the establishment of the modern State of Israel; the quantum leaps of science and technology that are making the vast world into a "global village"; the deep ecumenism that is bringing diverse people ever closer together; the serious concern about ecology and the preservation of the planet.

At the same time, human consciousness is expanding to ever-greater awareness.

There has been a dramatic awakening to the knowledge that the universe is so much more than what we can see, feel, hear, or experience at this moment in time. There has been ever-growing recognition that we are continually developing the capacity to perceive and receive that which has been there all along but is still to be revealed.

The universe continues to unfold bit by bit, revealing its mysteries, divulging its secrets. The veil is lifting. The distinction—and the distance—between this side and the other side is ever fading.

Some call it the world of intuition or perception, some call it the world of the psychic or the mystical, some call it the world of the spirit. We call it the world of God.

⚜

With all of these sweeping changes in our world, in our behavior, and in our psyches, the once innovative and comfortable world of Rabbinic Judaism is no longer enough for most of us. Its simplistic, innocent answers no longer fully satisfy our expanded minds; its insistence on the primacy of the law no longer speaks to our spiritually questing hearts and souls.

So, just as Biblical Judaism once gave way to Rabbinic Judaism when its ideas and forms no longer worked, contemporary Jews have brought Judaism to the brink of a new age, the cosmic moment when Rabbinic Judaism, whose time and purpose is in the midst of completion, gives way to a third era of Jewish religion and civilization.

The writer-historian Chaim Potok describes this, our moment on the stage of history: "At some future time, eyes will gaze upon us. They will perceive that we were once in an inter-face between civilizations. And they will say of us that we used our new freedom . . . either to vanish as a people or to re-educate ourselves, build our broken core from the treasures of the past, fuse it with the best in secularism, and create a new philosophy, a new literature, a new world of Jewish art, a new community, *a third civilization of Jewish people.* That is the adventure that lies before us" (italics mine).

The seeds of Judaism's coming third era have been planted in the last few decades by what is now called the Jewish Renewal Movement.

Birthed and nurtured through the vision of Rabbi Zalman Schachter-Shalomi and cradled in the sweet melodies of Rabbi Shlomo Carlebach זצ״ל, the movement has been described best by writer William Novak as "a new Judaic impulse fed by the best qualities in each of the recognized branches of Judaism: the authenticity of Orthodoxy, the liberalism of Reform, the scholarship of Conservative Judaism, the social awareness of Reconstructionism [and] the excitement of Chasidism."

Jewish seekers have created and found early manifestations of the movement in places like the three *Jewish Catalogs;* the establishment of *chavurot* and *minyanim* as small, intense places for prayer, learning, and the creation of community; in Reb Zalman's B'nai (then P'nai) Or, now ALEPH: Alliance for Jewish Renewal; in the National Chavurah Conference; in a few of the synagogue-based *chavurot,* first established by Rabbi Harold Schulweis; in the early days of the CAJE, the Coalition for

Alternatives in Jewish Education; in Elat Chayyim, the summer retreat center; in the writings of a few God-inspired teachers who are
contemporary Judaism's true spiritual guides and leaders.

Yet until now the movement toward Jewish renewal, the entryway
into Judaism's third era, has been rather loose and amorphous, little ac-
claimed or promoted by its adherents, and consigned to the shadowy,
"fringe-y" underground of Jewish life by the uninitiated—and too
often perplexed and conservative (small *c*)—members of the so-called
Jewish establishment.

But now the time is right.

The identity, the purpose, the direction, the focus, and even a
name can be given to Judaism's coming new age.

There are, right now, surely, more questions than there are answers.

And surely, from these first beginnings, tremendous evolution and
growth that will take place, over hundreds of years, from these first beginnings.

But now the questions are finally being asked.

The answers are slowly but assuredly being formulated.

The birthing has begun.

A new Judaism is being born.

Neshamah Judaism

We call Judaism's coming new era, Judaism's
third era, Neshamah Judaism: Soul Judaism.

Just as Biblical Judaism was characterized by its source and Rabbinic Judaism was characterized by its leaders, Neshamah Judaism
will be defined by its core manifestation, the intimate, spiritual soul-
connection of each person with God, and by its forgers and shapers,
precious individual souls.

Neshamah Judaism will be grounded in the covenant of spirit
made between God and Abraham and in the ever-resounding covenant
of love and law made at Sinai. Despite striking changes in the human
experience and condition, and despite the dramatic evolution of

human consciousness, God's word and will—our sense of *mitzvah*—will continue to command and inspire us. Our commitment to fulfilling God's ethical mandate will remain unchanged and unchanging.

Yet coming into Neshamah Judaism will mean returning to Judaism's original roots, to the ever-possible reality of direct revelation, of personal prophecy, of deep and sacred communication. It will mean returning to the intimate one-to-one relationship between God and each individual human being.

Jews will once again be able to turn to all of Judaism's resources—spiritual practice, prayer, meditation, language, music, and storytelling—for help in going on the spiritual journey, in joining the spiritual quest, in finding and knowing God.

In our time and place, we—each in our own, unique, individual way—can be like Abraham and Moses and Jeremiah. We can hear God's voice calling out to us, and we can know that God hears our voice when we call.

Judaism's coming new age, Judaism's third era, will be characterized at the same time by a deep connection to other members of Judaism's faith community.

In community, there is shared memory, unity of purpose, mutual commitment, reciprocal responsibility, and common destiny. In community, there is powerful energy that heightens awareness, supports unfolding consciousness, strengthens cosmic connection, enhances prayer, deepens meditation, and affirms transcendent experience.

In community there is sharing of tragedy and triumph—joy enhanced, sorrow eased. In community, there is support for personal healing—the pain and suffering of physical disease and emotional trauma tempered and soothed. In community there is encouragement and energy for global healing—the task of transforming and perfecting the world advocated and empowered.

As it always has been, the collective whole of the Jewish community will continue to be the place of origin and the ever-present, ever-supportive nurturing source for the innermost personal spiritual quest.

Yet in the coming new era, the definition and function of community will be even broader and more encompassing than ever before.

In the 1920s, Rabbi Mordecai Kaplan articulated what was already intuitively known: Judaism is much more than a religion. Judaism is "an evolving religious civilization" where, tribelike, clanlike, nation-like, Jews are deeply connected to one another and to Judaism through peoplehood, through collective consciousness and collective memory, through ethnicity and culture.

While traditionalists denounced Kaplan as a religious blasphemer and heretic, time and evolving wisdom have affirmed his teaching. Many Jews, especially the vast majority of Israeli Jews, feel deeply and passionately connected to Judaism and the Jewish people without accepting Jewish religious beliefs or practicing Jewish ritual observance, for while religion is at the core of the Jewish experience, Judaism creates a community that is deeply rooted, strongly bonded, and passionately loyal.

So in the coming new era, many, many Jews will be an integral part of Judaism and the Jewish people but will not be involved in Judaism's spiritual practices, for while Jewish religion and peoplehood are deeply intertwined, each element has its own separate and unique characteristics and can, if need be, stand independently from the other.

There will be deep connection to Judaism not only through God's world of the spirit, but also through ethnicity, history, culture, community, a commitment to the land and to the people of Israel.

How odd!

Here comes Judaism's new age, which will be most characterized by the renewal of deep spiritual practices, by deep soul-connection to God. Yet, at the same time, there will be a visible denial of the God-quest, a deep attachment to Judaism based solely on connection to community.

Odd, perhaps, but readily explained.

The hallmark of Judaism's coming third era is the uniqueness of each human being, the sacredness of each human soul.

Each person will relate to God in his or her own way. Some will come through a deeply spiritual personal connection. Others will come by being part of a greater whole, a community that nourishes and nurtures their humanity. Either way, God is there, manifest in the intimacy of personal dialogue or in the midst of the crowded, busy world, ready to welcome and embrace all children.

⭒❖⭒

Some, of course, will resist change and desperately cling to the past.

Change is scary—and threatening.

Once, the Sadducees bitterly opposed the coming of Rabbinic Judaism, and the Karaites insisted on the validity of only Torah Law for close to eight centuries after the Oral Law took its rightful place.

Today, some who still find Rabbinic Judaism personally fulfilling and satisfying or who are committed to it by belief, choice, or habit will insist on its continuing validity. Others will be frightened by the need to revamp old, comfortable forms. A small but vocal minority will dismiss the coming of Judaism's new age as inauthentic and foolish.

But when new light is ready to come, even the strongest forces of opposition or darkness cannot keep it away.

In the pluralism of modernity, Neshamah Judaism will forge and take its rightful place because Jews have brought us there, because it is the inevitable next step in Judaism's evolutionary process.

The change will be brought and the new era will be shaped by Jewish seekers—by those who know that our own spiritual quests are centered in the soul-connection with God that Judaism can provide and by those who know that Judaism's very survival depends on its ability to, once again, be flexible enough to adapt to changing times and open enough to meet its people's soul-cries for meaning and purpose in life.

While it will take decades, if not centuries, for Judaism's third era to grow, develop, and fully define itself, one thing is certain: the new Judaism will look and feel and be very, very different from the Judaism we know now, just as Rabbinic Judaism was dramatically different from Biblical Judaism. Yet many of the practices and techniques that will help shape Neshamah Judaism have been within Judaism all along. They will be rediscovered and reclaimed in a joyous and profound celebration of Jewish renewal.

Neshamah Judaism, most probably, will be far less structured, far less formalized, and surely far less unilateral than the Judaisms that have come before.

And it, most probably, will not come through the synagogue as we currently know it, for no formalized institution, no matter how noble its intent, can hold the radiant light of the spirit, the reflected and reflecting light of God. Instead, the renewed Jewish spiritual quest most likely will come from within small groups of seekers and from within individual Jewish hearts and souls—where it was supposed to be all along.

In the Beginning

DANCING WITH GOD IS AN INVITATION TO RENEW our spiritual connection to God and to our higher selves, and to bring deeper meaning, worth, happiness, and satisfaction to our lives. It offers an opportunity to join with others in our faith community to renew Judaism and to help shape and enter Judaism's coming new era.

In eighteen chapters—brief meditations, reflections, and musings—we will consider Jewish beliefs, rituals, and observances that we may have known about and even practiced all our lives but that may now seem empty or meaningless and may not touch us in any significant way.

Here we will reinfuse them with their original meaning and purpose, with their spiritual center. Here, simply and practically, they can come alive again, giving us newfound awareness and understanding, providing us with newfound pathways to our soul-connection with God.

For source and guidance, we will rely both on the vast richness and warmth of authentic Jewish tradition and teachings and on the best of the contemporary culture. For resources in creating new paradigms, we will turn to the storehouse of Judaism's mystical experiences, especially the ones that have been lost or hiding.

These spiritual practices are tentative yet decisive steps into Judaism's new era. More and more practices will be developed over the years, shaping and forging Neshamah Judaism as an ever-evolving soul-journey to God, as ever-unfolding expressions that bring Jews ever closer to the light of God.

❦

No matter what your place on the Jewish spectrum or what your level of Jewish belief, learning, or practice, no matter how close or far you feel from your God and your people or what your feelings about the world of the spirit, here is a pathway to personal growth and Jewish renewal, to the enrichment and ennoblement of mind and spirit.

This book is also an invitation to seekers of other faiths to explore Judaism's worldview, beliefs, and practices, Judaism's vocabulary, idiom, and rhythms. Just as many Jews have found spiritual direction and comfort in your faith, you may very well find meaningful spiritual encounter in ours.

❦

At this most exciting and awesome moment in Jewish history, a moment that comes but once every two thousand years, we stand at the birthplace of Judaism's coming new age.

We bear witness as both the heirs of the past—"how great our inheritance, how pleasant our lot"—and the fashioners of the future—"God called the world into being, and the call goes on; every instant is an act of creation."

Judaism's history and destiny come in us, because of us, and, now, through us.

We take our mission and our challenge from Rav Avraham Kook, the first Chief Rabbi of Israel, who taught, הישן יתחדש והחדש יתקדש, *Hayashan yitchadesh, v'hechadash yitkadesh,* "The old must be made new, and the new must be made sacred."

And we take our energy and our inspiration from our God who taught, "You shall be holy, for I the Lord your God am holy. I have filled [you] with the spirit of God. Be strong and of good courage. Fear not, for I am with you, and I will bless you" (Leviticus 19:2; Exodus 31:3; Joshua 1:6; Genesis 26:24).

Part One

Connecting with God

The prime concern of the religious quest is to bring individual human beings into personal, intimate relationship with God.

It is not an easy task, for there seem to be so many barriers: How can we mortal, finite human beings come to know the infinite, all-powerful, all-knowing God? How can we hope to understand God's vast, unrevealed plan? How can we affirm a perfect, loving God when there is so much imperfection, so much evil in the world? How can we hope to communicate with God, who seems so far away, so grand, so awesome? How can we talk to God and know that we are heard? How can we cry out to God in joy or pain and know that God will listen? How can each one of us—all of us tiny, individual souls—hope to have a personal, one-to-one relationship with God, who must be so busy with the immense, boundless universe?

From its very beginnings, Judaism has acknowledged and honored the tremendous effort and energy that it takes to forge a personal relationship with God. The very name by which the Jewish people and the Jewish land are known,

Yisrael—*Israel*—means *"to wrestle with God,"* indicating that it is an ongoing struggle for each person, in his or her own time and place, to find and know God, to carve out a satisfactory and satisfying bond with God.

So from its very beginnings, through its ever-developing spiritual practices, Judaism's core mission has been to be the clear pathway, to provide the open channel, for Jews—for all human beings—to connect with and communicate with God, to feel joy and fulfillment from knowing God.

The spiritual practices in this section—some ancient, some newly conceived—can take us on the journey to God.

In the words of the ancient sage, Tarfon, "The work is great . . . but the reward is much, and the Master is eagerly waiting" (Avot 2:20)

I

God Within

FOR MOST OF US, THE GOD WE MET IN CHILDHOOD is "up there" in heaven, while we live "down here" on earth.

Bible stories tell of an all-powerful God looking down from on high. Many prayers, especially in the High Holiday liturgy, create the poetic metaphor of an almighty God sitting on His heavenly throne, meting out Divine reward or punishment to His children who follow or transgress His commands.

For many children, the image of God is of an all-knowing, all-wise old man whose grandfatherly love and compassion hardly mitigates His awesome strength, His untouchable grandeur, and His stern sense of justice.

While God may be addressed through prayer, for most, He seems distant and remote—too far away to ever be close or intimate, too splendiferous to ever be truly approachable.

We grow in education, wisdom, and emotion; we become experienced and worldly wise, sophisticated, and cultured, but many of us never outgrow our childhood notion of God. We still envision old man God "up there" grandly overseeing the universe.

Of course, as it should, our rational intellect soundly rejects this naive, simplistic, conception of God. But rather than struggling to re-define God, rather than doing the work to form a realistic, mature, adult relationship with God, many find it easier to just ignore—or re-ject—God.

But without God we sense something is missing; there is an empti-ness, a void in our lives.

We want to know God; we want to be sure that God knows us. We want an ongoing, personal, intimate relationship with God. We want the certitude, the assurance, the inner peace that knowing God brings.

⋟✦⋞

The Kabbalists taught that there are ways to lessen the distance between the infinite God and finite human beings. If God is indeed "up there" and we are "down here," then at least we can bridge the gap.

The Kabbalists taught that there are ten emanations or steps—which they called *sefirot*—between God and humankind. Through prayer, contemplation, and meditation, the steps can be climbed in both directions, up from us to God and down from God to us, so that "holy sparks" of God's fiery light and the glint of the Divine within us can touch, and we can meet God in intimate dialogue.

Here is one way to meet God, to bring God into our lives with im-mediacy, with ever-evolving place and purpose.

Life begins with a cry or perhaps a whimper, the very first breath of earthly existence.

Life ends with a whimper or perhaps a cry, the final breath of earthly being.

From where does that first breath come? To where does that final breath go? And what of all the breaths in between—more than twenty-three thousand every single day?

A modern prayer affirms an eternal truth:

"You send forth Your breath, O God, and we are created. You take away our breath, and we die and return to the dust. We are ever in Your merciful power."

From God. To God.

Breath is the life force, the life energy. Without it, we human beings are no more than a lump of clay, a collection of chemicals worth no more than a few dollars.

But with breath, we are living human beings, precious children of the universe, created in the image of God, just a little lower than the angels.

Every moment, we are just one breath away from the end of our earthly sojourn. Yet how often do we appreciate—how often do we even notice—the life-gift of breath that flows within us?

Snorkelers and scuba divers report a greatly heightened awareness of life when hearing their own breathing. Old yoga techniques and modern rebirthing therapies teach concentration on the very act of breathing. Buddhists speak of "mindful" or "conscious" breathing as the most basic practice for touching peace.

Focus on breath is focus on being—on creation and on existence.

The Hebrew word for breath is *ruach,* which is the very same word for spirit.

And to whom does original breath, original spirit, belong? What is the source of breath, of spirit, of life itself?

In its opening sentences, the Bible reports that in the beginning the earth was "unformed and void, with darkness upon the deep; and *ruach Elohim"*—the spirit, the breath of God—"hovered over the water." And then God began to create.

What, then, is the source of creation? *Ruach Elohim,* the spirit, the life-breath of God.

Later on, in the second version of the creation of man, the Bible says, "The Lord God formed man from the dust of the earth, and He blew into his nostrils the breath of life, and man became a living soul" (Genesis 2:7).

Aha! There it is!

The breath of God is the breath, the life force, of human beings.

We exist, we live, we are, because our breath is the breath of God.

Every day we can feel God's intimate presence and can affirm our inseparable intertwined oneness with God.

Every day we can merge our breath with God's, with the life force of the universe. And we can feel God's breath, God's spirit, fill us with life, with energy, with love.

Every day—perhaps when we awaken in the morning to a dawning new day of life, perhaps for a few minutes in the middle of a busy day as reconnection to the source, perhaps as quiet darkness marks the end of another day—every day we can say, over and over again, *ruach, ruuu-ach, ruuuu-ach.*

(The "ach" sound at the end of *ruach* may be hard to pronounce. To "get it," remember how to pronounce the name of the great musician Johann Sebastian B*ach*.)

The very sound of the word—*ruuuu-ach, ruuuu-ach*—evokes the feeling, the whoosh, of breath. So as you say *ruach,* feel the spirit, echo the sound: breathe in; breathe out: *ruuu-ach.*

Breathe in. Breathe out: *ruu-ach.* Breathe in. Breathe out: *ruuuu-ach. Ruuuu-ach. Ruuuu-ach. Ruuuu-ach.*

As you breathe, you get in touch with that very first moment of creation. As you breathe, you get in touch with the Creator, God. As you breathe, you imitate God, who breathes life into you every moment. As you breathe, you can feel God's breath, you can feel God within you, infusing every particle of your being with life.

Singing the word *ruach* in a quiet, contemplative way helps the word, the feeling, resonate and reverberate deeply within.

To focus your soul-song, here is Rabbi Shlomo Carlebach's simple yet beautiful melody for chanting *ruach.*

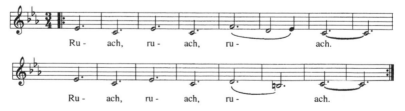

Ru - ach, ru - ach, ru - ach.

Ru - ach, ru - ach, ru - ach.

Ruach—the spirit, the breath of God; the life force of your being; God's living presence within you.

✒✦✒

Here is another way to bring God close.

The holy Kotzker Rebbe taught, "God is everywhere—everywhere you let Him in." God is simply waiting for you to call, and when you do, He will answer.

In contemporary times, this Chasidic notion of God being everywhere seems, to many, to be a sweet but impractical idea. It is an appealing intellectual concept to think that God, who created the entire world, resides everywhere in the universe rather than just in the heavenly realm. It is easy—and lovely—to assert that "God is in the beautiful sunset; God is in the majestic mountain; God is in the cry of the newborn infant."

But how is it possible for any one person—for all people—to see God everywhere, to experience God all around, and, especially, to feel God within?

How is it possible to truly grow beyond the innocent childhood notion of God above into the full-grown, felt-sense knowing of God everywhere?

There is a way that we can feel and know God within us, that we can feel and know God filling up our whole beings.

One of the earliest biblical names for God is made up of four Hebrew letters: ׳ *yud*, ה *hey*, ו *vav*, and ה *hey*. It is taken from the root word that means "to be," affirming that God was, is, and always will be.

The real pronunciation of this most sacred name of God has long been lost, so it is most often pronounced by its combined letter sounds, יהוה Yahweh. (Since we do not want to ever trivialize the pronunciation of this most holy name of God, we now use a substitute pronunciation for this four-letter name. We now pronounce God's name as Adonai, which means "our Master.")

By seeing these letters as symbols—what all letters really are—fully standing for and representing God, we can bring God within.

Instead of seeing these letters as Hebrew letters are usually written, right to left, see them written from top to bottom. Thus יהוה, *God*, looks like this:

יְהוָה

The first thing we notice is that the letters form the shape of a person: the *yud* is the head, the top *hey* is the shoulders and arms, the *vav* is the torso, and the bottom *hey* is the legs.

While God has no physical shape, no corporeal being, it is no coincidence that we human beings, who are created in the image of God, are shaped in the way that the letters form God's name.

When we close our eyes and visualize our human self, we can see the letters of God's name giving us form and shape, and we can see God within us.

The next thing we notice is that the letters represent the masculine and the feminine: the *yud* is the male seed and the *vav* is the male phallus; the two *heys,* the female womb. The letters take the form of man and woman, the giver and the receiver, the planting and the nurturing—the ongoing act of creation.

Just as God has both male and female attributes, we human beings, who are created in the image of God, have both male and female attributes. One attribute becomes dominant, making us, in this lifetime, a man or a woman. But the opposite characteristic is always a part of us.

When we close our eyes and visualize our human selves, we can see the letters of God's name giving us both our gender characteristics and our sexual drive, assuring the continuity of humanity. We can see God within us.

Finally, we can use these letters to bring God within us, to feel God's presence and nearness, to feel God's being in ours.

Try this spiritual practice of visualization.

Close your eyes.

See these four letters as hot, white fire.

See them sparkling and pulsating with the being—with the passion—of God.

Breathe the letters into you, one at a time.

Breathe in the *yud*. Breathe in the *hey*. Breathe in the *vav*. Breathe in the *hey*.

Again. Breathe in the *yud*. Breathe in the *hey*. Breathe in the *vav*. Breathe in the *hey*.

Let the letters fill you up.

Now see those hot, white letters fringed in gold, bright sparks of gold radiating out from each letter to the very ends of the universe.

Breathe in those letters. Let them fill you up.

Feel the hot fire, feel the passion, feel the radiance of God filling every particle of your being, from the very top of your head to the very bottom of your feet.

Inhale. Exhale. Inhale. Exhale.

God is within you.

Now, breathe in the *yud* and breathe out the *hey*. Breathe in the *vav* and breathe out the *hey*.

Again. Inhale *yud*. Exhale *hey*. Inhale *vav*. Exhale *hey*.

Feel the air flow through you. Hear the sound of the *hey* as it is expelled from your lungs.

Feel God's continuous flowing—in you, through you; in you, through you.

Feel the continuous flow of the universe—the never-ending flow of creation, of life, of being—flow in you, through you.

God flows within you. God flows through you.

Eternity flows within you. Eternity flows through you.

Now, you can go far beyond and far deeper than the childhood notion of God "up there." You know that God is everywhere, because you have let God in you.

Happy will you be, filled with God's presence.

Happy will you be in the presence of God.

2

In Her Image

We — you and I — are created, according to the biblical account, "in the image of God" (Genesis 1:27).

Like God, we have been given the capacity to think and know, to reason and remember. Like God, we have been given the ability to love, to form relationships, to make the life of another as precious as our own; to demand justice and righteousness, to feel compassion, to act with grace and mercy, to pursue peace. With God, we have been given the task of transforming, healing, and perfecting our world.

What a grand—and humbling—condition!

How good it would be if our ancestors, those who bequeathed to us the form and the language of relating to God, had been able to fully help us capture our "image of God," our image of ourselves.

Instead, they reflected the simple and acceptable images and language of their times to describe God, thus circumscribing God and, by extension, our image of ourselves.

Born at a time when religion was moving from the notion of feminine goddess to masculine god, and at a time when the society was rigidly patriarchal, Judaism adopted the image of God as a powerful, male, authoritarian figure.

The traditional prayerbook still calls God "Our Father who is in heaven"; "Our Father, our King"; "Father of mercy"; and it asks, "Bless us, O our Father, all of us together. . . ."

✤

In our time, feminists of both genders have made us sensitive to the almost exclusive male name-designations for God and to the continually dominant male imagery in prayer.

Many women feel shut out of much of Jewish life by exclusive rather than inclusive prayer language, by lack of a Godly role model— a God in whose image women are created—to whom to relate.

In response, many have begun to eliminate some of the sexist language from prayer translations and have added new words to some Hebrew texts. Rather than speaking of "mankind," many now say "humankind"; rather than saying "God of our fathers," many now say, "God of our ancestors." Rather than invoking the memory and the merit of only Abraham, Isaac, and Jacob, many now also remember Sarah, Rebecca, Leah, and Rachel.

✤

While gender-sensitive prayer language solves part of the problem, for many it is still not enough.

Many women—and men who understand the entirety of God's being—want an "image of God" to which to relate fully and unequivocally.

We understand that the archetype of many ancient gods is both masculine and feminine, with a duality often existing within the same entity. We understand Christianity's acknowledgment of the feminine aspect of God when it taught of God as Father and Son and taught also of the Madonna, Mother.

We wonder why Judaism's experience and language still limits the possibility of relating to, and reflecting, the full image of God.

Continuing limitations of vocabulary further compound the dilemma. In both Hebrew and English, the third person pronoun is either masculine *or* feminine, "he" or "she." There is no one word that addresses a being of either gender, a being with no gender, or a being with both genders.

So some have insisted that all masculine name-designations and images of God be entirely eliminated from prayer language. In this way, those who want to be able to fully relate to an unconflicted "image of God" will have no problem.

The most popular solution that has been embraced in contemporary times—found in a few places in the book of Psalms and brought down and taught to us by Reb Zalman—is to address God as יה Yah, as in הללויה HalleluYah, "Praise God," which seems to have no gender designation.

But the problem with this solution is that by eliminating God's male designations—by *always* calling God by a genderless name—what is really accomplished is the neutering of God. By not acknowledging any of God's masculine characteristics, we also eliminate the possibility of acknowledging any of God's feminine characteristics.

What we really want to do is acknowledge within God *both* God's masculine characteristics and attributes *and* God's feminine characteristics and attributes—the entirety of God, the whole image of God in which we all, male and female, are created.

⋆❖⋆

Quietly, subtly, Judaism has always acknowledged the masculine and feminine aspects of God.

The dominant imagery is of God as *Adonai* and *Elohim,* the powerful Creator and Ruler of the universe, and *Av,* the authoritarian Father.

Yet, just as significantly, God is known as *Shechinah,* the enveloping, caring, nurturing, protecting Mother.

When the Jewish People were ripped from their land and sent into exile, the texts relate that it was the *Shechinah,* the Sheltering Presence, who accompanied them to comfort them in their pain, to protect them from harm's way.

Later texts describe two of God's many attributes: *midat hadin,* the attribute of judgment, balanced by the *midat harachamim,* the attribute of compassion and mercy. The Hebrew root word of *rachamim,* "compassion and mercy," is *rechem,* which means "womb." God's overwhelming sense of compassion is instinctively connected to the female womb, the place of all life, the place of nurture, growth, and protection.

The Talmud records that when the sages wanted God's counsel and advice, direction and guidance, God often spoke to them in a *bat kol,* the heavenly voice or echo, the Divine voice of God in its gentle, enveloping feminine expression.

One of Judaism's most beloved rituals dramatically underscores the existence of God's masculine and feminine characteristics and the need for them to work in harmony.

During the fall harvest festival of Succot, we wave a *lulav,* a palm branch combined with willow and myrtle leaves, together with an *etrog,* a lemonlike citron. We hold those objects in our hands and shake them in all directions.

The traditional—and safe—explanation of this ritual is that the *lulav* represents the strong backbone of the Jewish People, the willow and the myrtle, the eyes and the mouth; and that the *etrog* represents the warm heart. Holding them together and shaking them in every direction is, according to this interpretation, the Jewish People's acknowledgment and celebration that God is everywhere.

It makes a good story to tell the children.

But a much more plausible explanation is that on the harvest festival, we, in imitation of our ancient ancestors, are imploring and thanking God for a full and abundant crop and for good seeds to be planted and to take root for the next growing season. So we hold the *lulav,* symbolic of the male phallus and testicles, and the *etrog,* symbolic of the female breast and womb, and shake them all over, asking that the reproduction of the earth imitate the reproduction of human beings; that God display and use the male aspect of planting the seed, and the female aspect of receiving and nurturing it.

~~◆~~

If we do not rob God of His maleness in order to acknowledge Her femaleness, we recognize that within God is both the masculine and the feminine. Then we can all better relate to God as both Father and Mother, powerful ruler and compassionate nurturer.

When we see in God His/Her fullness of being, then we can begin to see within ourselves—created in God's image—*our* fullness of being, for within every human being—just as within God—is both the masculine and the feminine. Every man has feminine attributes within; every woman has masculine attributes within.

The great psychologist Carl Jung explained it this way: in the collective unconscious, there is an inheritance of our universal experience as human beings, encoded in a multitude of archetypes. Every archetype has its polarity, its opposite, so that in each one of us there is both the *animus,* the male, and the *anima,* the female.

So as we acknowledge, get in touch with, and honor both the masculine and feminine of God, at the same time, we acknowledge, get in touch with, and honor the masculine and feminine within us. Women can touch their masculinity and be empowered; men can touch their femininity and feel compassion.

Then, regardless of historical, linguistic, or emotional limitations, we can know that we are relating and praying to God the Mother and God the Father, in whose image we are created. We can know that God will protect us with His strength and wisdom and envelop us in Her compassion and love.

Then, we can find and touch that most deep and intimate place within ourselves, that hidden place that makes us who we are, that sacred place that tells us of what we are made and what we might become.

By acknowledging the masculine and feminine in God and by seeing the reflection of God's masculine and feminine within each of us, we can affirm and celebrate an irrefutable fact of modern Jewish life: that so much of Judaism, which for so long has seemed closed off to so many women, is now fully open and accessible, for in all its aspects, ever-evolving Judaism now requires and rejoices in the absolute equality of every human being.

There is no way to excuse or make up for the historical dominance of the Jewish male or for the pain brought to bear on Jewish women by the exclusiveness of the past. But evolving consciousness and moral right make it imperative that contemporary Judaism—and, surely, Judaism's coming new era, which proclaims and honors the inherent and infinite worth of each human being in relationship with God—be completely inclusive and unequivocally egalitarian.

In learning, in prayer, in ritual, on the pulpit, and at every level of participation and leadership, women and men stand equally before God and as equals within the Jewish community.

Created in God's image and reflecting God's all-encompassing being, we recognize that we are all God's children and that we are all God's humble, joyful—and selfsame—partners. With this newfound understanding, which goes far beyond its original intent but uses wisdom gathered and refined by the ages, we confirm and celebrate the Talmud's teaching that "what is permitted one Jew is permitted all Jews" (BT Betzah 25a).

To help us call upon God—and in some reflective way to call to ourselves—beyond the boundaries and limitations of old language, we can call God *Shechinah*. Sweetly and gently chant Her name over and over again, and She will come.

Again, Reb Shlomo's music helps.

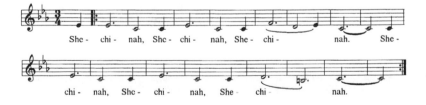

Once we expand our God-sense by bringing *Shechinah* into our beings, we can come to know God in many, many more ways—by many more names and attributes, by the fullness of His/Her being.

Connecting with God

This modern prayer calls us to the multidimensional, multifaceted God.

O God, because You are the source of all life and being,
We call You Creator.

Because we know the history of Your presence among Your people,
We call You Lord.

Because we know You intimately as parent,
We call You Father.

Because You are present at the act of birth, and because You shelter,
nurture, and care for us,
We call You Mother.

Because You give us strength and courage when we are in need,
We call You Sustainer.

Because we have known You in our pain and suffering,
We call You Comforter.

Because beyond pain lies Your promise of all things made new,
We call You Hope.

Because You are the means of liberation and the way to freedom,
We call You Deliverer.

Because You guide us to a world of goodness and peace,
We call You Redeemer.

Confident that You will hear, we call upon You
With all the names that make You real to us.

The names that create an image in our minds and hearts,
An image that our souls can understand and touch.

And, yet, You are much more than all these names,
You are more than we will ever know or comprehend.

You are our God, in heaven and earth.
You are our God, now and forever.

When we touch God in all His/Her fullness—and reflect God's being in our own beings—we can feel part of the wholeness of the universe and come much closer to achieving the holiness that comes from being one of God's precious children—created in God's image—here on earth.

3

The Jewish Mantra

A STORY FOR THEN AND NOW.

The date: October 1913. The place: Berlin, Germany. The time: the eve of Yom Kippur, the Day of Atonement, the holiest day of the Jewish year.

A twenty-six-year-old man named Franz Rosenzweig resolutely walked into an Orthodox synagogue.

Rosenzweig had been born a Jew, but his highly secular academic training, which had recently earned him a doctorate in philosophy, informed and influenced him far more than the faith of his heritage. As many of his relatives and friends already had done, he was on the brink of converting to Christianity, for being part of the prevailing religion and culture, he reasoned, would be far more advantageous to his intellectual pursuits and academic career than remaining part of a tiny minority mired in ancient beliefs and practices.

Yet he did not want to come to Christianity casually or by default. He wanted to come, as he understood it, authentically—not as a "pagan" or as a Jew "breaking away" from Judaism, but rather as a Jew "coming through" Judaism to embrace the "new covenant" of Christianity. So, like many of the first-century Christians who had come to the church through the synagogue, Franz Rosenzweig determined that his path to Christianity should lead through the synagogue, where he would say farewell to Judaism during Yom Kippur services.

But something happened.

Perhaps it was the powerful words of the liturgy; perhaps it was the haunting melodies; perhaps it was the inspiring message of Rabbi Markus Petuchowski, the grandfather—he so delighted in telling us—of our late and much-beloved rebbe and teacher, Dr. Jakob Petuchowski. But whatever occurred in that synagogue during the long hours of Yom Kippur utterly transformed Franz Rosenzweig.

When he left that synagogue and those services, he dismissed his plans to convert to Christianity and instead lovingly embraced his Judaism.

Franz Rosenzweig went on to become one of the leading and most influential Jewish thinkers and theologians of the twentieth century. His classic work, *The Star of Redemption,* became the blueprint for the understanding and practice of modern non-Orthodox Judaism. At the same time, it opened the doors to meaningful theological dialogue between Jews and Christians.

Franz Rosenzweig, the German intellectual who was ready to utterly forsake Judaism, became, instead, the "grandfather" of the modern Jewish renaissance—all because of a Yom Kippur service.

Wouldn't it be wonderful if the synagogue service, the liturgy, the prayers, the music could have that kind of effect on us?

We come to the synagogue seeking the sacred, we come to the synagogue wanting to connect with God, but few of us ever have that kind of powerful experience that transcends and transforms.

A good part of the problem is that we have ignored or we have forgotten what prayer really is and what it is supposed to do.

Prayer has two main purposes, two main functions: to help the pray-er connect to God, and to help the pray-er communicate with God.

It was for exactly these two purposes that the Jewish worship service was originally structured.

The Jewish service has two main components: the recitation of *Sh'ma Yisrael*—"Hear O Israel, the Eternal is our God, the Eternal is One"—which is for connecting to God, and the recitation of the *amidah* (more about this prayer in the next chapter), which is for communicating with God. Everything else in the Jewish service leads up to or away from these two elements.

The modern problem is that both *Sh'ma Yisrael* and the *amidah* have lost their purpose, their role, their meaning.

Here is the instruction so often heard from the pulpits of American synagogues during the past several decades (page numbers differ depending on the denomination and prayerbook):

"Turn to page sixteen. We rise to recite the 'declaration of our faith,' *Sh'ma Yisrael.*" (The congregation stands, sings, sits, reads the next paragraph in unison—sometimes in Hebrew, sometimes in English translation, sometimes in Hebrew followed by the English—and then sits in silence for a moment or two while the more traditional folks mumble some more Hebrew.) The rabbi continues: "We turn to page eighteen and read responsively, 'True and certain it is. . . .'"

Sh'ma Yisrael whizzes by, recited almost entirely by empty rote and dull routine, with little thought and little meaning.

Most worshipers understand *Sh'ma Yisrael,* as we have been taught to do since childhood, as the affirmation of the existence, the eternal unity, and the indivisible oneness of the Eternal God; the declaration of the Jewish People's faith and belief, enduring commitment, and unswerving loyalty to our God, the God of our ancestors, the God of our descendants—the God of always and forever.

The problem is that a "declaration" is merely a statement based in intellect and reason. Declaring belief, commitment, and loyalty may be intellectually satisfying, but it does not necessarily touch heart or soul; it does not necessarily respond to the yearning of the spirit.

The real purpose and the real role of *Sh'ma Yisrael* have been forgotten.

For when it is used correctly, when it is used as it was originally intended, *Sh'ma Yisrael,* with its simple words holding tremendous energy and power, can be the channel into the world of the spirit. It can be the gateway, the connector, to God.

Sh'ma Yisrael is the Jewish mantra.

A mantra—best known from the Eastern religions, especially the Hindu *ohm*—is a phrase to be repeated over and over again that enables focus and concentration, that helps the pray-er or meditator come into connection with the higher self and with God.

Some contend that *Sh'ma Yisrael* should be recited once and only once, for a "declaration of faith" is firm and unequivocal and need not be repeated. But when *Sh'ma Yisrael* is seen, instead, as the Jewish mantra, to be repeated over and over again, it is understood and used as the way to connect to God through clear focus and deep concentration.

Intuitively, traditional Jews have always understood *Sh'ma Yisrael* in this role. If it were a simple declaration of faith, it would be said standing tall and proud, chest puffed out, eyes straight ahead. But when traditional Jews recite *Sh'ma Yisrael,* it is with hands over eyes, with eyes closed. Concentrating on connecting with God is not to be disrupted by any outside distractions.

Reciting *Sh'ma Yisrael* over and over and over again has the soothing and the compelling purpose of quieting the mind and focusing its attention, of moving the mind from the level of mundane thought to the level of higher consciousness. It is the way to concentrate on finding and sustaining the connection to God, entering into God's presence, coming into deep and intimate relationship with God. Reciting *Sh'ma Yisrael* not just once or twice but over and over and over again is the way to touch and be touched by God.

Together as a community—for there is great power and energy in a prayer community—and alone in quiet, intimate quest, we can invite God into our lives.

To slowly, meditatively move into "God-space," some may choose to first invoke God's universal and eternal presence by calling Him *Ribono Shel Olam,* the Master of the World, thus acknowledging God's masculine attributes of power and strength; and then by calling Her *Shechinah,* the Sheltering Presence, thus acknowledging God's feminine attributes of nurturing and compassion.

Close your eyes, breathe deeply, and, then over and over and over again, quietly, sweetly, compellingly sing *Ribono Shel Olam,* and then over and over again, sing *Shechinah.*

Rabbi David Zeller's music helps us. Here is his chant for *Ribono Shel Olam.* Reb Shlomo's *Shechinah* chant is the same as the one we learned in the last chapter, invoking the feminine aspect of God.

Sing each musical motif, with each name of God, five, six, ten times.

Ri- bo- no shel o - lam,   Ri- bo- no shel o- lam,   Ri-

bo- no shel o- lam,   Ri- bo- no   shel o - - - lam.

Now, sing *Sh'ma Yisrael* over and over and over and over again, five, ten, twenty times or more.

Speak, at the very same time, to your community and to yourself:

"Sh'ma Yisrael," "Hear, O Israel . . . ": "You, my friends, and me, my heart, my soul, my being: Listen up; listen carefully; pay closest attention."

"Adonai Elohenu," "The Eternal is our [my] God . . . ": "I call upon You, O God, to come to be with me; to let me come into Your presence; to fill my being with Your light and Your love."

"Adonai Echad," "The Eternal is One": "I feel the complete unity of all things—You, O God, and me and every human being, every living thing, the earth on which we live, the stars and the planets, and

every particle of Your creation. You are One and everything is One with You."

Sing *Sh'ma Yisrael* in *nusach America,* the familiar *Sh'ma* prayer melody that is used in almost every American synagogue. Or, better yet, sing it in the original Torah cantillation. Feel the power of the music itself enhancing the experience—its poignant sound resonating across the millennia, its rich desertlike sound vibrating deep within you, its ancient sound as familiar as your own name, as intimate as a lover's gentle caress.

Finally, over and over and over again—ten, twenty, fifty times say the name *"Adonai Elohenu,"* "the Eternal our God."

Calling God by name, invoking God's being, not only acknowledges God's identity but also asks God to come close, to enter into intimate relationship. Calling God by name asks God to be your friend, your counsel, your comfort, your guide.

After reciting *Sh'ma Yisrael* in this way over and over and over again, using it mantralike to focus and concentrate on connecting to God, then, *sit in silence.*

Sit in silence for five, ten, fifteen minutes or more.

Give the connection enough time to take hold; feel God's all-enveloping presence; be bathed in God's radiant light; let your heart and soul be touched by God's overwhelming love.

You are with God.

Begin to formulate the words that you want to speak to God, and attune your hearing so that you can listen when God speaks to you.

Come up from the depths of silence slowly and gently, but do not let go of the connection.

You are with God.

From out of the sounds of silence, quietly remind yourself of your place and your mission: "You shall love the Lord your God with all your heart, all your soul, all your might . . . and you shall teach your children . . ." how to find God and how to be with God.

You are with God—and God is with you.

With *Sh'ma Yisrael* as the Jewish mantra, we, as Franz Rosenzweig once did, go back to our source and find ourselves there waiting to be found.

With *Sh'ma Yisrael,* we recapture the purpose, the meaning, the wonder of Jewish prayer.

With *Sh'ma Yisrael,* we come into God's presence; we make the delicate connection; we forge the powerful bond.

With *Sh'ma Yisrael,* we are assured that we can "dwell in the house of the Lord all the days of our lives" (after Psalms 23:6).

Now we are ready for the next step, the communication with God, the talking and the listening, the being and the doing.

Now we are ready to ask God to "listen to our voices" and to "answer us when we call."

4

Jewish Meditation

When was the last time you spoke to God?

When was the last time God spoke to you?

Talking to God, hearing from God, can be an everyday occurrence for every one of us, just like communicating with our husbands or our wives, our parents or our children, our neighbors or our friends.

It is just that the form and the format of Divine conversation is a bit different from human discourse.

When God talked with our ancient ancestors, it was most often through nighttime dreams or visions, and it was always at a time that was ripe for hearing.

It is highly unlikely Isaiah or Jeremiah was just walking down the street, going about his everyday business, when God called out, "Yo, Isaiah. Listen up. Jeremiah. I'd like to have a word with you."

Rather, when God appeared to them, the prophets and seers were most likely in a deep meditative state, with their thoughts and minds focused and concentrated on making connection and hearing God.

To hear God for the first time, Moses, the greatest prophet of them all, had to be drawn to a bush that burned and burned but was not consumed. He had to gaze steadily and deeply into that never-ending flame, focusing his entire being on the wondrous sign, before he could hear the voice of God.

❧

The long-ago sages who articulated the Oral Law knew that each one of us wants to talk to and hear from God, but, in establishing their own authority as the sole inheritors of God's continuing revelation, they also wanted to squelch individual claims of direct prophecy.

So, as they structured the thrice-daily worship service (which took the place of the animal and agricultural sacrifices at the Holy Temple), they set aside times for quiet meditation, for personal communication between each one of us and God. They hoped that these fixed periods of carved-out time, dedicated to entering into a meditative state, would provide the sacred time and the holy space for communicating with God. Their theological agenda was clear: personal communication with God could still be possible—and even encouraged—but it would be well controlled and regulated.

At the same time, the sages understood the vagaries of human nature. They knew that on some days we might be busy or tired or out of sorts, and that we would not have the time or the energy to talk to God. They knew that on some days, even if we tried hard, we just might not be able to feel the connection with God. And they knew that on some days, we just might not have anything to say to God.

And the sages reasoned that if we did not connect and talk with God often enough, we might become frustrated or we might lose interest, and we might give up trying to talk to God altogether. So the sages prepared a fixed set of words for us to say to God on the days when we just could not or did not have anything to say ourselves. In these words, they tried to reflect the whole of the human condition and to encapsulate the whole of the human relationship with God: our desire to offer praise and thanks, our need to petition and request.

This portion of the service became known as the *amidah,* which means "standing," because when we come before the awesome and holy God, we stand in respect and reverence.

The problem is that over the centuries, the recitation of the fixed prayer of the *amidah* took on a life of its own. People forgot that the *amidah* was just a replacement for their own direct and personal conversation with God. The *amidah* prayer began to be treated as the supreme spiritual exercise, while the true intent—the spiritual uplift that comes from coming to God with our own words and our own yearnings—got lost.

That is why, like its partner in the prayer service, *Sh'ma Yisrael,* the *amidah* has become for many—especially in our generation—little more than a rote and empty recitation: the long-ago written words do not resonate within us, and we have forgotten, or we never knew, that this was the rubric where we are to come to God with our own words.

For many of us, our "God-talk" remains unspoken, and "God's talk" remains unheard.

Yet our souls still yearn for those deep and intimate moments when we can come to God with the outpouring of our hearts and when we can hear the love-filled voice of God enveloping our beings. We fervently want the real and immediate experience of God.

So to learn how to communicate with God, to enter into dialogue with God, we return to our roots; we learn from Moses and Isaiah and Jeremiah how to be sourced by God, how to talk to God, how to listen when God talks to us.

Like our ancestors of old, we can come to God through meditation.

To many, *meditation* sounds like a very New Age word and concept. It conjures up images of people in long beards and sandals sitting cross-legged on the floor.

Actually, meditation is practiced in many different forms by people of various faiths and cultures.

Many meditators seek to quiet and clear the mind by "turning off" the constant flow of thoughts that pass through. These random and spontaneous thoughts, which some have termed "monkey chatter," come from the unconscious, the part of the mind that is not controlled by the will. If these thoughts can be controlled, the unconscious mind can be tamed, and more and more of the thought process can reside in the conscious mind. Thus the meditator achieves more and more self-mastery and, by will, can direct thinking. With greater control over the thought process, the meditator can develop the ability to focus and concentrate more fully. Since by most estimates we use no more than

15 percent of our mind's capacities, through meditation, more and more of the conscious mind, our brain power, can be used.

Other meditators use contemplative meditation to focus concentration, to purge the body and mind of its chaotic energy, to clarify the mind, and to rebalance the physical, mental, and spiritual. In this way, the mind is left clear to perceive in a more refined way, and deeper clarity emerges. Coming out of the meditation, the meditator can affirm the future—be it the next hour, the next day, the next plan—from the higher state of consciousness achieved through the meditation.

Still other meditators, especially those in the Buddhist tradition, use the meditation process to dissolve the illusion—as they understand it—that there is any permanency to self and to life. The goal of this kind of meditation is to be fully mindful and aware of all that life has to offer but to remain detached and uninvested.

For many, meditation also provides heightened awareness of sight, sound, smell, touch, and human experience. It also helps the meditator reach for the higher consciousness, the higher self, where universal truths and universal archetypes reside.

✺

We Jews can admire and honor all the meditative forms and practices of the other faiths and cultures, but we need not turn to them in order to meditate. For meditation is not for them alone. Meditation is actually very, very Jewish.

We learn in the book *Jewish Meditation,* from the great scholar and mystic of our time, Rabbi Aryeh Kaplan, the revered rebbe who died at such a young age—because, his disciples feel, he was revealing too much too soon, and God said, "Not yet": "There is ample evidence that meditative practices were widespread among Jews throughout Jewish history. References to meditation are found in major Jewish texts in every period from the biblical to the modern era. . . .

"One reason that this has not been universally recognized is that the vocabulary of meditation has been lost to a large degree, especially during the last century. Until the rise of the Jewish Enlightenment, mysticism and intellectualism had equal status within Judaism. The ostensible goal of the Enlightenment was to raise the intellectual level of Judaism. . . . [but] it was often at the expense of other Jewish values. The first values to fall by the wayside were Jewish mysticism in general and meditation in particular. Anything that touched upon the mystical was denigrated as superstition and occultism. . . . All references to meditation vanished from mainstream Jewish literature about 150 years ago. . . .

"When I speak to young Jews and ask them why they are exploring other religions instead of their own, they answer that they know nothing deep or spiritually satisfying in Judaism. . . . I tell them that *there is a strong tradition of meditation and mysticism, not only in Judaism, but in mainstream Judaism. . . .*

"Furthermore, since Judaism is an eastern religion that migrated to the west, its meditative practices may well be those most relevant to western man . . ." (italics mine).

For Jewish meditators, all meditation-purposes are worthy and worthwhile. But Jewish meditation has an even greater goal.

Through Jewish meditation, we strive for what the sages called כונה *kavanah,* the directing of consciousness; the aiming for higher consciousness; the true, deep spiritual intention; the highest spiritual connection.

Jewish meditation is our pathway to God.

We are always in the presence of God, for as the late great Abraham Joshua Heschel taught, "All it takes is God, a soul, and a moment. And the three are always here."

But through Jewish meditation, we come into alignment, attunement, at-one-ment with God. We come into God's "energy field": we get onto God's "wavelength"; we enter into God's "light-sphere." We open ourselves to become a conduit to God and a clear channel from God. We become a sacred vessel to be filled up by God.

Through Jewish meditation we can achieve the highest state of closeness and unity, what the sages called דביקות *devekut,* "cleaving to God," blending and melding with the Divine.

We need, of course, to be cautious.

In our journey to God, Rabbi Heschel warned that we do not want to become the mystic who seeks to become one with God. We seek to know God, to communicate with God, to be part of God's whole-world design of infinite unity. But becoming one with God would make us God, and that, of course, is impossible. This is a place where the Jewish mystical quest is clearly distinct and divergent from some of the so-called New Agers who seek undifferentiated oneness with God.

Heschel also warned that we do not want to be the ecstatic who seeks to separate mind from body in finding God. Nor do we want to be the psychotic who goes mad in the quest. We even need to be cautious about being the poet, lest we confuse our intent with God's intent, lest we think that our will is God's will.

We want to be what Heschel taught that we can all be—prophets who can find God, know God, be in relationship with God, be sourced by God, talk to God, hear the word and will of God, and be God's messengers here on earth. Or, if at the beginning that sounds too grandiose or unattainable, then the Talmud reminds us, "If they are not prophets, then at least they are the children of prophets" (BT Pesachim 66a & 66b).

≈❖≈

In-depth study of Jewish meditation can come, first, from sacred texts, and can be enhanced by modern-day masters. The finest contemporary teaching is from Rabbi Aryeh Kaplan's book *Jewish Meditation: A Practical Guide.*

The very best way to learn to meditate is to get a *rebbe,* a teacher—an expert in meditative practice who is steeped in Jewish learning, someone who has a fully developed, intimate relationship with God.

There are many Jewish meditation practices and techniques that have been developed over the centuries, especially by the Kabbalists and the Chasidim. Here are but a few of Jewish meditation's basic principles, some general ground rules and beginning techniques.

One of the strands of Jewish meditation is known as התבודדות *hitbodedut,* which is best translated as "self-isolation." Meditating means carving out the time and the place to be away from any external distractions. But, even more, meditating means moving beyond the internal surface level from which most of us conduct our lives and "going deep inside" to the deepest and most sacred place beyond ego and identity, character and disposition.

The Chasidic Rebbe Nachman of Bratslav taught, *"Hitbodedut"*—inner-directed, unstructured, active self-expression before God—"is the highest path of all. Take it."

Conversation with God through Jewish meditation does not happen haphazardly or casually. It takes both desire and discipline.

Meditation will take at least fifteen or twenty minutes a day; a half hour or more is optimum.

Meditation should be done every day, at the same time each day. Make it a habit, a routine.

Pick a quiet place for meditation, a place to be alone without any disturbance from the "outside world," such as a ringing telephone or crying children.

This meditation place should be comfortable and airy. Some may choose a place amid the beauty of nature, which inspires lofty thought. For others, it will be a stark, plain room, without visual distractions. For still others, the room will be embellished with color, paintings, or drawings that direct the senses.

There are some powerful symbols that can be used to help focus thought and direct meditation. The six-pointed star, especially when it is in the center of a circle, is an ancient symbol of mystical and magical powers. Because its points, formed by the intersection of two interconnected inverted triangles, emanate out in every direction, the star is thought to encompass and envelop the entire universe. Since the six-

pointed star has been popularly known, for almost three thousand years, as the Star of David or the Jewish Star, its inherent power and its Jewish association make it a very useful and compelling symbol for guiding thought and entering into meditation.

One of the yantras, well-known Hindu symbols that help focus meditation, is a set of six-pointed stars superimposed on one another and interconnected with one another. Obviously, there is no original Jewish meaning or connection to this symbol, which belongs to another religion. Yet it can be no accident that two seemingly disparate faiths have found inherent power and spiritual energy in this universal, yet particularly identified, symbol. By staring at the interlinked, seemingly infinite star pattern, and by being drawn

into its center core, thought can be directed toward the infinite source, and meditation can be enhanced and intensified.

The most authentic Jewish symbol for guiding thought and enhancing meditation is a שויתי *Shiviti,* which means "I place," from the psalm that says, "I place God before me always" (Psalms 16:8). It is a beautiful artist's rendering of the four-letter name of God. By staring at the *Shiviti,* thoughts can be directed right toward God, for God is "placed right before me." This *Shiviti* by the contemporary artist Betsy Platkin Teutsch is especially compelling.

Wherever it is—and whatever symbols best facilitate the meditative quest—pick the environment that is most comfortable and supportive and make it your regular setting for meditation.

꙳꙳꙳

Know that coming into communication with God and, certainly, coming into intimate relationship with God will not happen with the first or second or, perhaps, even the tenth meditation. It takes time; the relationship unfolds and develops slowly. Have patience; have determination. Do not give up. Keep meditating; keep trying to reach God. Let the practice engulf you; let the process flow through you.

Begin each meditation by breathing deeply and slowly. Feel *ruach,* the breath of the universe, the breath of God, filling you up. Breathe in time, in sync, with the universal breath.

Use the *Sh'ma Yisrael* mantra to focus, to concentrate, to guide, to lead toward God. Say the words, sing the words over and over and over again, gently, sweetly, compellingly.

Choose, if you wish, your own additional mantra—another name of God, a Hebrew letter, a Hebrew word, a short biblical or liturgical phrase—that brings you more and more focus, that deepens concentration, that brings you closer and closer to God.

Do not be discouraged when "monkey chatter" gets in the way; it always will, even for the most experienced and adept meditators. Come back to the *Sh'ma Yisrael* mantra, come back to your own mantra. Refocus. Go deeper inside so that you can go higher.

If it helps, visualize where you are going. In your mind's eye, see your journey. There is a long way to go; obstacles get in your way, but the destination glitters and beckons. See God's dwelling as you conceive it. Perhaps, as the holy Zohar has it, it is a grand palace or a heavenly paradise; perhaps it is at a beautiful seashore, a cool forest, or a soaring mountaintop; perhaps it is in the wispy clouds of the blue, blue sky. Your rational mind knows that you are anthropomorphizing, since God doesn't look like us or live where we might. But the image may work for you; it may make the journey and the destination more real.

Before listening, talk. Talk your "God-talk."

Tell God your gladness and your joy; tell God your sadness, your hurt, your pain.

Tell God your doubts, your worries, your fears.

Tell God your needs, your wants, your desires.

Tell God your hopes, your yearnings, your aspirations.

To hear answers, first ask questions.

Ask about the great mysteries of the universe, the vast unknown, the hidden and secret, the perplexing and as yet unanswered questions of life and death.

Ask about the purpose of existence and about your own purpose, your task, your mission here in this lifetime on earth.

Ask for a melding, a unity, with all that is wise, all that is beautiful, all that is meaningful.

Ask for what the sages, in another strand of meditative practice, called התבוננות *hitbonenut,* "self-understanding." Delve deeply into your psyche and your soul; come to understand what drives you, what motivates you; understand your hungers, your passions. Examine who you are and why you are what you are. Ask that a measure of all of God's positive attributes be reflected in you.

Ask the way toward health and well-being.

Ask for guidance and good counsel.

Ask for wisdom and enlightenment, harmony and inner peace.

Ask to be bathed in God's light; and ask to be a reflector of God's light.

And, then, listen.

Listen very carefully, because God's answers, "God's talk," can come in many different ways.

You may hear God's voice.

Or you may hear the voice of one of God's angels.

Or you may hear the voice of one of your spirit guides.

Or you may hear your own voice—the voice that you think is yours but that may really be God's.

Or you may hear your own thoughts—the thoughts that you think are yours but that may really be God's.

Or you may hear God-inspired words or thoughts that come through your hand to paper or canvas.

Or you may hear God through the sounds of silence.

Or you may see God's word in a dream or a vision.

Or you may see God reflected in the face of another.

Or, looking in the mirror, you may see God reflected in your own face.

You may experience God through what seems to be chance or co-incidence, and you will know that, for God, there is no such thing as chance or coincidence.

We do not want to leave God's immediate presence abruptly or rudely, so we will want to come out of meditation gently and gracefully. As we slowly return to fully conscious wakefulness, we can remind ourselves where and with whom we have been by softly reciting the words of Psalm 121, *Esa Enai.*

I lift up my eyes unto the mountain. From where comes my help?
My help comes from the Lord, Creator of heaven and earth.

The words echo deeply within when they are quietly sung in the well-known melody of the sweet singer Reb Shlomo Carlebach.

Does Jewish meditation work?

Jewish meditation sends energy out to the universe and brings that energy—life-affirming, life-enhancing energy—back to us.

Jewish meditation puts us into God's presence, and in God's presence, anything—everything—is possible.

We now have scientific proof for what we already intuitively knew about meditation, about meditative prayer. In his pathbreaking book, *Healing Words: The Power of Prayer and the Practice of Medicine,* Dr. Larry Dossey documents case after case where prayer and meditation worked in bringing higher rates of healing, swifter regression of disease, and even faster and better growth of seeds and plants.

Jewish meditation assures that we can truly communicate with God: that we can always talk to God, that God will always listen, and that God will always answer.

The answer that God gives may not be what we wanted or expected, and we may very well feel confused, hurt, rejected. While we may not know or understand God's eternal plan (and while a complete discussion of the question of God's response to prayer is in "An Essay on Prayer" in my book *Living Judaism: The Complete Guide to Jewish Belief, Tradition, and Practice),* when we are in continuing conversation and mutual relationship with God, then God will often give us a glimpse of the unknown, a hint of the secrets, an inkling of the infinite, and we will know that there is a cosmic order to all that happens, that there is perfection in God's grand design.

Jewish meditation is the pathway and the channel by which we can come to know God as our creator and protector, our strength and comfort, our confidante and friend.

We can ask God for a full measure of Divine knowledge, wisdom, insight, courage, and compassion.

We can bring God our anguish and our yearnings, our dreams and our commitments.

We can share with God our joys and our triumphs; we can ask God to share the burdens of our sorrows and tragedies.

We can turn to God for instruction, guidance, and direction.

We can feel God touching us with Divine spirit.

And we can be filled with God's light and love.

We can know that God knows us and cares about us and cares for us and watches over us and wants the best for us.

We can hear God's words of advice and good counsel; we can hear God's words of encouragement and support.

We can experience God hugging us in celebration and catching our tears of sadness.

We can listen to God calling to us with our destiny, challenging us with our life-task, and inspiring us with our life-mission.

We can be absolutely sure that God is our constant companion, our best friend, our greatest and most ardent ally.

And always, always, we can know that God loves us—unconditionally, passionately, overwhelmingly.

≈✦≈

And, so, our prayer is the prayer of our ancestors of old. It is spoken with the same sincerity and the same urgency; it is spoken with new understanding and new passion:

> *May the words of our mouths and the meditations of our hearts*
> *be ever acceptable unto you, O God.*
> *Accept our prayerful meditation, O God,*
> *and answer us with Your great mercy and with Your saving truth.*

And to our prayer, we hear God and all the Divine beings joyously and fervently proclaiming:

> *Amen and Amen.*

Jewish Ecstasy

WHERE DO WE FIND THE MOST VIBRANT, THE most inspiring, the most soul-satisfying worship services?

For a long time the answer was simple: at Jewish summer camps, at youth group gatherings, and in a few Junior Congregations.

There youngsters sing and learn together, they clap their hands to the music, grasp shoulders and sway to the melody, and feel the joy of coming before God. They experience what the psalmist of old advised:

Shout out to the God all the earth.
Serve the Lord with gladness.
Psalms 100:1–2

And then?

Then they come back home to their own synagogues where—despite the rare soul-inspiring moment or the occasional intellectually stimulating sermon—the service is usually formal and cold, where they are sung at and preached to, and where almost no one smiles.

They learn well how to be serious and sad, how to lament, mourn, and say *kaddish,* but they rarely learn how to be lithesome and happy, how to rejoice, celebrate, and say *hallel.*

And they are bewildered. "Where," they ask, "is the fervor, the excitement, the joy, of the services at camp or convention? Isn't there some way we can translate the warmth, the exhilaration, the spirit, of those services into our synagogues, into our daily lives?"

The answer can be a resounding yes.

If synagogue worship services remain dreary and dull, then, individually and collectively, in our small prayer and meditation groups, we can set out to recapture the spirit that inspires us and moves us toward God. Our questing hearts and our yearning souls can be uplifted and inspired, transformed and transcendent.

We now know that one of the ways we can come to God is in the quiet of contemplative meditation.

But just as well, just as meaningfully, just as powerfully, we can come to God in jubilation, in exultation, in ecstasy. We can animate our own souls with gladness, and we can come to God in the fullness of joy.

Come into God's presence with songs of joy.
Psalms 100:3

The prophet tells us that the angels in heaven stand at opposite ends of the firmament and, back and forth to each other, shout out praise of God: "Holy, holy, holy is the Lord of hosts. The whole earth is full of God's glory" (Isaiah 6:3). By singing this praise, these angels— the seraphim, by name—create the vibration of love that emanates from God's throne and fills the universe.

The first way to approach God in ecstasy is by singing with throbbing excitement, with unleashed jubilance, with a rapture that transports you to the heights of passion.

We already know the importance of Jewish song. The *nusach,* the mode and melody of prayer, is deeply entrenched and embedded in the Jewish psyche. While there are differences between Ashkenazic and Sephardic musical settings, the *nusach* establishes and identifies the day, the time of day, and the observance of Shabbat, holy days, and festivals. Many Jews who may not know the words to a certain prayer will know its familiar melody, a melody that evokes the whole of the Jewish experience, that deeply touches spirit and soul, and that inspires a joyful journey to God.

Sing.

Rabbi Nachman of Bratslav taught, "The most direct means for attaching ourselves to God from this material world is through music and song, so even if you can't sing well, sing. Sing to yourself. Sing in the privacy of your own home. But sing."

Sing from the depths of your being, at the top of your voice. Clap your hands to the rhythm; stomp your feet to the beat. Let loose; throw away your inhibitions and your restraints. Let the pulse of the music become your pulse. Feel the resonance deep inside, and let your spirit and your soul soar to the greatest heights.

Sing the words of the prayers, sing the *nusach,* the traditional mode and melody of prayer; or sing the modern melodies and tunes that have been composed in recent years.

The words and the intent of some of the prayers of the traditional liturgy beg to be sung in joyous melody. For example, the introductory, warm-up prayers of the morning service are filled with words of praise and thanksgiving to God. These prayers are not to be hurriedly mumbled but to be warmly and richly sung. On festivals, the *hallel* psalms are added to the service to acknowledge and celebrate the specialness of the day. They are not to be chanted in a slow, stately manner; rather, they are to be sung in upbeat tempo with sounds of jubilation.

Sing to God, in a manner rooted in the ancient psalms and as contemporary as the spontaneous expression of our hearts, by singing the word הללויה *HalleluYah*, which means "Praise God."

This melody, which repeats the word *HalleluYah* over and over again, pulsates in song and praise. As you become more and more involved in the melody, as you get deeper and deeper into the song, singing louder and louder, faster and faster, with more and more passion, your enthusiasm, your soul-involvement, your love go right to God.

Ha- lle- lu- Yah, ha- lle- lu- Yah, ha- lle- lu- Yah, ha- lle- lu- Yah, ha- lle- lu- Yah, ha- lle- lu- Yah, ha- lle- lu- Yah, ha- lle- lu- Yah, ha- lle- lu- Yah, ha- lle- lu- Yah.

If you have no words, no words at all, then sing a wordless *niggun,* a lilting, joyous melody. Sing any one of the hundreds of Chasidic *niggunim,* or sing a modern chant. Without words, sing the sounds; sing "La-la-la-la"; sing "Ya-ba-ba-ba"; sing Hy-di-de-die di-de-die." Make a happy noise.

A *midrash* teaches that all the prayers that are recited to God are caught by the angels who encircle God's heavenly throne. The angels take the prayers and weave them into a crown—a golden crown that they place upon God's head. What better way is there for God's children to crown God than with shouts of gladness and songs of joy?

> *Praise God with the sound of the horn . . . with the psaltery and harp*
> *. . . with tambourine . . . with stringed instruments and the flute . . .*
> *with clanging, loud, resounding cymbals.*
> Psalms 150:3–5

From that moment when the Children of Israel stood dry and safe on the other side of the Sea of Reeds—when Miriam the prophetess took timbrel in hand—Jews have praised God with the sound of musical instruments.

There are at least nineteen specific musical instruments mentioned in the Bible. They were used throughout the liturgical life of the people: when the Ark of the Covenant was brought to Jerusalem; during the dedication of the Holy Temple services; during the coronation of kings; as part of spontaneous prayer, often led by women; and, most certainly, during the Second Temple period, as part of the worship rites. The majestic words of the psalms, most often attributed to King David, are best heard as they were probably written, reverberating to the soft sounds of David's harp.

With the destruction of the Second Holy Temple and the exile from the Land of Israel, musical instruments were banished from the emerging synagogue worship services. זכר לחרבן *Zecher l'chorban,* "in remembrance of the destruction," and in recognition that this people had been ripped away from its spiritual center and sent off to wander the earth, the joyous sounds of musical instruments were not to be heard as part of formal Jewish worship. Only with return and restoration would musical instruments once again take their rightful place in "making a happy noise" to God.

There are those today who still wait for the Holy Temple to be rebuilt before permitting the use of musical instruments during worship.

But for most the joyous, uplifting, and inspiring spiritual mood that music can produce brings the use of musical instruments back into our prayer places.

In the mid–nineteenth century, some liberal Jews began using the stately and full-voiced pipe organ to musically enhance worship. In recent years, stringed instruments such as the guitar and the cello and wind instruments such as the flute and the ancient *chalil* have been added.

What glorious sounds musical instruments make! How grand and majestic, how sweet and beautiful, how joyous they make prayer!

To your worship bring your guitar. Bring your drum. The drum is not only for Native Americans or for contemporary men who go into the woods to get in touch with their masculinity. The repetitious, syncopathic sound of the drum can be a spiritual call to all of us, for it reaches deep into our primal beings and sends through us ripples of Godly vibrations. Bring your trumpet, your tambourine, your flute, your cymbals, your bells. Bring instruments with soft, tender voices; bring instruments with full, loud voices; bring instruments that throb with cadence and tempo; bring instruments that pulsate with jingle and beat.

Be like our ancestors of old who "to the blessed God offered sweet melodies." Come to God with the melody, with sweet harmony, with rhythm. Pound out the sound; feel the sound. Feel the joy that the sound brings to you and to God.

Add the voice of the instruments to your own voice, for, as the mystics teach, "there is a palace in the heavens that is opened only through music."

Praise God with dance.
Psalms 150:4

There is a time for dancing.
Ecclesiastes 3:4

We know the feelings of deep joy and happiness that come from whirling around the bride and groom in the wedding dance. We know the unrestrained joy we feel dancing with the Torah Scrolls on Simchat Torah, celebrating the completion of another year of hearing and learning Torah and the privilege and honor of beginning all over again.

We know how the movement of dance makes us feel: light and airy, rising above the ordinary, floating above and beyond ourselves.

Why not use movement and dance to approach God every day? Why not make dance one of the sacred and joyous pathways to God?

In dance, as in song and in music, there is the pulsating beat and rhythm of existence, the excitement and jubilation of great rejoicing. But there is more. For dance involves the entire body; it is a whole and a holistic experience; it calls on every bone and muscle, every sinew and cell to praise God.

Traditional Jewish worship already involves a good deal of movement—bending, bowing, rising up on tiptoe. And during many of the prayers, especially those that are recited while standing, many Jews do not stand still but sway and move back and forth or side to side. This movement, called *shokeling*—usually much more spontaneous than planned—engages the whole body in the act of meditation and prayer.

In a more coordinated way, there are a number of well-known and popular Israeli dances that can be danced as part of a prayer service.

For example, on Friday evening the centerpiece prayer of the *Kabbalat Shabbat* service, the psalms and songs for welcoming the Sabbath, is *Lecha Dodi,* "Come my beloved . . . welcome the Sabbath bride." When this prayer was composed by the mystics, in the sixteenth century, in the town of Tzfat in the mountains of northern Israel, it was the custom to go out to the fields to greet the approaching Sabbath. Some four hundred years later, as the setting sun marks the beginning of Shabbat, these joyous dances are still danced by many sects of Chasidim. We, too, can dance—in the aisles of our synagogues, in the auditorium, in the sacred space of our prayer places, outdoors on the sidewalk, in the streets, in a park, or at the beach—to lovingly welcome the Sabbath day.

When singing the prayer *Mi Chamocha,* the prayer of praise to God that the Children of Israel sang at the Sea of Reeds, we can imitate their actions by dancing in joy and thanksgiving.

On Shabbat and festival mornings, when the Torah Scroll is taken from the Holy Ark, we can encircle it in song and dance.

As our worship services end, we can grasp hands in prayer and song, and we can break into joyous dance.

Our Oneg Shabbat or Kiddush, the time of greeting and socializing following the service, can be an extension of the worship. We do not just have to stand around drinking coffee and eating brownies, for we can continue to celebrate the day and praise God with dance and song.

Beyond the traditional dances, we can engage our bodies in new and meaningful movement.

An organization based in Seattle, Washington, called Dances of Universal Peace, unites groups of people throughout the world who regularly come together to dance using the sacred phrases, chants, music, and movements from the varied religious and spiritual traditions of the earth. The hope is that by combining people and practices from so many different yet, ultimately, similar traditions, universal life-energy and peace will take root.

Many of the dances taught by Dances of Universal Peace are sourced by Hebrew phrases from the Bible and the liturgy, including *Evdu HaShem B'Simchah,* "Serve the Lord with Gladness," *Kadosh, Kadosh, Kadosh,* "Holy, holy, holy is the Eternal," and *Baruch Kavod,* "Blessed is the glory of God." One of the simplest yet most powerful dances is to the continually repeated word *Shaddai,* a biblical name of God.

These simple circle dances, coming to us from an organization that honors our tradition as a source of joy and peace, are worth finding, exploring, and trying. They can bring newfound joy—as seen and affirmed through the eyes of others—to our heritage and traditions. And they can help us understand the truth articulated by the founder of the Dances of Universal Peace, Samuel L. Lewis, that "The dance is the way of life, the dance is the sway of life. What life gives may be expressed with body, heart, and soul to the glory of God and the elevation of humanity, leading to ecstasy and self-realization."

And we can visualize dancing with God.

We can see the letters of God's name floating sensually before our eyes, beckoning to us, enticing us to hold and hug God in the covenant of love.

We can embrace God in dance.

יהוה יהוה

The story is told that the holy Baal Shem Tov was dancing with the Torah Scroll on the joyous festival of Simchat Torah. He handed the Torah Scroll to someone else, but he continued to dance. His disciple said, "Our master has laid aside the visible dimensional teaching. He has taken the spiritual teaching unto himself."

Dancing with the invisible God may seem uncomfortable or awkward or even silly to some. But joyously dancing with God alters our consciousness; it brings us into close and deep relationship with God. It affirms God's ever-present place in our lives, and it confirms God's ever-enduring immediate and intimate involvement in our lives.

The old proverb teaches that they who dance are thought mad by those who do not hear the music. We hear the music. We can dance with God.

✼

Nachman of Bratslav insisted, "If you don't feel happy, pretend to be. If you are downright depressed, put on a smile. Act happy. Genuine joy will follow." For, Reb Nachman counseled, "Always remember: Joy is not merely incidental to your spiritual quest. It is vital."

You shall rejoice before the Lord your God.
Deuteronomy 12:12

Smile. Laugh. Cry tears of joy. Sing. Dance. Make beautiful music. Celebrate. Clap your hands. Stomp your feet. Let your soul soar to the heights of bliss and ecstasy.

For, as the modern philosopher taught, "Ecstasy means living in another. . . . You are living (if you have eyes to see) in God."

6

Body and Soul

TWO POWERFUL AND PROFOUND PRAYERS, WHICH are recited by traditional Jews each and every morning, tell us of our place in the universe and of our relationship to God.

> *My God, the soul you placed within me is pure. You created it, You fashioned it, You breathed it into me. You preserve and safeguard it within me. Eventually, You will reclaim it from me, but You will restore it to me in a time to come. As long as the soul is within me, I gratefully thank You, O God, my God and God of my ancestors, Master of all worlds, and of all souls. . . .*

And,

> *Blessed are You, O Eternal our God, Ruler of the universe, who fashioned human beings in wisdom, and created within us* נקבים *נקבים חלולים חלולים n'kavim, n'kavim, chalulim, chalulim, openings and cavities. It is obvious and well known before Your throne of glory that if but one of them were to be ruptured or but one of them were to be blocked, it would be impossible for us to survive and stand before You. . . .*

Of dust we are created. Our bodies are nothing more than a collection of earthly chemicals. Yet if our bodies did not function properly—if any of the cavities or openings were ruptured or shut—we would die, and we would not be able to do God's work here on earth.

At the same time, we are created "in the image of God" (Genesis 1:27), "just a little lower than the Divine" (Psalms 8:5). Our soul—that which makes us living, breathing human beings—is a spark of Divine light. "The candle—the spark, the light—of God is the soul of human beings" (Proverbs 20:27).

Judaism teaches no dichotomy of mind and body, no separation of flesh and spirit, no sense of superiority of one component over the other. Body and soul may be separate entities, but they are inseparably intertwined. They are, in the words of the poet Walt Whitman, "like two waves rolling over each other and inter-wetting each other."

The body without the soul is an empty, lifeless vessel; the soul without the body is energy unable to manifest purpose or direction here on this earth plane.

To exist, to be, we need both body and soul.

God has neither body nor soul as we know them.

The Kabbalists called God *Ein Sof,* which means "Without End." This God without beginning or end, this Infinite God, created the universe and everything in it, including us.

How are we finite human beings, with all our earthly limitations of time, space, and capacity, to know the limitless God? How are we to close the gap, to make the journey, between finitude and infinity?

We connect with God, we come to God, with both body and soul; we connect with God, we come to God, with the fullness of our being.

The mystics teach that there are four distinct yet completely interconnected worlds in which we live, four worlds between us and God. Understanding the place, process, and power of each of these four worlds helps us begin to transverse the distance between us and God.

ASSIYAH, which means "action," is the world of our physical body. Here, we live in and experience the material world of physical survival, needing things such as air, food, and water; manifesting the sexual urge to reproduce; and having very real sensations of pleasure and pain. *Assiyah* is our rootedness in the third dimension, the reality of being in body.

YETZIRAH, which means "formation," is the world of our emotional body. Here, we experience feelings and deep emotions; we are imaginative, creative; we dream and we perceive. *Yetzirah* is our gateway to the fourth dimension, to the level of psychic knowing.

BERIYAH, which means "creation," is the world of our mental body. Here we think, contemplate, and discern. *Beriyah* is our leap into the fifth and sixth dimensions, our attempt to understand and know God's plan and blueprint of creation

ATZILUT, which means "emanation" or "intuition," is the world of our spiritual body. Here, we go to the highest planes of pure being; we come to union with God, to beingness with God. We enter into the realm of God's Divine light; we are bathed in the emanation, the glow of that light; intuitively, we know the innermost hidden secrets of the universe; and then we reflect the light of God's presence. *Atzilut* is our merging with eternal, universal, knowledge; it is our being at one with God.

The soul is that which leads us on our inner journey to God, for our soul corresponds to—and, in one instance, expands upon—and reflects these four worlds of existence.

The soul has not four, but five, levels, radiating from the innermost level, the level of physical existence, to the outermost level, the level of union with God.

To best understand these five soul-levels, picture a candle.

NEFESH. At the base of the candle flame, the place closest to the wick, the fire burns hot blue. This is like the first level of the soul, the *nefesh,* the physical being, the place where the soul is filled with the energy of the universe and the vitality of being. This is our "felt-sense" and our action.

RUACH. The next level of the soul is *ruach,* the spirit of humanness, the qualities of uniqueness—of place, of presence, of self; our potential and our growth; the parts of our beings that are stirred by majestic sounds and sights in "soul" music, "soul" food, "soulful" love. It is our affect and our emotion. On the candle, *ruach* is the bright yellow and gold flame, which grows, expands, and illumines.

NESHAMAH. The third level of the soul is *neshamah,* human inspiration—our ability to think, to reason, to remember, to innovate, and to create. *Neshamah* is that which separates us from the animals, from anything else that is living; it makes us distinctly and uniquely human. It is our knowing through thought, our rational intellect, our evolving human consciousness. On the candle, *neshamah* is the flickering red-orange of the outer edge of the flame.

CHAYAH. The fourth level of the soul is *chayah,* the life force. *Chayah* is "isness," the nonverbal level of direct experience. How do we describe the color orange? How do we explain the unending vastness of the ocean? How do we tell about the love we feel for our children? *Chayah* is life beyond our current understanding, but it is, surely, the powerful life force, the will not just to live but to prevail. It motivates the soul not just "to do" but "to be." On the candle, *chayah* is the tiny flickers of black at the very, very edge of the flame. These flickers are part of the candle flame, but they are separate, already reaching toward eternity.

YACHIDAH. The fifth and final level of the soul is *yachidah,* the knowing beyond knowing, the intuition, the self of the self. *Yachidah* is the place where the singular, unique oneness of each soul crosses the abyss and knows that there is no distance to *Yachid,* the Infinite Oneness of God. It is, in the image of Martin Buber, the ultimate I-Thou, the eternal union, the merging of the human soul with God. On the candle, *yachidah* is the white-silver shiny glow that the flame creates around and above itself, being at one and the same time part of the fire and completely separated from the fire; part of the flame and part of the air; part of nothing except itself—flickering, glowing, reaching, stretching its way to the greater beyond where infinity's journey begins and never ends, over and over and over again.

To help visualize your soul—the source of our being, the vehicle for our journey to God—light a candle.

Look deeply into the multidimensional flame and flickers, and see your soul, see yourself, see your God.

For to know your soul is to know yourself.

To know your soul is to know your grand and glorious place in the universe, your precious spirit, your sacred journey, your holy destiny, your ultimately infinite and eternal being.

To know your soul is to know your God.

⚜

All the while that we are traversing the four worlds and the five levels of the soul on our journey to reach God, at the very same time, God is working to bridge the gap between the Infinite and the finite by reaching to us.

The mystics teach that between the Infinite and the finite—between God and us—are ten emanations or steps, which are called *sefirot.*

The word *sefirot* may simply come from the Hebrew word meaning "count," because we count the steps to God, but it may come from the Hebrew word meaning "sapphire," because the mystics visualized God's radiant light as the illumined brightness of a precious sapphire gem.

Many different images are used in an attempt to define and describe the *sefirot:*

- the spheres of light sent forth by God in the process of creating the world
- the aspects or the qualities or the powers that God used in creating the world
- the aspects or qualities or powers that God uses to continually govern the world
- the Divine powers of God as they appear to human beings
- the steps that emanate from God to the earthly world, in descending order
- the steps that are the pathway from us to God, in ascending order

- the links in the chain, or the rungs on the ladder, that connect God and human beings

The Kabbalists visualized these *sefirot* in a structured order and form, which they called the Tree of Life.

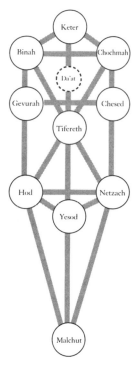

Since so much of mystical practice has been hidden away for so long, there is no one definitive understanding or interpretation of the *sefirot*. Indeed, some would say that there is more confusion than accord about the names, places, purposes, and meanings of each and all of the *sefirot*. Yet there is enough general agreement to make exploration and basic understanding possible, all the while knowing that there are those who offer differing or alternative designation and interpretation.

KETER, which means "crown," is the highest of all the *sefirot*. *Keter* is the will of God, and it is the acknowledgment of God as King of the Universe. The universe was created when God exerted the will to create.

CHOCHMAH, which means "wisdom," is God's contemplation, God's thought. There were many possible ways for God to create the universe. *Chochmah* is the process of God's choice through thought.

BINAH, which means "understanding," is God's decision of how best to create the universe, God's specific plan and course of action. *Binah* turns the contemplation of *chochmah* into implementation, into the act of creation.

This first triad, these first three *sefirot* combined, represent the mind of God.

In the image of the four worlds in which we live, these three *sefirot* reside in the world of *atzilut,* the spiritual world, the highest plane of pure being, the eternal oneness with God.

Some say that there is an unseen and uncounted "shadow" *sefirah,* or vessel of energy, just below the first triad, in the middle of the Tree of Life. This *sefirah* is called DA'AT, which means "knowledge," and is understood as the intermediary that synthesizes the qualities of the first three *sefirot.*

Below the first three *sefirot* on the Tree of Life, and below the shadow *sefirah* if it exists, is a set of three more *sefirot.*

CHESED, which means "mercy" or "lovingkindness" or is best translated as "unconditional covenantal love," is God's deepest love and widest compassion. *Chesed* is God in all God's goodness.

GEVURAH, which means "strength," is God's power of discernment between right and wrong, between darkness and light. *Gevurah* is sometimes known as DIN, which means "judgment," and in that sense is God's attribute of absolute justice. In its *din* context, *gevurah* is God's inscrutable—and, most often, stern and unrelenting—rectitude and punishment. Because it is on the left side of the Tree of Life, the left side of God, the side that is known as the *sitra achra,* the "other—or the dark—side" of God, in its *din* context, *gevurah* accounts for the existence of evil in our world.

In its own sense, *gevurah* is God's self-judgment, the giving, receiving, and balancing of often conflicting forces. *Gevurah* is the internal, inherent strength that it takes—even for God—to do self-evaluation and self-judgment, to discern between good and evil, to find the light even in the darkest moment. In this context, *gevurah* reminds us of the Talmudic account of the prayer that God says to Himself: "May it be My will that My attribute of mercy outweighs My attribute of strict justice" (BT Berachot 7a). Being on the left side of God, *gevurah* takes in, evaluates, and mediates the deep love and wide compassion coming from *chesed* on the right.

These two *sefirot* in opposition represent the didactic tension in our world, the constant struggle between evil and good, between justice and mercy, between chaos and order, between bewilderment and discernment, between vulgarity and refinement, between darkness and enlightenment. When the *sefirot* are in balance, the world can function, because the fine line between opposing forces is in delicate harmony. When they are out of balance, the world tips to one side or the other. If the world tips toward *gevurah,* then a tempest of unrest and upheaval can dominate. But if the world tips toward *chesed,* then God's goodness infuses existence.

TIFERETH, which means "beauty," is the harmony between *chesed* and *gevurah. Tifereth* balances the polar opposites, harmonizes the tensions, and brings equilibrium to the world. In addition to balancing and anchoring the five *sefirot* above it, *Tifereth* centers the four *sefirot* below it.

Some say that *Tifereth,* beauty, is the highest manifestation or presence of the Divine that human beings can glimpse during life on the earthly plane.

This second triad, these second three *sefirot* combined, represent the principles that God uses to rule the world, the basic principles of an ethical, moral world.

In the image of the four worlds in which we live, these three *sefirot* reside in the world of *beriyah,* the world of our mental body, the place where we contemplate and think, where we try to understand and know God's eternal plan.

Below these middle three *sefirot* on the Tree of Life is a set of three more *sefirot.*

NETZACH, which means "victory," is the attribute of God's everlasting endurance and mighty powers. It is the male aspect of God's being, the eternal aspects of form, and it represents nature's ability and power to increase and expand.

HOD, which means "glory" or "majesty," is the female attribute of God's being. It is the limiting aspect of nature, the reigning in of increase and expansion by decrease and contraction, the specific shape and appearance of eternal form.

Netzach is God's out-breath, the powerful energy of expansion and growth. *Hod* is God's in-breath, the equally powerful energy of drawing inward, of coming together. In the imagery of some Eastern traditions, *hod* is *yin,* the feminine aspect of the internal, the innermost intimacy, while *netzach* is *yang,* the masculine aspect of the external, the outward, emanating force.

YESOD, which means "foundation," is the harmony of nature, the balance between *netzach* and *hod,* between *yin* and *yang.* If the right side of the Tree of Life represents God's male attributes and the aspects of power and increase, and if the left side of the Tree of Life represents God's female attributes and the aspects of gentleness, forbearance, and limitation, then *yesod,* in the center, is the harmonizer and synthesizer. *Yesod* is the life force and balance of nature.

This third triad, these third three *sefirot* combined, represent the principles that God uses to rule the natural, physical world.

In the image of the four worlds in which we live, these three *sefirot* reside in the world of *yetzirah,* the world of our emotional body, where we experience feeling and emotion and where we perceive and imagine.

Centered below this final triad of *sefirot* is the tenth and last *sefirah.*

MALCHUT, which means "kingdom," is the place of union between God, the King, and the People Israel, the Queen. This is the place of the climax of creation, where God and God's children meet. This *sefirah* is also known as SHECHINAH, the Divine Presence, the feminine aspect of God replete with its sense of sheltering and nurturing. This is the place where God's male and female attributes blend and where we human beings, created in the image of God, touch both the masculine and the feminine within us. This is the place where the transcendent, Infinite God—the *keter,* the crown, the highest of all *sefirot*—comes into communion and relationship with the finite human beings who are the "crowning" work of creation.

In the image of the four worlds in which we live, this *sefirah* resides in the world of *assiyah,* the world of our physical body, where we exist in the material world of physical need, experience physical sensation, and know the reality of being in body.

Looking at the entire Tree of Life, we see the emanations, the steps, the rungs of the ladder, between finite corporeal humanity—being at the *sefirah* of *malchut*—and the Infinite God—being at the transcendent *sefirah* of *keter.*

We see that the Tree of Life provides an internal system of checks and balances. The right side represents the male, and the aspects of expansion and increase; the left side represents the female, and the aspects of contraction and decrease. In the middle are the *sefirot* that provide the centering, the balancing. Even the holy pathway to the holy God can be fraught with imbalance, contradiction, and struggle, which must be synthesized and harmonized.

✦

It is clear how the *sefirot* can provide a pathway to God. By meditating on each of the *sefirot,* each of the attributes or aspects of God, we can come closer and closer to bridging the gap between us and our finitude, and God and God's Infinity. For in meditation we come to understand and embrace each of the *sefirot,* each of the emanations of God, and in knowing God's attributes, we come—in the best way we human beings with all our human limitations can—to know God.

Some may want to meditate on each *sefirah* individually and progressively. Meditate on *malchut* today, this week, this month, this year, and then go up to *yesod* until, eventually, the meditation centers on *keter* and the transcendent God.

Others may want to meditate on the entire Tree of Life each and every time, spending a few minutes of meditation at each *sefirah,* moving slowly but decidedly from the finite to the Infinite, from the earthbound to the transcendent, from us to God.

The mystics have aided our journey, our quest to meet God, by associating a different name of God with each of the *sefirot.* These names reflect the place and the role of each *sefirah* on the Tree of Life, and move us from the most basic to the most esoteric understanding of and relationship with God.

As we might imagine, neither mystics nor students of mysticism have one standard, established rubric that assigns a specific name of God to a specific *sefirah.* Throughout the centuries, there have been many differing associations. But there seems to be one basic agreement: the name of God associated with *malchut* is *Adonai.* Many of us know God best in this name-designation, because it is the name of God we use in the standard formula of blessing. *Baruch Atah Adonai,*

"Blessed are You, O Eternal. . . ." Since the name *Adonai* is the most simple and familiar way we know God, it makes sense that *Adonai* should be associated with the first rung on the ladder of the Tree of Life, the step that is closest to us, the *sefirah* where God meets us in the physical world.

The other general agreement is that either *keter* alone, the highest of the *sefirot,* or *keter, chochmah,* and *binah* together, the triad of the top three *sefirot,* is associated with the name of God that is *Ehyeh Asher Ehyeh.* Loosely translated, it means an ever-present "I am that I am" or "I will be what I will be."

This is a God-name laden with inherent power and with deep mystery. When God charged Moses with the task of going back to Egypt to liberate the Hebrew slaves, Moses asked, "When I come to the children of Israel and say to them, 'The God of your fathers sent me to you,' they will say to me, 'What is His name?' What shall I say to them? And God said to Moses, 'Tell them, *Ehyeh Asher Ehyeh,* I am that I am' " (Exodus 3:13–14).

What kind of God name is this? What does it mean? What does it represent? What does it signify?

This name of God is based on the verb *to be.* It is the acknowledgment of God's eternal existence. God "was," "is," and "will be" forever and ever. This is the God-name of timelessness, of "before there was a before" and of "after there is an after"; of "never-beginning" and "never-ending"; of God immutable, imperishable, infinite.

Since *keter,* either alone or with the companion *sefirot, chochmah,* and *binah,* represents God's pure being, union with God, and being-ness with God, it makes sense that *Ehyeh Asher Ehyeh* should be associated with the highest rungs on the ladder of the Tree of Life, the steps that are closest to God, the *sefirot* where God resides in the transcendent, Infinite world.

Associating the names of God with particular *sefirot,* and meditating on these names, is one more way that we can come closer to understanding the nature of God, closer to understanding God's aspects and attributes, closer to being with God.

✦

It will not always be easy to traverse the *sefirot,* to focus and concentrate and move up the pathway to God. We know—we want—the rewards of coming into the reflection of God's light, of coming closer and closer into God's presence, of understanding more and more of the mysteries of the universe. But there are so many distractions, so many diversions, so many disruptions—and so many excuses—that our pathway to God may be littered with good intentions but little progress.

So to inspire our journey, we can remember this story told in the name of the holy Baal Shem Tov.

A king built a grand palace and surrounded it with guards. Many of the people came to see the king, but when they saw the guards, they departed. Others gave gifts to the guards and were permitted to enter the palace. But when they saw the furnishings and the ornaments in the great halls, they stopped to look at them and forgot their mission to see the king. Still others looked neither at the guards nor at the decor but went straight to the throne room to see the king.

The Baal Shem drew the obvious but persuasive parallel. Some who seek God retreat at first hindrance. Others bring gifts of charitable acts or good deeds, but they become engrossed in the trivial, the mundane, and even in the glitter of the material world. But there are the ones who concentrate on their task, who refuse to be diverted by any distraction, no matter how appealing. They are the ones who enter into the throne room and come into the presence of God.

God is waiting for us to traverse the *sefirot,* and come into the Divine presence. Can we let anything impede us or keep us away?

✦

The Tree of Life is our way of connecting with God, by moving up the steps, by traversing the *sefirot* from us to God.

But it is much more.

By superimposing the *sefirot* of the Tree of Life onto ourselves, onto our own human form—onto Adam Kadmon, the image of the

first and primal human being—we can come to greater and deeper understanding of who we are in our being, our nature, our needs, our de-

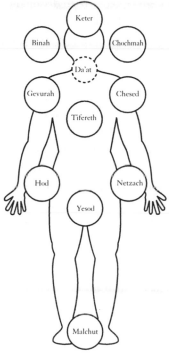

sires, our imperfections, our healing,
our renewal.

We who are created in the image
of God can see ourselves reflected in
God. We can see the *sefirot,* the emanations coming from God, as signposts
and pathways in our own lives, and we
can use them to enrich and ennoble our
own existence.

Much like the Hindu concept of
chakras, the *sefirot* are energy centers.
Each *sefirah* corresponds to a specific
place on the body, to an aspect of our
being, whether physical, emotional,
mental, or spiritual, and to a particular
life-purpose. And each *sefirah* can have
a sound vibration and a color associated
with it.

As we understand the *sefirot* in our
bodies, we understand ourselves.

When a *sefirah,* an energy center, is fully developed and fully realized and when it is functioning at an optimum level—when the energy
is pure and flowing without obstruction—then the corresponding
place in the body is healthy and well. If that *sefirah* is underdevel-
oped or unrealized or if it is not fully functioning—if the energy is
blocked—then physical disease or emotional, mental, or spiritual disease can result.

It is, of course, the goal of human existence to have all ten *sefirot*
fully developed and functioning at full capacity—to have continual,
unobstructed energy flow. For the blockage of one *sefirah* can bring imbalance to the entire being, but all ten *sefirot* working and functioning
in holistic harmony brings health of body and mind, and alignment
and at-one-ment with self and with God.

Some say that each *sefirah* has a particular and unique sound and tone. If even one of the sound vibrations is off-key or the tone is out of frequency—if the energy of the vibration is blocked—then dissonance comes to body and soul. But when the sound vibration of each *sefirah* works in harmony with the sound vibrations of all the other *sefirot*, then harmonic balance comes to our beings.

Through meditation, "inner hearing," and "the sounds of silence," each of us can become aware of our own vibrations, can resonate to our own sounds and tones, and can be in harmony and attunement with ourselves and with God.

There are those who say that each *sefirah* also has a color. Some of these color designations come to us from the mystics, and, as usual, there is no definitive designation but a good deal of general agreement. The encompassing imagery is that of water flowing through the *sefirot*, a water that in itself is clear with no color at all but that takes on its hue from the reflection of the meaning and function of the individual *sefirah* through which it passes.

Some color designations are "traditional," such as white for compassion and red for judgment. Thus *chesed*, lovingkindness and mercy, is seen as white, and *gevurah*, power and judgment, is seen as red. *Keter*, the crown of transcendence, the ultimate "isness" and "beingness" of God, is seen as either pure white or deepest black. *Chochmah*, wisdom, is seen as blue, for it emerges out of black; and *binah*, understanding, is seen as green. The tenth *sefirah*, *malchut* or *Shechinah*, the place where God and human beings connect in the earthly realm, is seen as a rainbow, for it is here that all the forces and all the colors of the universe are interwoven into one tapestry of brilliant color.

There are those who say that in superimposing the *sefirot* on the human body, each *sefirah* of each individual takes on a particular and a unique color. Whatever a person's *sefirot* colors, it is important to keep each one sharp, clear, rich, and in visual harmony with all the other *sefirot* colors.

Through meditation, it is possible for each of us to visualize and see our own *sefirot* colors and have one more way of bringing internal balance to our physical, emotional, mental, and spiritual planes.

In working with the inner *sefirot,* we begin at the bottom of the Tree of Life, at the place where God and human beings intersect, and we move up the tree toward ultimate transcendence. We associate each *sefirah* with its corresponding body part, we place it in its proper world, we delve into its meaning for our lives, our personality, and our character, and we engage it in dialogue.

We begin with MALCHUT, the kingdom, also known as SHECHI-NAH, the Divine Presence, the place where we human beings can encounter God.

MALCHUT is the physical realm, our sense of rootedness and grounding with the physical world. *Malchut,* which is the one *sefirah* that resides in the world of *assiyah,* the material world, affirms our connection to the very planet on which we live, the ground on which we walk, the animals and minerals and plants with which we share existence. We ask the *malchut* in ourselves: do I feel one with all of God's creation, with all of God's creatures, or do I flaunt my alleged human superiority? Do I appreciate the marvelous wonders of the universe, or do I take awesome nature for granted? Do I have the will, the energy, to embrace life with joy, or am I constantly tired and bedraggled? Do I earn my living with integrity and gratification, and do I have a satisfactory relationship with money, or do I hate my job and struggle with finance? Is the world of my *malchut,* my physical, material world, obstructed and blocked, or it is open with free-flowing energy?

We move up the Tree of Life to the three *sefirot* that in the descent down the Tree from God to us reside in the world of *yetzirah,* the world of our emotional body, but in the ascent up the Tree from us to God reside in a specialized category of *assiyah,* the aspect of spiritual *assiyah,* our way of functioning in a spiritual mode in the physical world.

YESOD, the foundation, is the genitals and the reproductive system, the dimension of human sexuality. *Yesod* is the intimacy of human connection, human relationship, and shared human emotion. *Yesod* is the energy of creation and regeneration, the energy of human survival. *Yesod* is the physically primal yet highly spiritual realm of love and sex. We ask the *yesod* in ourselves: Is my imagination, my creativity, at peak performance? Is my desire to perpetuate the human race strong and sure? Is my commitment to children unwavering? Is my most intimate relationship rooted in respect and honor? Do I love deeply and unconditionally? Is my sexual relationship mutually satisfying and fulfilling? Is the world of my *yesod,* my sexuality, obstructed and blocked, or it is open with free-flowing energy?

NETZACH, the victory, is the right leg and the muscular system. Its counterbalance, HOD, the majestic glory, is the left leg and the skeletal system. *Netzach* and *hod* deal with the functions and the basic instincts of our body—the food and drink we consume, the level of physical activity we maintain, the natural or chemical substances we choose to ingest or to reject. *Netzach* on the right, the powerful male energy, determines how expansive we are in our appetites. *Hod* on the left, the delimiting female energy, determines how we curb our desires. We ask the *netzach* and the *hod* in ourselves: Do I eat to live or do I live to eat? Do I respect my body, or do I fill it with harmful substances? Am I able to exercise self-control and self-discipline, or do I give in to whim and impulse? Do I maintain the freedom to choose, or am I plagued by dependence and addiction? Am I able to balance my wants with my needs, my fantasies with reality? Is the world of my *netzach* and my *hod*, my counterbalanced world of expansion and contraction, obstructed and blocked, or it is open with free-flowing energy?

We move up the Tree of Life again to the three *sefirot* that in the descent down the Tree from God to us reside in the world of *beriyah,* the world of our mental body, but in the ascent up the Tree from us to God, reside in the world of *yetzirah,* the world of our emotional body.

TIFERETH, beauty, is the torso with its respiration from chest and lungs, and with its central nervous system emanating from the spinal cord. *Tifereth* is the world of the spirit within us—our sense of beautiful music and art, our appreciation of fine literature or stirring words of speech, our esteem for moving drama or graceful dance. *Tifereth* is our awe and honor for people of wisdom and experience and our respect for inherent worth regardless of outward appearance. We ask the *tifereth* in ourselves: Do I discover and appreciate beauty in my world, or am I satisfied with the conventional and the mundane? Do I see the world through the prism of vivid color, or do I settle for dull grayness? Do I still marvel at the awesome, the wondrous, the miraculous, or do I take the extraordinary for granted? Do I see the sublime even in the ordinary, or have I become jaded and cynical? Do I tap into the soul-spirit within me, or do I live in shallow superficiality? Do I rightly balance the aesthetic with the active, the inner with the outer? Is the world of my *tifereth,* my sense of beauty and wonder, obstructed and blocked, or it is open with free-flowing energy?

CHESED, lovingkindness, is the right arm and the right hand. *Chesed* is our sense of self and our relationship to others, the aspects of our personality and character, the qualities and attributes that manifest in our attitudes and our behavior. Rooted in the concept of unconditional love, *chesed* is our sense of compassion, mercy, kindness, decency, and dignity; the ability to be selfless, sharing, and generous; understanding, accepting, and forgiving. *Chesed* is our outward conduct—how we treat others; and *chesed* is our inward conduct—how we treat ourselves.

GEVURAH, strength and justice, is the left arm and the left hand, the counterbalance to *chesed. Gevurah* is the discernment, the evaluation, the inner judgment, the setting of boundaries and limits. *Gevurah* balances selflessness and selfishness, self-interest and the common good. *Gevurah* is self-awareness and consciousness of self, the ability to reach out and to hold back in just the right proportions. *Gevurah* is the "inner policeman" who tells us whether or not we are doing what is right, whether or not we are treating those around us and ourselves as we should.

We ask the *chesed* and the *gevurah* in ourselves: Am I open and sharing, or am I closed and selfish? Am I altruistic and other directed, or am I self-centered and egotistical? Am I charitable and generous—in both resources and spirit—or am I miserly and greedy? Do I open my heart and my hand to those in need, or am I self-indulgent and stingy? Am I kind? Do I feel compassion, sympathy, and empathy for others, or am I hard-hearted, self-concerned, and caring only about myself? In the face of another, do I see a friend or a stranger? Does communal responsibility and the common good outweigh my own self-interests? Does my forgiveness outweigh my need for revenge, my mercy outweigh my sense of strict justice, my love outweigh my hatred? Is the world of my *chesed,* my lovingkindness, and my *gevurah,* my strength and justice, obstructed and blocked, or is it open with free-flowing energy?

We move up the Tree of Life again.

CHOCHMAH, wisdom, on the right side of the Tree, is the brain—its ability to perceive and to think at the highest and most profound levels. *Chochmah* is the realm of the "aha" experience, the moment of revelation, of clarity, of understanding. *Chochmah* is the place where we get our first glimpse into the mysteries of the universe, into universal and eternal truth. On our ascent up the Tree of Life toward God, *chochmah* resides in the world of *atzilut,* the world of our spiritual body, the world of emanation and intuition.

BINAH, understanding, on the left side of the Tree, is the brain—its ability to feel, to discern, to know. *Binah* is the intellectual process and the mental evaluation, the ability to remember, think through, analyze, and come to conclusion. *Binah* is the confirmation of knowing, and *binah* is how we feel about what we have learned and what we know, how it affects our mind, our psyche, and our spirit. *Binah* balances *chochmah* by integrating the revelatory, illuminating spiritual moments with grounded thought and rational analysis. On our ascent up the Tree of Life toward God, *binah* resides in the world of *beriyah,* our mental body, where we think and discern, where we try to understand in a rational way God's plan for the universe, where we "make sense" of the glimpses of the eternal truths we have discovered through *chochmah.*

We ask our *chochmah* and our *binah:* What do I know, and when did I know it? Am I wise, or am I just educated? Am I both a thinking and a feeling human being? Has the world of my rational, analytical intellect shut out the world of my spirit? Has the world of my spirit overwhelmed my ability to function in the world of the everyday? Is this world as we know it all there is, or is much hidden that is still to be revealed? Am I open to illumination and revelation? Am I open to experiencing spiritual awe? What are the secrets; how did I forget them; when can I know them again? Is the world of my *chochmah,* the wisdom of my thought, and my *binah,* my deepest inner understanding, obstructed and blocked, or it is open with free-flowing energy?

KETER, the crown, the crowning *sefirah* at the very top of the Tree of Life, is transcendence. *Keter* is the highest place in our inner world, the very edge of the brink, the place where, at those rare and precious moments of illumination and revelation, we can meet God. *Keter* is the ultimate gateway to God. *Keter* is not *malchut,* or *Shechinah,* the gate way that is at the bottom of the rungs of the ladder of God's *sefirot,* the place where God comes down to meet us at the point where the human realm intersects with the Divine. Rather, *keter* is the gateway at the very, very top of the *sefirot,* the place where God dwells, the place where—in that incredibly unique flash of insight and in-sight—we go up to meet God.

On our ascent up the Tree of Life toward God, *keter* is said to re-side in two concurrent worlds. Some say that *keter* is in the world of *atzilut,* the world of our spiritual body, for it is the place of ultimate transcendence, the place of ultimate merging with God. Others say that *keter* is in the world of Adam Kadmon, the image of the first and primal human being, for it is in the world of the spirit, in the world of God's emanation, that God first conceived and created human beings. Thus, Adam Kadmon is both at the very top *and* at the very bottom of the Tree of Life—the place where human beings were created, and the place where human beings reside. Adam Kadmon is in the place where God formed us, and the place to which we can return in mo-ments of transcendence and to which we will return at the end of our days on this earthly plane. And Adam Kadmon is in the place where, in the course of our daily being, we intersect with God, the place where God comes to interact with us.

We ask the *keter* in ourselves: Do I possess, am I developing, the highest spiritual energy, the God-energy, so that I can experience revela-tion, so that I can encounter God? Is the world of my *keter,* my gateway crown, obstructed and blocked, or it is open with free-flowing energy?

～✦～

Entering and traversing the Tree of Life through deep contemplation and meditation can be a sacred pathway—the holy journey of interconnected body and soul—both toward God and to-ward self-understanding and personal growth.

Meditation on the *sefirot* and their psycho-spiritual elements can be a daily *cheshbon hanefesh,* a soul-inventory, a personal psychological profile. By encountering each *sefirah's* psychological and spiritual meaning, and by asking the questions of self-evaluation that each *sefirah* poses, we can confront our flaws and our failings, and we can challenge ourselves to be and do the highest good.

The Tree of Life is the perfect metaphor for our journey of self-examination and our quest for transformation through wholeness and holiness. For the closer we come to human perfection, the closer we come to God.

⤙✦⤚

The Kabbalists have given us a most powerful image of a Tree of Life, with its *sefirot* emanating from God to us and from us to God. It is reminiscent of another precious image in the Jewish experience.

When he fled in fear from his father and his home, our ancestor Jacob dreamed a dream. In it, he saw a ladder reaching from his stone pillow on earth up to the very heavens. And Jacob saw angels of God ascending and descending the ladder. And he heard God say, "I am the Lord . . . and behold, I am with you, and I will watch over you wherever you go . . . and I will not leave you" (Genesis 28:13, 15).

"And Jacob woke from his sleep, and he said: 'Surely, the Lord is in this place, but I, I did not know it. . . . How full of awe is this place! This is none other than the house of God, and this is the gate of heaven" (Genesis 28:16–17).

Like Jacob, we can find God.

By traversing the ladder, by embracing the *sefirot*—in our wholeness and holiness of unified body and soul—we can come into God's presence, we can encounter God, we can come to know God, and we can be assured God will be with us always.

One of the earliest texts of Jewish mysticism teaches us just how much is at stake and how very much we can achieve.

> *The righteous One [God] stands gazing out at humanity.*
> *When God sees human beings engaged in Torah, seeking to refine themselves, and conducting themselves in purity, then the Righteous One expands,—filling Himself with all kinds of flow-*

ing emanations from above, to pour into the Shechinah, *the Divine Presence. . . . The entire world is blessed by those righteous humans, and the* Shechinah *is blessed through them.*

But if, God forbid, humans defile themselves by distancing themselves from Torah, by perpetrating evil, by injustice and violence, then the Righteous One . . . sees, gathers inward, contracts Himself and travels higher and higher. The flow of all the channels stops, and the Shechinah *is left dry and empty, lacking all good.*

One who understands this secret understands the immense power that a human being has to build or to destroy.

Now come and see the power: You can unite all the sefirot, *balancing and harmonizing the upper and the lower worlds.*

Part Two

Connecting with Jewish Tradition

Almost every religion and faith community has a set of
rituals and rites that serve to reinforce, enhance, and
intensify its belief system.

Participating in religious ceremonies can provide a link
to the history and practices of a people. Rituals can bring
rhythm and cadence to life; they can bring beauty and meaning to existence; they can make the ordinary holy and make
the everyday sacred; they can be an avenue to faith.

But rituals and rites, customs and ceremonies, are so
very much more. Rituals are performed to bring us to a
deeper place in the human psyche than words can touch.
Rituals are without words, before words. They provide a
physical experience, a "felt-sense," that goes beyond intellectual "knowledge" to metaphysical, intrinsic "knowing."

꘠꘠꘠

Jewish rituals are especially rich because they are rooted in
the sense of mitzvah—in the commands that God issued.
The notion is that if we follow all of God's injunctions—if

*we observe God's ritual laws as the instrumentality that will
lead us to observe God's ethical laws—then we are rightly
headed to the fulfillment of the mandate and the promise,
"You shall be holy because I the Lord your God am holy"
(Leviticus 19:2).*

*For some, Jewish rituals remain as they were intended—
deeply satisfying and richly fulfilling. For some, the ceremo-
nial has taken on such paramount importance that all of
Judaism seems to rest on the almost slavish performance of
the most minute details of ritual law.*

*But for many, if not most, ritual holds a theoretical place
of power, and the performance of ritual brings back warm,
nostalgic memories. But most traditional rituals have been
dismissed or ignored, and the few that are observed are
quickly performed out of habit or by rote.*

*Yet without ritual, without ceremony, there is an emp-
tiness, a hollowness, to our lives. We are without anchor
at points where life insists on rootedness and source, without
touchstone when we long for the familiar; we are without
identity in a world where our sense of unique meaning and
purpose is easily lost.*

*We can recapture the meaning and the beauty and the power
of Jewish ceremonies and rituals for our lives.*

*Some Jewish rituals can be newly conceived in response
to our evolving consciousness, to our evolving life situation.
But the many Jewish rituals that have been lost or become
remote, that have given way to rote performance, can come
alive again when we tap into their original purpose, when we
reinfuse them with their original spiritual center, when we
give them back their original vibrational energy.*

*Then we will enrich ourselves with the "felt-sense" of
knowing beyond knowing, for we will understand that the
rituals we perform are the signposts on our journey to knowing God.*

7

The Holy Tongue

WHEN HARVARD COLLEGE WAS FOUNDED IN 1636, one of the required courses in the curriculum was Hebrew language and literature, and until 1819 the Harvard graduation exercises included an oration given in Hebrew.

As other colleges such as Yale, Columbia, Brown, Princeton, Johns Hopkins, and the University of Pennsylvania were founded, they, too, required the study of Hebrew.

The seals of at least two of the oldest and most prestigious universities in America, Yale and Dartmouth, include Hebrew phrases, and Columbia's seal has the Hebrew name for God at the top center.

It is even rumored that there was such strong anti-British feeling and such interest in Hebrew in the American colonies at the time of the revolution that certain members of the Continental Congress proposed that the use of English be formally prohibited and that Hebrew be substituted as the national language.

What is it about Hebrew that so captured the imagination of colonists and academics and political leaders while birthing the United States of America? What is it about Hebrew that was so invigorating that a language that had remained virtually unspoken for almost two thousand years should inspire such affection?

The power of Hebrew may have been best described by Martin Luther, who, despite his virulent anti-Semitism, was a biblical scholar and the first to translate the Bible into German. Luther said, "The words of the Hebrew tongue have a peculiar energy. It is impossible to convey so much so briefly in any other language."

The modern French thinker Aime Palliere affirmed the notion. "Many have known the indescribable charm that the language of the Bible holds. . . . Through the Hebrew syllables with their sonorous cadence, something of the soul of Israel reached me . . . an emotional and religious value that I could never again find in French or Latin."

The modern poet Danny Siegel captures the essence of the grandeur of the "holy tongue."

> I'll tell you how much I love Hebrew
> Read me anything—
> Genesis
> or an ad in an Israeli paper
> and watch my face.
> I will make half-sounds of ecstasy
> and my smile will be so enormously sweet
> you would think some angels were singing Psalms
> or God Himself was reciting to me.
> I am crazy for her Holiness
> and each restaurant's menu in Yerushalayim
> or Bialik poem
> gives me peace no Dante or Milton or Goethe
> could give
> . . . .
> That's the way I am.
> I'd rather hear the weather report
> on Kol Yisrael [the Israeli radio station]
> than all the rhythms and music of Shakespeare.

God understands all languages.

God understands the power and the majesty of each and every word of human speech. But, as Professor Louis Ginzberg explained,

"The recollection that it was the Hebrew language in which the Revelation was given, in which the Prophets expressed their high values, in which generations of our fathers breathed forth their suffering and joys, makes this language a holy one for us."

Hebrew is the Jewish language.

It is the language that our ancestors heard at Sinai; the language in which God's word and will were recorded for all humankind. It is the language of our history, our sacred and our everyday, our enduring values, our ultimate destiny. It is the language of our literature and our holy texts; and it is the language in which we learn to talk to God. In its modern revival, it is the language of our land and our people, our independence and our identity.

Hebrew's sounds and tones and cadence resonate deeply within our souls, in our Jewish genes, in the DNA that wraps its strands from Abraham to Moses and Miriam to King David to Rabbi Akiba to the Rambam to the Ari to Theodore Herzl to Anne Frank to Golda Meir, to each and every one of us at the core of our beings.

～✥～

Surely, it is possible to be Jewish—to delve into Jewish learning and involvement, to have an appreciation of Jewish life, to create a personal relationship with God—in the vernacular, in English or Russian or Greek or in any one of hundreds of languages. But trying to experience Judaism without Hebrew is like try to read a good book in a poor translation, or like seeing a beautiful painting in a black-and-white reproduction.

Hebrew holds the wonders and the secrets and the mysteries and the sweet pleasures of communicating with the whole of the Jewish experience and of intimate conversation with God.

We Jews need Hebrew because it is the key to unlocking the great storehouse, the great treasure house, of Judaism.

Yet, sadly, few contemporary Jews—we who have studied Latin, French, and Spanish; who do business in Japanese and Korean; who have become experts in Chinese literature—know Hebrew. Many "people of the Book" cannot read the Book in its original. Many are unfamiliar and uncomfortable with the chants of Hebrew prayer.

Many cannot understand a simple Hebrew greeting or a word from an Israeli newspaper.

Danny Siegel, the great lover of Hebrew, once had the same problem. He writes:

The day I discovered
Aryeh's dog
understood more Hebrew
than all the phrases I had memorized
through years of Hebrew school—
that day I bought the books and records
I would need to read, speak,
understand and write
everything my heart desired
in the words of Moses.
That day I began
with Aleph *in the dictionary*
through the Fall to Mem,
And finally to Tav
. . . .
All because of Kushi the Kelev [dog]
late of Jerusalem.

It's not our fault that we don't know Hebrew. Hebrew school was boring; it wasn't relevant; the teachers were old-fashioned and mean. We had much more fun playing Little League or taking ballet lessons.

It's not our fault that we don't know Hebrew. But it is our loss. It is our loss because so much of Judaism is closed off to us. So much of Judaism remains untouchable, foreign and fuzzy, because, as much as we might like, we just don't have the words to speak or to understand.

The good news is that it is never too late. It is never too late to learn Hebrew.

Fortunately, Hebrew is a very concise and relatively simple language. It has an alphabet of twenty-two consonants with seven accompanying vowels. Each letter and vowel has its own distinct sound, and almost every Hebrew word is phonetically regular and consistent, making pronunciation and reading fairly easy. Certainly, like all other languages, Hebrew has its complex grammatical constructions and a few seemingly unfathomable irregularities. But we don't have to study for long or become linguistic scholars in order to acquire the basic Hebrew reading and verbal skills, vocabulary, and grammatical principles that will open the world of Judaism to us.

Many different and varied programs exist for studying Hebrew: videotapes, audiotapes, computer programs, and texts designed especially for the adult learner; courses emphasizing reading skills, modern conversational Hebrew, or more formal diplomatic Hebrew; courses to understand biblical Hebrew or prayerbook Hebrew or modern Israeli newspaper Hebrew. There are opportunities everywhere: at synagogues and Jewish schools and Jewish community centers; at colleges, universities, and community learning centers; in adult education programs in a variety of settings; by mail, by fax, and on the Internet.

Some courses take a year or a semester or an evening a week for ten weeks. Others are page-a-day texts that promise ability to read with simple comprehension in less than a month. One program even guarantees basic reading skills in a single twelve-hour-day marathon session. And, of course, as with all learning and personal growth, Hebrew study can fill a lifetime—a new word today, a new grammatical principle tomorrow, greater comprehension the next day, another new word the day after.

When we decide to learn Hebrew and to continually upgrade our Hebrew knowledge and skills, we pledge to ourselves to know at least as much Hebrew as that little dog in Israel. When we decide to learn Hebrew, we give ourselves the great gift of the Jewish tradition that can come only through the "holy tongue," only through the language of Sinai and Jerusalem. When we decide to learn Hebrew, we touch who we are. For, at the very depth of our beings, we know the truth that Chaim Nachman Bialik, the national poet of our people, taught, "Hebrew is our very flesh and blood, and each encounter with it is an encounter with our soul."

⚜

There is great power in Hebrew and, by extension, in Yiddish words. Many Hebrew and Yiddish words hold centuries of wisdom and discernment; they often carry a meaning, an essence, that goes far beyond, far deeper, than the simple definition. One word can convey untold levels of recognition, connotation, implication, and significance. In one word can reside a whole world of insight and understanding.

With apologies to the late-night comic David Letterman for making serious what he always makes funny, here is the "Top Ten List of Words Jews Should Always Say." These are words that will wrap us in the Jewish tradition and open our hearts and our spirits to Jewish values; these are words that, in the image of the sages, "when spoken from the heart will enter into the heart."

10. SECHEL, *literally, "wisdom." Sechel means more than book learning, more than acquired knowledge. Sechel means deep understanding and insight; the ability to perceive and discern. Sechel means having common sense and "street smarts"— having the capacity to meet any challenge and to prevail through wisdom and wile. Every day we need to use our own sechel and to surround ourselves with people who have sechel.*

9. FARBRENT *(Yiddish), literally, "burning." In the idiom,* farbrent *means passionate, deeply involved, committed, as in "I am* farbrent *for God, for Torah, for* mitzvot, *for justice, for peace, for faith, for love." Into every life must come a passion, a cause, a commitment. Mine—yours—can be our God and our people. Farbrent is a good thing to be. We can say it—we can be it—proudly, zealously.*

8. EMES, *literally, "truth." "Zog* dem emes, *tell the truth." Our honor, our good name, our reputation all depend on our words being believable and believed. So each and every moment, we must speak the* emes. *At the same time, we have to be wary of people who rise up to full height, stare us straight in the eye, hold up their right hands, and say, "I swear, it's the* emes." *It probably isn't. When our word is our bond, we don't have to say the word* emes *very often; we just have to speak the truth always.*

7. KAVOD, *literally, "honor." The imperative, the command, comes to each and every one of us: honor your parents, honor your spouse, honor your children, honor yourself. Honor your dreams. Give* kavod *where* kavod *is due. By your words and your deeds, bring* kavod *upon yourself. Stenciled into the walls of the subway train in Haifa is a quote from the Talmud, "Rise up before the hoary head [the elderly]." Get up and give your seat to an older person who needs it. That's* kavod.

6. ZIESKEIT *(Yiddish), literally, "sweetness," usually used in speaking to a baby (while pinching a cheek), as in "Oh, what a* zies, *what* zieskeit, *what a sweet child." Children come by their* zieskeit *naturally, but as we grow older, life's challenges and hardships have the tendency to knock the* zieskeit *out of too many of us. But our* zieskeit *remains, waiting for us to recapture the innocence and the sweetness of our youth. When we look for and speak of the* zieskeit *in others, we usually find and touch the* zieskeit *in ourselves. And we are reminded just how sweet life can be!*

5. TZEDAKAH, *usually mistranslated as "charity" but, literally, "justice/righteousness." Not only out of the goodness of our hearts, but because it is our obligation, we give* tzedakah, *we share what we have with those in need. Be it our material resources or the work of our hands, giving* tzedakah *means that we provide food for the hungry, shelter for the homeless, education for the illiterate, hope for the downtrodden, because it is the sacred responsibility of every human being to care about and for every other human being. We give* tzedakah *because it is the right thing to do.*

4. CHEIN, *literally, "grace." A traditional Jewish prayer asks God to grant peace, goodness, blessing,* chein—*grace—lovingkindness, and mercy to the world.* Chein *is dignity, graciousness, virtue, providential care. If* chein *is what we want from God, then* chein *is what others want from us—and what we can graciously provide. We can bring* chein *to every word, to every act, to every relationship, to every moment. We*

can wrap ourselves and everyone around us in a mantle of
care and an aura of gracefulness.

3. RACHMONES, *literally, "compassion," from the word meaning*
"womb." We ask God to deal with us not only with a sense of
justice, but with an overwhelming sense of mercy and com-
passion. We, who are created in God's image, can do no less
with our fellow human beings. We need to develop and feel
compassion, caring, sharing; we need to speak compassionate,
loving words and do compassionate, kind deeds. We need to
have rachmones *and give* rachmones. *There are so many*
who need our rachmones, *so many who need our compas-*
sion, our empathy, our decency. We need to have rachmones
for them. And we need to have rachmones *for ourselves, for*
we, who are often so harshly judgmental of ourselves, need
our own compassion. We need to be kind to ourselves.

2. NACHES, *literally, "pleasure/satisfaction/pride," most often*
used by saying, "I get such naches *from the* kinder, *such*
pride, satisfaction, joy, from my children"; often used as a
prayerful—and hopeful—invocation to God: "May You have
naches *from Your* kinder." *Yet for God, and for us, there is a*
caution. Our children are not here on earth to be "naches
machines," living in ways just to please their boastful parents.
In the words of the poet Kahlil Gibran that we all read (over
and over again) in college, "Your children are not your chil-
dren / They are the sons and daughters of Life's longing for it-
self. / They come through you, but not from you, / And
though they are with you, yet they belong not to you." Far
better than depending on our children for naches, *we need to*
seek naches *from ourselves—certainly from our accomplish-*
ments and achievements, but more from our sense of self, our
innermost and deepest satisfaction. We can shep naches *from*
who we are and from the wonders that life so happily gives.

1. *And the Number One Word That Jews Should Always Say:*
MENSCH, *literally, "man." But a mensch is much more than*
a man. A mensch *is a person—of either gender—who is de-*
cent, kind, and honest, a good person who is fully human

and fully humane. A mensch is an honorable person who al-
ways acts with complete integrity, who has chein *and* rachmones. *To say that "he's a* mensch, *she's a* mensch" *is the*
highest praise and the greatest compliment that can be ac-
corded. Far, far more important than saying "My child, the
straight A *student, my son the doctor, my daughter the lawyer"*
is being able to say, "My child, the mensch." *For every one of*
us, for all of us, the charge and the challenge is the same: Let
menschlichkeit *be your guide and your goal. Zei a mensch,*
be a mensch. *It is the greatest and most worthy thing you*
can be.

Everything we do—everything that is important, everything that
forms our personal existence, everything that shapes the world in which
we live—depends on what we say, on the images we create through the
words we speak. And every word we speak ripples into eternity.

Our Jewish heritage gives us wise words, words of goodness and
greatness. So take these top ten words as a precious gift from your tradition, and use them, be them. Speak these words about others, speak
them about yourself. For when we embody and live these top ten
words, our humanity is enhanced, our existence is enriched, our lives
are ennobled.

~~~

There are a few Hebrew words and phrases that have a
power all their own, an inherent power that comes not from meaning
but from the sound, the rhythm, and the cadence. When these words are
spoken, their very utterance creates an aura of mystery, magic, and awe.

For example: the litany of the six opening words of every Jewish
blessing is, *"Baruch Atah Adonai, Elohenu Melech HaOlam. . . ."*
"Praised are You, O Eternal our God, King of the Universe."

Listen to the sound; listen to the cadence—"Da-da, Da-da, Da-da-
da; Da-da-da-da, Da-da, Da-da-da. . . ."

The words carry an important meaning, but the meaning almost
does not matter. What matters is the sound, the rhythm, the beat. The
intonation of the sound creates its own intent, its own essence. In these

sixteen syllables, the sound creates invocation and manifestation—invocation as we call upon God, and manifestation as God responds openly, graciously, and generously to our petition and our praise.

It is as when a child calls out to a parent in a familiar way: "Mommy, please come here. I need you." "Daddy, Daddy, you're home, you're home." After a while the words do not matter—the words are not even heard. Rather, the parent hears the child's voice—the sound, the tone, the pattern of the rhythm—and the parent knows the child is calling. And the parent responds in the fullness of love.

It is the same with us and God. The words of the call have little import. The sound of the call carries the magic of connection.

The best example of the inherent power of the sound of the word is in one of the most well known Jewish prayers, the *kaddish*. The *kaddish* is a doxology, a prayer of praise to God: "Magnified and sanctified be the name of God throughout the world. . . ."

In one of its forms, the *kaddish* is a prayer recited by mourners during their bereavement at the death of a loved one. The original purpose in having mourners recite *kaddish* is clear: even in the face of tragedy and grief, the mourners are still able to stand and declare continuing faith in God. But because, in this form, the prayer is now known as the "Mourner's *Kaddish,*" and because many do not know the meaning of the words or the intent of having mourners recite a prayer of praise, the *kaddish* has come to be closely associated not with praise but with death.

Yet it really does not matter whether the mourners understand the meaning of the words or the original intent of reciting the prayer. It does not matter that highly rational, intellectual people might object to reciting words of praise while grieving over death. The sounds of the *kaddish* have a power all their own.

Listen to the sound, the rhyme, the cadence—in either Sephardic or Ashkenazic Hebrew:

יתגדל ויתקדש שמה רבא
Yitgadal v'yitkadash sh'may rabbah.

or

Yisgadal v'yiskadash sh'may ra-boh.

The words are syncopated—Da-da-da, Da-da-da-da, Da-da, Da-da.

There is an internal rhyme, a natural cadence, a flowing beat.

The sound of the *kaddish*—not the words or their meaning, but the sound—is deeply etched into the Jewish psyche. The sound of the words brings a natural order to the chaotic, bewildering moment of burying a loved one. The sound of the words brings familiarity to a very foreign experience. The sound of the words brings comfort in the midst of great pain and anguish.

The order, the familiarity, and the comfort come from the sounds that reverberate, not just in the moment, but backward and forward through the centuries and millennia; they come from the very deepest place in Jewish memory and consciousness.

To a Jew, the words of the *kaddish* hold magic. It doesn't matter what the words mean, because the power is within the words themselves. The word is spoken, the sound resonates, and the magic happens. For the mourner, by making the sounds of the *kaddish,* the magic of transformation from raw grief to gentle healing begins.

And for the soul, the sound of the words carries a vibration, an energy, that assists the soul in departing this earthly plane and going to the Other Side.

At the very same time, the sound *and* the words of *kaddish* join together to play a vital role for the departing soul. The soul of the deceased may be lingering on this earthly plane. Leaving loved ones behind, especially loved ones who are grieving or who do not understand how thin the veil really is, can be sad and traumatic for the soul. The journey to the Light on the Other Side can be scary; going to the vast unknown of the Other Side may be frightening.

So the soul waits for a sign, for an indication from this side that it is all right to go, that it is safe on the Other Side. And what does the soul hear? The soul hears the mourners—even in their longing, even in their grief—saying, "Magnified and sanctified is the name of God. . . . Exalted and honored is the name of the Holy One; blessed is God whose glory transcends. . . . May there be abundant peace from the heavens and life for all of us. . . ."

The soul hears the praise of God; the soul is caught up in the sound and the cadence of speaking to God; the soul is assured that the greatness of God envelops the whole of creation; the soul is promised that there is life on both sides; and the soul knows that it can pass over the veil, come into the Light, and be with God. The words of *kaddish* are the blessing and the affirmation from the souls on earth to the soul that has departed from earth saying, "Go and be not afraid; go and know that we will always remember and love you; go and be with God, for it is good there; go in peace."

We know that these words and sounds work as they are supposed to, because those who have the gift of "seeing," the gift of true "sight," report that at the graveside, at the very moment the mourners are reciting the *kaddish,* the soul can sometimes be seen rising up and moving toward the Light.

⚜

There is one more Hebrew word that holds incredible power in both its meaning and its sound. It is such an important word, a word so integral to Judaism and the whole of the Jewish experience, that is has to be added to the "Top Ten List" as the "Extra-Special Bonus Word That Jews Should Always Say."

It is the word *shalom.*

Shalom is probably the most well known of all Hebrew words, because it is used so often, and is now known and recognized all throughout the world. Whenever people meet, whenever people depart, the greeting is *shalom,* for *shalom* means "hello" and it means "good-bye."

Most of all, *shalom* means "peace."

We all desperately want peace—within ourselves, in our relationships, in our families, in our workplaces, in our organizations, in our communities, in our country, in our world.

That is why *shalom* is such an oft-repeated word. For, even as a simple greeting, it embodies deep yearning and solemn promise.

So the ancient sage Hillel insisted that it is not enough to simply want peace, to hope for peace, even to pray for peace; he taught us to "love peace and actively pursue peace" (Avot 1:12).

In a world that seems so filled with strife, in a country that seems so filled with dissension, in our families, which are so often beset with contention, in our souls, which so often swirl in conflict and dis-ease, how do we bring *shalom?*

We begin with the root word of *shalom, shalem,* which means "whole" or "complete."

Peace comes not when there is diffusion or fragmentation, not when there is emptiness or hollowness, but when there is wholeness, fullness, unity of being. Peace comes to each of us when we feel solid at the core, when we feel inner contentment, inner harmony.

And when there is peace within, it radiates from each person and spreads outward to every other human being, and ripples to every corner of the earth. Nations do not make wars, governments do not make wars, presidents and generals do not make wars. People make wars; somebody's daddy or mommy or grandpa makes a war. Wars happen when hatred or bigotry or contention or fear—lack of wholeness—resides in a person's heart and soul and then gets translated into government policy and, eventually, international conflict.

But, in the words of the sixties campus slogan, "What if they gave a war and nobody came?" Then, paraphrasing the words of the ancient prophet, "Nation could not lift up sword against nation, and they would not experience war anymore."

Simply and profoundly, peace among nations begins in one heart, in one soul. As the old folksong so correctly and so poignantly understood: "Let there be peace on earth, and let it begin with me."

From the simplest human interaction to the most complex multinational negotiation, whether as a nation, a community, or as individuals, when we fill up our souls, when we fill up our hearts, when we fill up our beings—when we are not hollow and empty, but whole and complete—then *shalom* comes.

So the next time—every time—that life seems too hard, the next time you are stuck in the five o'clock traffic jam or you are late picking up the kids from Little League or the boss has heaped a new pile of work on your desk or the cleaner just ruined your best blouse or you just had a fight with your best friend or your husband forgets or your

wife tells you for the tenth time to take out the garbage or your children are acting like wild animals or the IRS calls with just one little
question or the synagogue board meets until midnight and still can't
balance the budget; the next time the nightly news seems too painful to
bear or the television screen is filled with warfare and violence around
the world or around the corner or you hear that another good friend
has cancer or one more old buddy dropped dead on the tennis court or
you celebrate still another birthday and wonder where all the years
have gone; the next time—every time—that life seems just too complicated and far too overwhelming, do not give in to disillusionment or
despair, but seek *shalom,* seek peace.

Peace may not be present in the painful and confusing elements
swirling around you, but, surely, you can find peace within you.

When you say the word *shalom* over and over again, it can help
bring *shalom,* for the very word itself has a soothing and healing sound
and powerful inherent energy. It is no accident that the Hebrew word
shalom sounds like the Hindu mantra *ohm.* Said over and over again,
ohm or *shalom* help focus attention and direct thought.

When life sets up its obstacles and stumbling blocks, when life pre-
sents its inevitable pain and anguish, go deep inside yourself and say
shalom. Say it over and over again. Elongate the word *shaaa-lommm,
shaaa-lommm, shaaa-lommm.* Let the sound resonate within you; let the
meaning enwrap you.

Like magic's *abracadabra,* Hebrew's *shalom* can work its magic on
your psyche and on your soul, and its reality and its promise can transform you.

We find, again, that one of Rabbi Shlomo Carlebach's beautiful
melodies can help us sing *shalom,* and we can be soothed by its sound,
healed by its hope, and invigorated by its promise.

Peace.
Peace for our planet. Peace for our world.
Peace among nations. Peace among people.
Peace in our streets. Peace in our homes.
Peace in our hearts. Peace in our souls.
Peace unto you.
Peace within you.
Peace.
Shalom.
Shalom.

8

Five Seconds a Day
That Can Change
Your Life

I HAD A PROFESSOR IN RABBINICAL SCHOOL whose task was to teach us Aramaic grammar. Now, truth be told, few rabbinical students were very interested in the subject. Even though much of the Talmud and the *ketubah,* the wedding contract, and a number of our prayers including the well-known *kaddish* are written in Aramaic, the fine points of linguistic grammatical construction were not high on our list of priorities.

The rabbi-professor, a wise man, was sympathetic to our attitude, and so he approached our study in a very astute manner.

"Gentlemen," he said (this was in the days before woman rabbis), "today we begin our study of Aramaic grammar. In order to pass this course, you will each need to know and master two hundred principles of grammar." We all groaned.

"Now I know," he continued, "that most of you consider this a nearly impossible task. And I want you to know that you are right."

We all gasped in amazement at this admission.

"Yes," he said, "to go from step zero, where you are right now, all the way up to step 200 is impossible. But to get from step 199 to step 200 isn't hard at all. So today we'll go from step zero to step one. Soon we'll be at step twenty-five, and then step fifty. Before you know it, we'll be at step 199, and then the jump to step 200 will be very easy."

Aramaic grammar is not the only seemingly vast and impenetrable thing in our lives. So many people look at the vast treasury of Judaism—the *mitzvot,* the customs and ceremonies, the rituals and observances, the ethical mandate—and say, "Impossible. Too intimidating. There is no way that I can possibly know and do all those things. And since I can't do them all, and since I don't even know where to begin, I'll just skip it all together. I won't do anything."

Yet we need only remember the wise professor's approach to grammar to know that Judaism can be embraced in the same way— one step at a time. We need not understand the vastness and the complexity of the system of Jewish law and observance. We need not do all the *mitzvot* or feel inferior or guilty just because we can't or won't.

We need just to feel that we want to encounter the *mitzvot,* because they will fill our hearts with happiness, enrich our spirits, and ennoble our souls.

And we need just to know that we can begin simply and easily, yet significantly, one *mitzvah* at a time.

Here is one way to begin, a simple plan to add a *mitzvah* to your life, a *mitzvah* that can be done in five seconds, a *mitzvah* that has the potential to change your life.

The plan is called the *Motzi Mitzvah.*

Here's how it works.

Each night before dinner, recite the traditional Hebrew *b'rachah,* the blessing for food. It's only ten words:

בָּרוּךְ אַתָּה ה'
אֱלֹהֵינוּ מֶלֶךְ הָעוֹלָם
הַמּוֹצִיא לֶחֶם מִן הָאָרֶץ

Baruch Atah Adonai, Elohenu melech haolam, hamotzi lechem min ha'aretz.

"Praised are You, O Eternal our God, Ruler of the universe, who brings forth bread from the earth."

or

"Eternal God, Source of all being, we praise You and we thank You for all Your many blessings and for the food we are about to eat."

That's it. Ten words. Easily recited in five seconds.

(You might want to photocopy these words of blessing and tape them to your refrigerator so that they are always before you, always reminding you to speak them.)

When you say these simple ten words in the moment before you eat, many things happen all at once. And when you stay aware of the many-layered, multidimensional power of these ten words, you will soon begin to see how much different and better your life can be.

1. When you say *motzi,* you can, if you choose, put on a *kepa,* the traditional Jewish head covering worn by Orthodox Jews at all times and by more liberal Jews when praying, studying, and eating.

For centuries the outward, visible, public, identifying symbol of a Jewish man, and in recent years of some Jewish women as well, has been a covered head. So when you put on a *kepa,* you automatically identify yourself as a Jew. You link yourself with generations of Jews who wore this "Jewish uniform" while eating, and you recognize your connection to every other Jew throughout the world today who wears the same kind of *kepa* to recite the same prayer.

You can keep your *kepot* in a kitchen drawer, always nearby, always ready for every member of the family and for mealtime guests. As with any uniform or piece of equipment, it's best to have your own special, favorite *kepa.* Over time, it becomes a part of you, an extension of your identity and your being; it's familiar, it's comfortable, it's you.

2. When you say *motzi,* you speak ten words of Hebrew.

As we have already discovered, Hebrew has an inherent magic that turns mere words into powerful incantations. By reciting even ten words of Hebrew a day, you not only link yourself to the ages by speaking the Jewish language and attuning to Jewish sounds and rhythms, but you invoke God's presence and celebrate God's manifestation in your life.

3. When you say *motzi,* you affirm your humanity.

Animals take any food that is in front of them and stuff it into their mouths. We human beings have the ability to exercise self-control and self discipline; we can choose the food we eat (for traditional Jews the laws of *kashrut* determine what is permitted and what is prohibited), and we can choose when and how to eat it. Even though we may be "starving to death," we have the holy power to pause for five seconds to say a prayer.

4. When you say *motzi,* you acknowledge the power of God and express gratitude to God for God's many gifts.

We human beings share in the process of creation by planting the seeds and harvesting the crop, but it is God, and God alone, who is the spark, the source, of creation, who gives life to the wheat and the apples and all the ingredients in a hot fudge sundae. In our highly scientific and technological world, where some seem to think that all the power is in our hands, it is good to spend five seconds a day remembering our real place on the cosmic totem pole. It is good to be able to say, "Thank You, God, for this food that you have provided me, that is going to nourish and sustain me. I gratefully acknowledge You as the source and the Creator of all that is in the universe, and I thank You for all Your goodness toward me."

5. When you say *motzi,* you can bring your family close together.

If you are eating together with your family, you can make the rule that no one may say *motzi* until everyone is seated at the table ready to eat. This means that no family member is the servant, still running between stove and table, while the others are already eating.

It also means that for at least five seconds a day you can be linked together in common purpose with every member of your family who is sitting around the table. Each of us has individual needs and activities; we are often in a hurry to get to a meeting or a game or back to our homework. But for those magical five seconds, you and the members of your family are bound together. Hopefully, saying *motzi* together will be the beginning of dinner table conversation, leading to new talk, new sharing, new understanding between parents and children, between siblings, between spouses.

If the *Motzi Mitzvah* were offered as a business deal, you would grab it before the ink could dry on the contract.

Your investment? Ten words recited in five seconds a day.

Your return? A link to the Jews of the generations and to every Jew in the world today; the Jewish language on your lips; a daily reminder of your humanity; a daily expression of gratitude to God; new family ties and closeness.

What a marvelous return for such a small and simple investment!

Commit to it while it is still fresh in your mind. Say *motzi* tonight, tomorrow night, every night. Add this easy, simple *mitzvah* to your daily routine, ingrain it as a habit, adopt it as a ritual, and in five seconds a day you can change your life and the life of your family.

Happy *mitzvah.*

Happy *motzi.*

Happy eating.

Happy you.

9

Shabbas Soul

GOD'S GREATEST GIFT TO THE JEWISH PEOPLE IS Torah, and the greatest gift in Torah is Shabbat, Shabbas, the holy Sabbath day.

It is hard to imagine what our ancestors who stood at Sinai must have thought when they heard the command, "Remember the Sabbath day and keep it holy" (Exodus 20:8). They who had been slaves, whose labor had been demanded and exploited, who had worked day after day, year after year, who saw rest as a luxury that only the free and the wealthy could afford, were now told that one day in seven—one day in seven!—was to be set aside for physical relaxation and spiritual rejuvenation. What a revolutionary concept; what an extraordinary acknowledgment of humanity and equality; what a supreme gift!

Throughout the generations, Shabbas has been the central, core observance of Jewish life. It has been the centerpiece of Jewish existence. Wednesday until Friday meant preparation for Shabbas; Sunday until Tuesday meant living in the sweet glow of Shabbas. When Jews were blessed with material resources, the finest table was set and the finest food was prepared for the Sabbath meal. When Jews were wretchedly poor, the few coins that could be scraped together went to buy for wine for *kiddush.*

The holy Shabbas is the bride, her weekly visit a time of fevered anticipation and deepest love. The holy Shabbas is the queen, her weekly visit a time for deepest happiness and unrestrained joy. Shabbas is greeted with song and dance; she is welcomed as a precious guest. Some say that the twenty-four-hour Shabbas is a foretaste of *masheachvelt,* the time of the messiah, for the quiet and tranquillity, the harmony and peace, the overflowing love of Shabbas that envelops us and our world, is just what it will be like in messianic days.

Shabbas is such a precious gift to body and soul because, in essence, it says to us, "You have control over your own life. You have the ability to stop work, to stop the unrelenting onslaught of time, to call a halt to the seemingly endless demands on your energy." In modern parlance, "You can run your business, your business does not have to run you." You can take twenty-four hours a week away from schedules and deadlines, and you can carve out time to rest your physical body, to reinvigorate your mind, to revive and restore your spirit. You can take time for your spouse, your children, your parents, your friends, your God, yourself. You can take time to eat, to sing, to talk, to make love, to sleep, to pray, to connect with community, to take a walk, to read a book, to take a nap in the middle of the day, to visit, to think, to watch the sun set and the stars come up.

Given a gift like this, who wouldn't grab it and hold it tight? Who wouldn't eagerly await the holy Shabbas and embrace her wholeheartedly?

Yet everybody knows that not many Jews observe Shabbas anymore. The freedoms and opportunities that America offers on Friday night and Saturday seem to have attracted more Jews than have the gifts of Shabbas. For many, the laws of traditional Shabbas observance— which were conceived as the "fence" to keep us from being tempted into our weekday habits—are seen as strict prohibitions and restrictions rather than as the life-affirming shouts of "Yes!" that they are really are:

"Yes, I can choose rest over work, family over business, God over my bank account,"

For many, the holy Shabbas has become just a memory, a shadow of what she used to be. Our grandparents said, "Gutten Shabbas." Our parents said, "Shabbat Shalom." We say, "Have a good weekend."

We have lost the beauty and the power of the day; we have forgotten what Shabbas can mean to us, what Shabbas can be for us. We have forgotten that one day a week there is time not "to do," but "to be." We have forgotten how our souls and our spirits can be touched by holiness.

It is time to recapture, to renew Shabbas—to give ourselves the gift of this precious day for revival of body and mind, soul and spirit.

As important as it is, "how to" observe Shabbas—how to make a Shabbas dinner, recite the Shabbas table prayers, attend Shabbas services, spend the Shabbas day—is something that can be learned by participation. Here, we explore just two aspects of Shabbas observance, the two deepest spiritual quests of Shabbas: on Shabbas, which celebrates the moment of creation, how do we get in touch with creation and the Creator? And on Shabbas, which celebrates the holiness of each individual soul, how do we raise our souls higher and higher to the realms of God?

First, consider the candle.

Consider the short, stubby, little white candles that we call "Shabbas candles."

They aren't particularly pretty. They aren't used as decoration to bring color or form as the centerpiece of the table; they surely aren't used to set the mood for a romantic dinner.

They aren't very unique. We can get them almost anywhere these days—at the Jewish bookstore, at the synagogue gift shop, at the kosher butcher's, even from the shelves of the local supermarket.

People often talk with nostalgia, pride, devotion, and love about the candlesticks they use to hold their Shabbas candles.

"These are the candlesticks that my *bubbe* brought with her on the boat from the old country."

"These are the candlesticks I inherited from my mother when she died."

"These are the candlesticks I received as a wedding gift fifty years ago."

"These are the candlesticks we bought in that little shop in Jerusalem."

"These are the candlesticks that were given to me by my in-laws when I converted to Judaism."

But rarely, if ever, does anyone speak about the candle.

We know of its origins.

The Children of Israel, the recently freed slaves, were commanded to light no fires on the Sabbath during their trek toward the Promised Land. In the desert, that meant that the bonfire, providing heat and light, could not be stoked during the twenty-four hours of the Sabbath.

When our ancestors became urban dwellers, they used oil lamps and eventually candles for the practical purpose of bringing light into an increasingly darkening household between sunset, when Shabbas began, and bedtime.

Over the centuries, the lighting of the Sabbath candles took on the religious symbolism of being the ritual that marks the beginning of Shabbas.

For traditional Jews, the lighting of the candles still signifies the exact moment when Shabbas begins each week. No matter what time sunset comes—as early as four o'clock in the winter or as late as after eight o'clock in the summer—the Sabbath begins precisely on time, with the lighting of the candles that usher in the day of rest.

Many liberal Jews light candles not at the precise moment of sunset, but when their own Shabbas observance begins—either when they sit down to eat Shabbas dinner, when they leave home to attend the late Friday evening service at the synagogue, or when the candles are lit as part of the congregational ritual as the worship service begins.

If truth be told, for most liberal Jews—and, it is suspected, for a good many traditional Jews as well—the lighting of the Sabbath candles has become rather routine, a thirty-second ceremony done almost by rote.

But consider the candle.

When understood and performed with its original spiritual intent, the lighting of the Sabbath candles can be a sublime moment, an ecstatic moment, a moment of supreme holiness.

For lighting the Shabbas candles can be our weekly connection to God, the Creator, and to the exact moment of creation.

The Sabbath prayers tell us that Shabbas is *zecher l'ma'aseh v'rasheet,* a "remembrance of the act of creation." Each week we commemorate and celebrate God's creation of the world and God's rest when the task was completed.

And what was God's very first act of creation? The Bible reports, "God said, 'Let there be light' " (Genesis 1:3).

The world, as we know it, began at the exact primordial moment when God created light.

Every particle of creation is infused with God's light.

Light is the symbol of God.

Light is the symbol of God *in us.* For, as the proverb teaches, "The candle, the flame, the spark of God is the very soul of humankind" (Proverbs 20:27).

That which makes this lump of clay that is a body into a living, breathing, functioning human being is the soul—and the soul is the light of God.

So what do we do as Shabbas begins, what do we do at the exact moment that is the weekly observance of the birth moment of our world, the "remembrance of the act of creation"?

We imitate God.

In that tiny second when we light the flickering flame of the Shabbas candle, we instantly transport ourselves backward through time; we connect ourselves and merge with that original primordial moment of creation.

God infused the world with light, and creation began.

We, who are created in the image of God, imitate God's act of creation by creating light.

Like God, we infuse our world with light: the light of God, the light of creation, the light of each human soul.

We renew creation in our time and place.

So, next time—every time—that you light your Shabbas candles, don't just see a routine ritual; don't just see stubby little white candles.

Look deeply into the flame; candle gazing is not just a New Age phenomenon. Stare at the light for ten seconds, for thirty seconds, for a minute or more.

In that light, see God; in that light, see the exact moment of creation; in that light, see the entire universe. In that light, see yourself and your children, and your children's children, and generations yet unborn. In that light, see the totality of existence—your deep connection to all that was, all that is, and all that will be. See your long-ago beginnings and your forever destiny.

To heighten the sense of seeing, and to enrich Shabbas, you may want to recite words of modern prayer as you light your candles.

Since we often welcome Shabbas within a circle of family or friends, this prayer—as are many Jewish prayers—is in the plural, *"we* see." If you are welcoming Shabbas by yourself, you may want to make the meditation-prayer more your own by shifting to the more personal *I.*

On this night
we see the world
in a new light.

On this night
we add a new spirit
to our lives.

On this night
we taste
a new time of peace.

We rest
from desire for gain,
ambition for things.

We raise our eyes
to look beyond time and space
toward eternity.

We
come to see the world
in a new light.

"Let a new light shine upon us
and may it be our blessing
to see its splendor."

Consider the candle.

Everything that is important to us at the very core of our beings—everything that is important to our world—is in its flame.

Open your eyes and see.

Close your eyes and see.

᠊᠊᠊᠊᠊

What a heightened sense of existence Shabbas gives us as it connects us to the magical moment of creation.

But there is even more. For on Shabbas we are elevated far beyond our everyday world, and we are able ever so slightly to touch the hidden secrets of the universe—all that we once knew and all that we will one day know again.

The Talmud teaches, "On the eve of the Sabbath, God gives each person an additional soul, and at the close of the Sabbath, God withdraws it" (BT Betzah 16a).

An additional soul? What is it? What does it do?

An additional soul—in Hebrew, *neshamah y'terah*—is an extra measure of God within us. It raises us up on every level—physical, mental, emotional, and spiritual—high above our normal state of being.

"In its descent, the additional soul bathes itself in the sweet perfumes of the Garden of Eden, after which it descends and rests upon the holy people" (Zohar Sh'mot 204a).

The *neshamah y'terah* comes on Shabbas, as the sweetest, sweetest gift from God, so that on the day that is different from all others, we can be different than we are on all other days.

Having an additional soul enhances everything we do, as if we had a double portion of all our senses and attributes. With this additional soul, the Shabbas soup is tastier, the *kiddush* wine is sweeter. Our singing is richer; our praying is deeper; our conversations, even our lovemaking, is more intense.

Having an additional soul means that "all sadness, gloom, and irritation are forgotten, there being only joy and gladness diffused through both the upper and lower worlds" (Zohar Sh'mot 204a).

Having an additional soul gives us a foretaste of the world to come, of the messianic time when harmony and peace will reign. As the Zohar teaches, "On the Sabbath, all sorrow and vexation and trouble is forgotten because it is the day . . . when an additional soul is imparted [to human beings] as in the future world" (Zohar Vayirka 95a).

The Talmud teaches that the future world, the world of *masheach,* the messiah, will come when "every Jew observes the Sabbath two weeks in a row" (BT Shabbat 118b). For when the heightened feeling of harmony and peace that comes with Shabbas observance envelops the whole world from one week to the next, the world will have come to perfection; the world will be ready for *masheach.* It is the *neshamah y'terah,* the additional soul, that elevates us enough to envision that future world. It is the *neshamah y'terah* that gives us the fleeting touch and the delectable taste of the future world, the incredibly fulfilling feeling of wholeness and holiness that *masheach* will bring.

By attuning ourselves to the presence of the *neshamah y'terah* within, we can almost "float above" our everyday lives. Our consciousness is expanded. We can see from one end of the universe to the other; we can see what is always "out there" but what the limitations of our single soul usually keep from us. We can feel the oneness of all of creation; we can feel at one with all creatures. We can remember some of the secrets of existence, some of God's great plan, that our soul once knew but that we had to leave behind when we came to this earthly plane. With the power of the double soul, we can catch a glimpse of what we have forgotten and be assured that one day all will be revealed again. We can touch the places deepest within us and soar to the grandest heights to feel richest happiness and satisfaction—what we call *simchah* and *naches,* what the Eastern traditions call bliss. We can experience the universal energy that brings us closer to the one world of God.

Is it any wonder that when Shabbas is about to end, when the *neshamah y'terah* is about to leave us for another week, we are sad? Some even say that we feel faint, for the departing additional soul leaves us empty and bereft. To keep the sweetness of Shabbas with us for just a few more moments and, some say, to revive our bodies after the departure of the additional soul, we sniff sweet-smelling spices as part of the *havdalah* ritual, the short prayers separating Shabbas from the rest of the week. "For when the additional soul departs, the soul and spirit are separated and sad until the fragrances come and unite them and make them glad" (Zohar Vayikra 35b).

What would it be if we could keep the *neshamah y'terah* with us for a few more moments, for an extra hour, for an extra day? What would it be if we could keep the *neshamah y'terah* for a week—from this Shabbas until next Shabbas?

It would, of course, be *masheachvelt,* the world of the messiah, the world to come.

So that becomes our goal—keeping the *n'shamah y'terah* for longer and longer until it remains from one week until the next, until *masheach* comes.

That is why, as *havdalah* ends, as Shabbas departs, we sing the song of Eliyahu HaNavi, Elijah the prophet. According to old Jewish legend, it is Elijah who will herald and announce the coming of the messiah, so we invite him into our midst to remind him that he now has six new days to bring *masheach.* We ask him to extend the presence of the *neshamah y'terah* for another minute, another hour, another day so that *masheach* can come.

☙❀❧

Shabbas does not just happen.

Without us, time cannot be sanctified, and Shabbas could be Tuesday or Thursday or not at all.

But when we "make Shabbas," Shabbas becomes a "holy happening."

And every Shabbas becomes a foretaste of the ultimate Shabbas, when Shabbas peace and love will envelop the whole world.

We can't let one more Friday night and Saturday go by as just another weekend, for Reb Shlomo was right: "The whole world is waiting to sing the song of Shabbas. And God is also waiting to sing the song of Shabbas."

10

Rejoicings

Reb Zalman tells the story of the Jews of Berditchev, when the czar was making life miserable not only for Jews but for all the people of the country.

One of the oppressive measures that had been imposed was a ban on Turkish tobacco. It was forbidden to import, sell, buy, or smoke Turkish tobacco, and anyone caught with it would be severely punished. This meant that a good smoke, one of the few simple pleasures left to the poor peasants, was no longer possible.

That year on Erev Pesach, just as the *seder* was to begin, Reb Levi Yitzchak of Berditchev called his chasidim together and said, "I cannot begin the *seder* unless I have two things. I need a pound of good Turkish tobacco, and I need a bit of *chametz*, a bit of leavened bread."

The chasidim were incredulous. Where were they going to get a pound of Turkish tobacco, the very tobacco that had been prohibited by the czar under threat of great penalty? And where were they going to get any *chametz*, any bread, when Pesach was about to begin—when all the Jews had surely discarded all their prohibited leaven? But Reb Levi was insistent, so the chasidim went out in search.

An hour later, the chasidim who had gone looking for the prohib-ited tobacco returned laden with pound upon pound of the banned substance. Even with the decree that the czar had issued, and even with the promise of severe punishment, hundreds of Jews had hidden away measures of the smuggled Turkish tobacco. But the chasidim who had gone looking for the *chametz* returned empty-handed. On the eve of Passover, there was not one scrap of bread to be found in any Jewish home.

Reb Levi smiled and said, "Now we can begin the *seder,* for now I know that we have no fear of the czar of flesh and blood and his silly laws. But our Jews stand in great awe before the King of Kings, the Holy One, blessed be God. It is God's laws we revere and obey."

⚜

Throughout the centuries, Jews have observed Jewish holidays and commemorations loyally and faithfully. No matter where or under what circumstance Jews lived, the observance of the festivals gave meaning, purpose, and rhythm to life; provided reason for rejoic-ing and celebration; and kept close connection and unity within family and community.

Adherence to the laws of the celebrations was so great that when the sages forgot whether a particular activity was permitted or prohib-ited on a festival, they decided to go out and see what the people were doing. The sages were certain that the people were so committed to proper observance that they were sure to be following the law correctly (BT Pesachim 66a & 66b).

In contemporary times, Jewish holidays do not engender the same kind of observance and the affection they once did.

In the Orthodox community, the holidays are still observed for their own sake, through a sense of *mitzvah,* of fulfilling the commands of God. But in the liberal communities, they seem to have taken up res-idence on the "Jewish smorgasbord." There they and their ritual obser-vances sit, waiting to be chosen by modern Jews who have so many other competing demands on their time and attention. Sociologist Dr. Rela Mintz Geffen contends that in order to be taken from the smorgasbord, embraced, and observed, the rituals of the holidays must somehow "make it" in the minds and hearts of the Jews by being interesting, engaging, and tempting enough.

As well, in order to be happily observed, the Jewish holidays must overcome the unwitting "baggage" that many now associate with them. For many, holidays are wrapped up in warm, nostalgic, wonderful feelings about childhood, home, and family. Yet for just as many, holidays are wrapped up in cold, bitter memories about childhood, home, and family. It is hard to joyously embrace holiday celebration if the very holiday itself triggers feelings of recrimination, remorse, or pain.

Finally, holiday observance has suffered the same fate as so much else in contemporary Jewish life—its significance, highly irrelevant; its ritual, dreary rote; its spirit, listless and uninspiring.

Recently, someone described the majority of Jewish holidays as having one recurring three-part theme: (1) Jews were hated and persecuted, and someone more powerful than we wanted to kill us all; (2) by reason of fortitude, strength, sheer luck, or Divine intervention, the enemy was defeated and the Jews lived to see another day; (3) we celebrate that, rather than dying, we lived.

Frankly, this holiday motif is enough to frighten our children and make them wonder what is so great about being Jewish if so many hate us so much. And, as praiseworthy as our continuing deliverance is, it is not enough to inspire great spiritual exaltation or enlightenment. We have created too many rites and rituals to herald our continued existence, but we are sorely lacking in ceremonies that acclaim and laud our inherent, unique, and worthy reasons for being.

Like so much else of Jewish life, our holiday celebrations need to be reinfused with spiritual meaning and enriched by spiritual rite. They need to speak to our questing minds and our yearning hearts; they need to bring uplift to our hungering souls.

Our holiday celebrations can become moments of deep and holy encounter not only with our history and our destiny, but also with our God when we come to understand some of their original sacred purpose and when we reclaim some of their sacred practice.

There are many, many ways to renew our holiday celebrations and revitalize Jewish life. Here is a small sampling. More will come from other Jewish renewal teachers and communities—and from your own experience, from your own heart.

Rosh HaShanah

ONE OF THE MOST POWERFUL PRAYERS OF THE Rosh HaShanah (and Yom Kippur) liturgy is the *Alenu.*

Regular worshipers are familiar with this prayer (and we shall have much more to say about it in chapter 16) because it is the prayer that concludes every Jewish worship service—evening, morning, and afternoon; weekday, Shabbat, and festival. *"Alenu l'shabayach la'Adon hakol...."* "We praise the Lord of all...."

In the middle of the prayer, we say, *"Va'anachnu koreem...."* "We bend the knee and worship and give thanks...." As we recite these particular words, we match our actions to our words by slightly bending and bowing.

At each service, this *Alenu* prayer serves as the capstone of our worship. In its center section—a part of the prayer that is usually recited silently so it is not as well known as the rest of the prayer—are words that encapsulate the whole of the Jewish experience: *"l'takain olam b'malchut Shaddai...."* "[We hope for the day when] the world will be perfected under the kingdom of God." And the prayer concludes with the eternal hope for ultimate redemption for ourselves and our world: "As it is written, 'The Lord shall be King over all the earth, and on that day, the Eternal God shall be recognized as One, and God's name as One.'"

It is no wonder that *Alenu's* ubiquitous presence in all our services and the powerful sentiments it expresses have made it one of the most beloved of all Jewish prayers.

But on the High Holidays—in its original spot in the liturgy, before it was made part of every service—*Alenu* commands a central place and purpose. It is recited at the beginning of the *musaf,* additional, service as the keynote prayer to all that will follow—on Rosh HaShanah, at the beginning of the three sections of worship, each containing the sounding of the *shofar,* and on Yom Kippur as the prelude to the *avodah* service, the reenactment of the Yom Kippur ritual when the Holy Temple stood in Jerusalem.

The *Alenu* prayer embodies one of the central themes of the High Holidays, the Kingship of God. Here, at a peak moment of the prayer service, we acknowledge God's sovereignty and figuratively place upon God's head the crown of leadership and authority.

When we come to the words, *"Va'anachnu koreem. . . ."* "We bend the knee and worship and give thanks . . ." we do not simply bend knees and bow, but it is traditional for the prayer leader, the cantor or the rabbi, to literally kneel and prostrate in front of the Holy Ark, dramatically and vividly demonstrating our acknowledgment of God's Kingship, our reverence for God, our loyalty to God, our submission to God's will.

When the prayer leader kneels, it is a moment of highest emotion, a breath-stopping moment of greatest awe.

So here is the *chiddush;* here is the new (but very old) way to bring a great, awesome moment of spirit to your life, to your relationship with God.

Kneeling for *koreem* on Rosh HaShanah and Yom Kippur is not just the job of the cantor or the rabbi.

Kneeling for *koreem* is the great privilege and awesome responsibility of every Jew—you and me.

Don't just watch your rabbi and cantor kneel for *koreem.* Join them.

When it comes time for *Alenu,* find your space in the aisle; say the words from out of the depths of your being; sing the haunting melody with passion. When you come to the words *"Va'anachnu koreem . . . "* bow, kneel, and prostrate yourself. Come before God in humility and in awe. Tell your God that even if you forget during the rest of the year, you give Him/Her the crown; that you submit to God's awesome power; that your life is in God's hands; that you are God's child, and that He/She is your God.

The first time you kneel and prostrate will be scary; it will feel funny; it will seem to defy the "suburban imperative" that we must be formal and dignified in synagogue. But once you have done it, you will recognize and anticipate its great power.

Over the years, I have invited worshipers in the service I conduct to join with me in the ritual of *koreem*. Now almost everyone—from our young Bar and Bat Mitzvah boys and girls to the most elderly in our *minyan*—kneels at *koreem*. People tell me that it is the High Holiday ritual they most eagerly await and love, for it brings so much satisfaction, so much spiritual joy.

As much as God will appreciate your words and your actions, you will feel the great power of prayer and ritual, the need for repentance, and the humble joy of forgiveness. You will experience Rosh HaShanah and Yom Kippur, the Days of Awe, as they are to be observed—with your full participation, your full awareness, your full heart.

Min hamatzar, "from the very lowest of depths," from the very lowest physical point you can be—stretched out full-length on the floor, face in the ground, body vulnerable and at risk—you will rise to the highest, the greatest, of spiritual heights.

You will call.

And God will listen and hear.

And God will answer your prayer.

✻

And then, on Rosh HaShanah afternoon, go out to a body of flowing water to perform the Tashlich ritual.

Tashlich—which means "to cast" or "to throw"—is a quaint ceremony that comes to us from the Middle Ages, but it so captures the human condition and the human spirit that it should be part of every Jew's Rosh HaShanah observance.

The premise is quite simple: into a body of flowing water—a river, a lake, a stream, an ocean—we symbolically "cast our sins and transgressions." With a number of short, poignant, and deeply personal prayers, we throw bread crumbs or pocket dust or pebbles, representing our sins, into the water, to be carried away by the gentle flow.

Until only a decade or two ago, the Tashlich ritual was most often performed by the pious few. But in recent years, more and more Jews have embraced the Tashlich service. Entire congregations now gather at the water, late on Rosh HaShanah afternoon. The sense of community, of belonging, of shared quest is almost palpable. The prayers are fervent; the singing is rich and sweet. In those places where the body of flowing water is in a beautiful setting, the gathering additionally becomes a celebration of the wonders of God's creation. Just imagine the glory that we on the West Coast feel as we participate in the Tashlich ritual just as the fiery red sun sinks into the rolling waves of the Pacific Ocean!

In places where there is no body of flowing water, people have begun to gather for Tashlich to cast small pieces of paper or—despite the rightful environmental concerns—colorful balloons to the winds.

Tashlich has been revived and has become so popular because it is a most vivid and dramatic way of doing *t'shuvah,* of doing repentance, and bringing *tikkun,* personal healing. Without having to know the words or the melodies of the prayers, without having to sit through a lengthy service, the real work of Rosh HaShanah—the work of personal introspection, reflection and repentance—can be done. In an informal setting, in comfortable clothes, we create an atmosphere that quickly ranges from the solemn task of admitting foible and failing to the joyous relief of hearing forgiveness. We follow the admonition and the invitation of the prophet to "cast away all our transgressions, and create within ourselves a new heart and a new spirit" (Ezekiel 18:31 and, similarly, 36:26).

Tashlich is Rosh HaShanah at its very best and its most powerful. At that supreme moment when we watch the water carry away all the hurts and the troubles and the anguish and the mistakes and the regrets and the failings of the old year, like the psalmist of old, we call out to God in our distress, and we know that God answers us and sets us free. And we say, "Turn us to You, O God, and we will return." And we say, "Thank You, God, for giving us another year to live and to love, another year to heal and to grow, another year to be Your partner here on this beautiful and magnificent earth."

Yom Kippur

YOM KIPPUR IS A GREAT PARADOX.

It is the most intensely personal and solitary of all Jewish observances, yet it is carried out in the midst of the largest Jewish crowd to gather all year. It demands internal scrutiny about external behavior. And it calls for public confession of the most private of acts.

However we regard its paradoxical contradictions, however we choose to observe or to ignore Yom Kippur—whether we choose to come close or to stay far away—there is no denying that it has a powerful effect on us. Is it nostalgia and warm memories? Is it family ties? tribal instinct? guilt? mind games? terror? hope?

Probably it is all these and more, mixed together in a potion that creates Jewish magic, that turns an otherwise ordinary date on the calendar into a momentous occasion of, in the words of the philosopher Søren Kierkegaard, "fear and trembling."

Yom Kippur, at its simplest and most profound, demands a *cheshbon hanefesh,* a soul-inventory, an accounting of the words and deeds of the year gone by. Only when we have honestly evaluated where we have been can we hope to enter into the new places where we would like to be.

Introspection and reflection are never easy; self-assessment takes candor and courage. Yom Kippur gives us the rubric, the structure, the long, often repetitious day, to accomplish the task. Yom Kippur, taken seriously, offers the opportunity for doing repentance and holds out the promise of hearing sweet forgiveness. But the real work, the deep, deep exploration into psyche and soul, is not dependent on a day or a gathering or a liturgy. It is ours and ours alone.

⚜

Here are two new ways—one external and one internal— to enrich the Yom Kippur quest and to renew the Yom Kippur journey.

On Yom Kippur we choose to fast, to not eat or drink for twenty-six hours so that our spiritual quest will not be interrupted by physical need.

Long ago, the prophet Isaiah warned that fasting itself is a hollow and empty gesture unless it is accompanied by ethical behavior. "Is this the fast I desire, A day for men to starve their bodies? Is it bowing the head like a bulrush, And lying in sackcloth and ashes? . . . No, this is the fast that I desire: To unlock the fetters of wickedness, And untie the cords of lawlessness, To let the oppressed go free; To break off every yoke It is to share your bread with the hungry, And take the wretched poor into your home; When you see the naked to clothe him, And not ignore your own kin" (Isaiah 58:5–7). Ritual—even the Yom Kippur ritual that supposedly sets the atmosphere for sincere repentance—is in vain unless it is matched by worthy and worthwhile action.

For Yom Kippur to be a holy day worthy of our soul's redemption, we must match our actions to our words of prayer and repentance.

One way to do this, in the midst of our own voluntary fast, is to help feed the hungry of our world, our country, our neighborhood, who fast on this day through no choice of their own.

In this world of five billion people, where we have the technology and the capacity to feed seven billion, only four billion people eat each day. One billion people go hungry every day! Each day, more than forty thousand children—that's more than fourteen million children a year—die of hunger or hunger-related disease.

On Yom Kippur, we can each make a small contribution to alleviating the suffering, to feeding the hungry.

Many synagogues, *chavurot,* and *minyanim* sponsor food collections on Yom Kippur, and if yours does not, then you can organize it. When you come to worship, bring with you your gift of nonperishable food—a box of cereal, a jar of peanut butter, a package of macaroni and cheese, a can of tuna fish. You and your fellow worshipers can collect hundreds and hundreds of pounds of food that you can contribute to your local food pantry, food bank, or shelter. With your Yom Kippur food gifts, you will not end world hunger, but hungry people in your own backyard will be fed.

As well, when you come to the Yom Kippur service, bring a check for MAZON: A Jewish Response to Hunger, made out for the amount of money you and your family save by not eating on Yom Kippur. This money no longer really belongs to you; it is *tzedakah* money, much like the corners of the field, which belong to the poor and the hungry. The money that MAZON collects is distributed to institutions and organizations throughout the country that feed hungry people and advocate and educate on their behalf. From a modest beginning in the early

1980s, MAZON now allocates almost two million dollars a year. That's real money; that's money going a long way toward alleviating hunger.

Almost eight hundred synagogues, *chavurot,* and *minyanim* in North America are MAZON Partners, and they will help you direct your gift to MAZON. If your prayer group is not a MAZON Partner, you can help it become one, or you can make your own gift directly to MAZON, which is headquartered in Los Angeles.

These small acts—giving food and giving money for food—give you the way to live the words you speak, to turn your Yom Kippur prayers into Yom Kippur acts of lovingkindness.

In the days before Yom Kippur, we wish each other a *tzom kal,* "an easy fast." May it also be a fast that is worthy and good.

✂✦✂

The task of going deep inside to honestly evaluate our words and our deeds can be daunting and intimidating. Our inner vision can become either blurred and hazy or too pristine and clear. Sometimes we tend to be too easy and too gentle with ourselves, overlooking, excusing, rationalizing away behavior that deserves a more critical view. Sometimes we are far too harsh with ourselves, becoming our own severest and unrelenting critic and judge.

Yom Kippur calls us to find the balance as the first step toward transformation.

In order to help ourselves see with clarity, here are two visualizations.

First, in your mind's eye, see a calendar with a separate tear-off page for each day of the year. Go through the calendar day by day. Try to remember where you were, what you did. Try to see the faces of the people you were with.

Many of the pages are, undoubtedly, filled with pleasant memories; with a sense of achievement and accomplishment; with kindnesses done and received; with love and affection given and returned.

Yet many of the pages, and many of the hours on some of those pages, are filled with sadness, with bitterness, with mistakes, with feelings of remorse, with deeds left undone and words left unsaid or better left unsaid. These are the days, the hours, the moments that beckon on Yom Kippur. These are the pages of the calendar that need different entries in the year ahead. In the image of the poet Ruth Brin, these pages "turning and returning . . . calling and recalling . . . return us to our past . . . and turn us toward the future . . . [they] call to us and change us."

There is one more visualization, which you can do privately or together with all the members of your prayer group.

Before Yom Kippur begins, set out three candles—one black, one red, one white. The black candle represents all the ills and evils that beset our world, the foibles and failings of human beings and the human condition. The red candle represents all our own personal mistakes and transgressions, all the wrongs that we have committed during the past year.

As the Kol Nidre prayer is about to be chanted, light the black and the red candles and let them burn throughout the Yom Kippur prayers. They are a vivid reminder of the work that we must do during Yom Kippur—to extinguish those flames, to rid ourselves and our world of all that is evil, of all that is wrong.

Staring into their flames reminds us of the five levels of our souls (which we learned about in chapter 6) and of how our process of introspection and repentance goes through those five levels from our physical being to our highest self and to our interbeing with God. In this way, Yom Kippur becomes, in the highest and greatest sense, a true *cheshbon hanefesh,* a real soul-inventory.

Let the white candle stand as the goal, as the symbol of the journey and the quest of the twenty-six-hour Yom Kippur experience—that after all the work of repentance is done, in the words of the prophet Isaiah, "Your sins that are red as scarlet shall turn white as snow" (Isaiah 1:18). Just as Yom Kippur ends, just before the *shofar* is sounded, blow out the flames on whatever remains of the black and red candles and light the flame of the white candle. The work has been done, the transgressions have been absolved, the process is complete, the vision is fulfilled. The white candle of soul-purity and of sweet forgiveness brightly burns.

Bathed in the light of God's mercy, grace, and compassion, we have but one more prayer to fervently whisper as we return to our homes and resume our everyday lives. In the words of the Kol Nidre prayer, "From this Yom Kippur until next Yom Kippur, may it be for us for good."

Succot

POOR SUCCOT!

Succot is one of the most delicious and "yummy" of all Jewish holidays. With its vivid and unique rituals—the *lulav* and *etrog* and the fragile booth—it seems to have everything going for it.

Yet Succot is one of the most underappreciated and—except in the Orthodox community—least observed of all Jewish festivals. Perhaps if it occurred in the cold of winter or in the middle of summer, when there is little else on the Jewish calendar to engage us, it would capture our imagination. But coming only five days after Yom Kippur, when so many of us are already all "holiday-ed out," and focusing as it does on agricultural themes, when so many of us consider ourselves to be sophisticated urban dwellers, poor Succot just doesn't "make it" for many modern Jews.

We may not be personally engaged in plowing and planting and harvesting the land; we may buy our bread in cellophane wrappers and our oranges in plastic bags, but our lives are inextricably linked to the land on which we live and the air that we breathe.

In recent years, we have learned the dire consequences of raping the land of her minerals and forests, of polluting the waters and the skies with our waste, of bombarding the ozone layer with our hair spray.

More, we have learned to listen to the environmentalists and, better yet, the Native Americans who teach us the wisdom that there is no separation between humankind and the place we live, that, in words attributed to Chief Seattle, "all things are connected. Whatever befalls the earth befalls the sons of earth. Man . . . is merely a strand in the web of life. Whatever he does to the strand, he does to himself."

We are one. We are the land; we are the waters; we are the skies; we are the air.

With this understanding, Succot can be reinfused with new and deep spiritual meaning. As it was for our ancestors, Succot can be for us the recognition and celebration of our merged oneness with our planet. Succot can be the acknowledgment of our awesome yet joyous responsibility to our place and to ourselves. Succot can be our yearly call to consciousness and to action.

In our *minyan,* we try to heighten our awareness of our planet earth by participating in what we have named the Earth Ritual.

Each year, when our members travel on summer vacation, they collect small vials of water and soil from the places they visit. On Succot, we pour all water and soil into one large container. It is quite a mix—water and soil coming from all across the United States and Canada, from Israel and Europe and the Far East. One year, a woman brought small bags of soil from a number of old, desecrated Jewish cemeteries from small towns in Russia and Ukraine, where she had gone searching for the graves of her great-grandparents.

By mixing together the soil and water from all over the globe and then by ritually pouring it out on the lawn in front of our prayer place, we symbolically yet vividly demonstrate that the whole earth is interconnected, that every grain of sand and drop of water comes from one source, and that we, who are made of the elements of earth, are part of the unified whole.

We recite prayers and blessings and sing songs and chants that affirm our commitment to the earth and the sacred oneness of all things. In one of our prayers, we join in the call of our Native American brothers and sisters.

We call upon the earth, our planet home, with its beautiful depths and soaring heights, its vitality and abundance of life, and together we ask that it:

Teach us, and show us the way.

We call upon the mountains, the high green valleys and the meadows filled with wild flowers, the snows that never melt, the summits of intense silence, and we ask that they:

>*Teach us, and show us the way.*

We call upon the waters that rim the earth, horizon to horizon, that flow in our rivers and streams, that fall upon our gardens and fields, and we ask that they:

>*Teach us, and show us the way.*

We call upon the land which grows our food, the nurturing soil, the fertile fields, the abundant gardens and orchards, and we ask that they:

>*Teach us, and show us the way.*

We call upon the forests, the great trees reaching strongly to the sky, with earth in their roots and the heavens in their branches, the fir and the pine and the cedar, and we ask them to:

>*Teach us, and show us the way.*

We call upon the creatures of the fields and the forests and the seas, our brothers and sisters the wolves and the deer, the eagle and the dove, the great whales and the dolphin and the beautiful salmon, and we ask them to:

>*Teach us, and show us the way.*

We call upon all those who have lived on this earth, our ancestors and our friends, who dreamed the best for future generations, and upon whose lives our lives are built, and with thanksgiving, we call upon them to:

>*Teach us, and show us the way.*

And, lastly, we call upon all that we hold most sacred, the presence and the power of the Great Spirit of love and truth which flows through all the universe, to be with us to:

Teach us, and show us the way.

And, in deep humility and with deep gratitude, on Succot we offer new words of praise to God, from this poem by Rabbi Vicki Hollander.

> *We who are made of heaven and earth, body and spirit,*
> *we, who are filled with water,*
> *so as to merge with the world*
> *and simultaneously,*
> *with flame,*
> *which lights our soul with fire;*
> *we praise You*
> *for breathing into us*
> *the breath of life.*
> *Praised are You, Holy One, who sculpts the moon and sprinkles*
> *the stars above, who shapes the world and life and time;*
> *who plants wonder in the world each day;*
> *who wipes our brow when we are weary, and*
> *gives us drink when we are dry;*
> *who lights our soul with dance and hope;*
> *who blows upon the flame within us;*
> *and delights in our glow.*

Chanukah

EVERYONE KNOWS THAT CHANUKAH IS A MINOR festival on the Jewish calendar. But everyone also knows that in modern times, especially in contemporary America, Chanukah has been elevated to tremendous out-of-proportion status because of its time relationship to Christmas.

We don't want to be left out of all the parties and celebrations and, surely, we don't want our children to feel left out from all the gift giving, so we have made Chanukah into much more than it is or was ever intended to be.

How ironic!

Chanukah is a celebration of the Maccabeean-led uprising for religious freedom—to protect the Jewish people from having to assimilate into the culture around them. And here we are, doing just what the Maccabees fought to prevent.

But there is no need for a polemic against how Chanukah is celebrated, no lament against living in an open society, for, after all, we have gained much by living with freedom, acceptance, opportunity. Rather, what we need is perspective; we need to recapture the deep spiritual meaning that is at Chanukah's core.

The greatest teaching of Chanukah, which may be trite but is surely true, is that it takes just one candle to light the darkness.

So on Chanukah, the best gift we can give ourselves, the greatest gift we can give our children, is the gift of learning how to light the candle, the gift of learning how to bring light where there is dark.

We have already given our children much—a place to live, food to eat, clothes to wear, schools to attend, lessons of every sort, camps, vacations. We buy them what they need and, often, what they want. And we expose our children to the vastness of this world; we give them the gift of knowledge and the love of learning.

But have we given our children the gift they most deserve, the gift they need most? They have big brains, but do they have big hearts? They have depth of knowledge, but do they have depth of soul? Have we given them the gift of knowing how to light the candle to illuminate the darkness?

Your Chanukah "gift list" may be entirely different; your list will reflect your concerns, your choices, your commitments, but let this list serve as a guide:

On the first night of Chanukah, take your children with you when you volunteer to serve meals at the local homeless shelter. Light one candle to illuminate the darkness.

On the second night of Chanukah, take your children to the local hospital, and show them how to give a teddy bear or a doll to one of the young patients. Light one candle to illuminate the darkness.

On the third night of Chanukah, you and your children take an old coat or an old blanket downtown and give it to a homeless person who is cold. Light one candle to illuminate the darkness.

On the fourth night of Chanukah, you and your children take a pair of socks downtown and give it to the same homeless person you met last night. If he needs a coat, he probably also needs a pair of socks, but no one ever thinks to give away a pair of socks. Light one candle to illuminate the darkness.

On the fifth night of Chanukah, take your children to visit some of the folks living at the local retirement home. Sing a few songs, tell a few stories, hold a few hands, and listen to the loneliness—and to the wisdom. Light one candle to illuminate the darkness.

On the sixth night of Chanukah, take your children with you to the local blood bank, and let them watch as you donate a pint of blood, as you give the gift of life. Light one candle to illuminate the darkness.

On the seventh night of Chanukah, take your children to play with the young ones at the local women's shelter. Light one candle to illuminate the darkness.

On the eighth night of Chanukah, take your children to an elderly neighbor's house and cook, straighten up, vacuum, scrub the bathtub and the toilets, clean the oven. Light one candle to illuminate the darkness.

On every night of Chanukah, invite friends and neighbors, teachers and classmates, relatives and business associates into your house. Make your home a place of learning and of light, of high purpose and of deep spirit. Hold your children, hug them tight, tell them how much you love them. Give your children the gift that will last a lifetime—the gift of compassion, of sweetness, of humanity, of soul. Light one candle to illuminate the darkness.

Torah teaches that when Moses came down the mountain with the Tablets of the Law, his face was glowing with light, for he had been with God, and he reflected God's light (Exodus 34:30). Every day we pray that we can be like Moses: "Bless us, O our God, all of us together, with the light of Your presence." We pray that we may encounter God, be bathed in God's light, and glow in the light of God's reflection.

On Chanukah, we receive and we give the gift of light. For on Chanukah we learn and we teach that it takes just one candle to illuminate the darkness.

Purim

WITH ITS COSTUMES, NOISEMAKERS, CARNIVAL games, and raucous merrymaking, we usually think that Purim is just for the children.

But, for all its frivolity, Purim is one of our most sublime holidays, for on Purim we touch the deepest within ourselves.

The four heroes of the Purim story—King Ahasuerus, Haman, Queen Esther, and Mordecai—are not just storybook characters. They are part of our collective unconscious, for they are, in Jungian terms, representative of four of the primary archetypes: the King, the Warrior (and their dark side, shadows), the Lover, and the Magician.

The Purim story is such an exquisite story because, through its archetypes, it takes us to the deepest part of our shared memories, our collective unconscious. Literally and figuratively, we get to put on the masks, and bring the internal to the surface.

That is why Purim creates such deep joy—our deepest human energy becomes external and we have incredible energy, we erupt into unleashed, uninhibited joy.

Further, by putting on the masks, by tapping into that primal archetypal energy, we become acutely aware of the very thin line between being a heroic magician and being a villainous warrior, the delicate balance between evil and good.

Even the most virtuous of people can be tempted, can err, can give up or give in.

Purim shouts out a warning: "Be careful. See what can happen if you lose your sense of right and wrong, if you get caught up in ambition or arrogance or hubris. Do not be a child of Haman; be a child of Mordecai. With your very being, bring goodness and light into the world."

And Purim also teaches us about trying to touch the deepest joy every day.

Eventually, we have to take off the masks, to return the archetypes that have come to the surface back to their internal home. But once we have been with them, once we have experienced the infinite joy that comes when we recognize them, we want to be energized like that and to feel that kind of joy as often as we can.

There are two kinds of joy in this world. The first kind is the one we can experience almost all the time, the kind of joy that says we look happy. We even act as if we are happy, but no one—sometimes not even ourselves—knows if it is real, if it is true joy.

"How are you?" Big smile. "I'm fine, thanks. How are you?"

"Can you handle this for me?" Big smile. "Sure, no problem."

"I'd like you to meet my friend." Big smile. "What a pleasure to meet you."

"How was your day, honey?" Big smile. "Great. How was yours?"

And then there is the other kind of joy, the joy that is at the deepest part of our being, the joy that touches the deepest part of our souls. This is the joy we feel when we are in touch with who and what we really are, with what "makes us or breaks us" as human beings: the joy we feel the moment our child emerges from the womb; the moment our son is called to the Torah as a Bar Mitzvah, the moment we walk our daughter to the *chuppah*. It is the joy we feel that is not dependent on any outside situation or circumstance, any other person or thing. It is the joy we feel when we've done our best and when we've been our best.

Purim teaches us to reach for this second kind of joy—to get rid of the masks of false joy and to reach for the inner joy that comes when inhibition is gone, when the real self is revealed, when we find and touch the deepest recesses of our being.

The sages teach, "Be happy—it's Adar, the month of Purim." And we add, "Sustain Adar's happiness, sustain Purim's joy, all the months of the year."

Pesach

PESACH IS THE MOST OBSERVED OF ALL JEWISH holidays—more than Rosh HaShanah, more than Yom Kippur, even more than Chanukah. More Jews come together for some kind of Passover meal, with or without the elaborate ceremonies of the *seder,* than participate in any other Jewish ritual throughout the course of the year.

What is it about Pesach that we love so much? Is it connection to family? Is it the special foods? the meal-centered rituals? the drama and the mystery of the story? the warm childhood memories?

It is, most probably, all this and more. For Pesach captures and encapsulates the whole of the human experience; it touches deeply both our personal consciousness and our collective memory.

The *haggadah* insists that "in every generation each person should feel as if he or she personally went out from Egypt." Somehow, we do. Somehow, Pesach is not just an ancient story but is our story; it is not just a disembodied recollection but a direct and very real experience. That is why, throughout the centuries, more than 2,500 separate editions of the *haggadah* have been produced. Each generation, in each place, remembers a long-ago tale and then rewrites it with compelling immediacy.

In our generation alone, new *haggadot* and additions to traditional *haggadot* have been written to reflect the quest for liberation and freedom for survivors of the Holocaust; for blacks and other oppressed minorities; for the people of the war-torn countries of Southeast Asia and the soldiers from all countries forced to fight there; for Soviet Jews; for women; for the children of Jacob and Esau, the people of Israel and her Arab neighbors who seek to live together in peace. And prayers have been added to the traditional text for personal liberation and freedom from the shackles that bind our minds and the addictions that hold our bodies.

❧✦❧

Bringing continuing renewal to Pesach, infusing it with deep spirit, is as real and as possible as each family, as each person.

Here are but a few new rituals, ceremonies, and texts that might be added to Pesach preparations and to the *seder.*

What could be more arduous than making a house ready for Pesach? All the *chametz,* the leavened, must be removed; all the cabinets and cupboards and major appliances thoroughly scrubbed and cleaned; all the *chametz* dishes and utensils put away, and all the Pesach dishes and utensils brought in from their storage places. Making a house "kosher for Pesach" is the ultimate spring cleaning.

This thorough preparation is reminiscent of how our ancestors readied their lands for the spring harvest. The silos and the storage containers had to be completely cleansed of any remaining grain, not only because room had to be made for the new harvest, but also because the last remnants of the old crop might spontaneously erupt in flames and destroy any newly cut crop that was placed with it. The long-term success of the spring harvest depended on how well the old was cleaned out in order to make place for the new.

The Pesach cleaning, whether on ancient farms or in modern homes, is insistent on letting go of the old and preparing for the new.

Yet it is not in our dwelling places alone that we must throw out the old in order to take in the new. It is in our indwellings, too. It is in our psyches and our souls that we must prepare for Pesach.

It is no accident that Pesach comes halfway through the year, directly opposite Yom Kippur. For Pesach asks of us a semiannual *cheshbon hanefesh,* a mini soul-inventory.

In the image given to us by Arthur Waskow, in order to truly come into Pesach, in order to truly touch the meaning of the observance, we have to clean up not only our homes but also ourselves. We must rid ourselves of the *chametz* that has accumulated within us, the puffed-up ego, the arrogance, the false pride, the harmful habits that debilitate us.

And we must confront our own Egypts—the behaviors, the attitudes, the fears, the addictions—that enslave both our bodies and our minds. We must break the shackles that bind us and keep us prisoners of ourselves.

Even during the hectic days and hours of preparing our homes, we must take time out for deep contemplation and deep meditation in order to prepare our hearts. We need to ask, "Who am I, and what is my life?" We need to "clean up our acts." We need to liberate ourselves from the internal Egypts that hold us down, and we need to throw away the internal *chametz* that fills us up and leaves little room for growth.

When we visualize the *chametz* within being swept away, we can enter into Pesach newly cleansed, and we can embrace our new hearts and our new spirits.

A new *seder* ritual.

It is told that when a very traditional Jew heard that women were being ordained as rabbis, he said, "A woman has as much place as a rabbi as an orange has on a *seder* plate."

Those who believe in the full equality of all human beings and the complete egalitarian nature of Jewish life and practice now add an orange to their *seder* plate.

One of the most beloved songs of the seder is *"Dayenu,"* "It Would Have Been Enough." Over and over again, God's interventions and miracles are enumerated, and the joyous refrain is *"dayenu,"* "it would have been enough" if God had done just one of these great things. But God never stopped. One great miracle piled on top of another until our ancestors were free people in a free land.

But as much as we love the song and its happy melody, the truth is that no single one of God's acts would have been enough. Then, as now, there was always more to be done, there was always one more step on the way to freedom.

So here is a new prayer to add to the *seder,* a prayer that you can amend to fit your circumstances and place, and that you can change every year as the situation warrants.

It is not enough!

> *There is always one more miracle right around the corner—*
> *a miracle of freedom, of liberation, of hope.*

*And there is always a miracle maker present—for God is always there.
And so are we.*

> *For God turns to us, partners in the ongoing process of creation
> and re-creation, partners in healing and transforming and
> perfecting the world, and God says, "My children, there is work to
> be done."*

*It would be easy to ignore the call, now that we sit in sunshine rather
than darkness, in freedom rather than slavery, in luxury rather than
degradation.*

> *It would be easy to ignore the call, sitting at our suburban seder
> in the "land of the free and the home of the brave."*

*It would be easy to say "Dayenu," it is enough that we have achieved
liberty and attained prosperity.*

> *But it is never enough!*

*So, at this seder, we add to the litany of bondage those who seek
freedom of body and soul, freedom from want and need.*

> *We say their names.*

> > *South Central L.A. and
> > Bed-Sty in New York, and
> > the homeless and hungry across America, and
> > those held down by race or creed, and
> > those enslaved to drug or drink, and
> > those in the jails of political prison, and
> > the captives in every land, and
> > Somalia, and
> > Bosnia, and
> > Southeast San Diego.*

> > Dayenu.
> > *It is enough already that anyone suffers,
> > that anyone is enslaved.
> > Release the captives, O Lord,*

Set free the enslaved, O God.
Do it for their sake, and for ours.

Do it speedily, and in our day.
Do it now.
Amen and Amen.

When we think of Pesach, we most often think about the exodus itself—the plagues, the angel of death passing over the houses of the Hebrews, the quick departure, the *matzah.* The second part of the story, when the newly freed slaves come to the sea, is just as important and just as compelling, and it has great lessons for our personal growth as human beings, as children of God.

There they stand at the edge of the sea. The mighty waters are in front of them; Pharaoh's chariots are behind them. They panic; they complain; they cry out in fear; they don't know what to do. They wait; they hesitate; they wait some more. Then, according to the *midrashic* legend, one man, a fellow named Nachson ben Ami'nadav, stepped out of the crowd and walked into the sea all the way up to his chin. Then and only then did the waters part and the Children of Israel pass through in safety.

Perched on the opposite shore, they watched the waters come crashing down on the enemy, and they broke out into songs of thanksgiving.

They had learned a powerful lesson: fear could not help, complaining could not help, waiting could not help. They and they alone could face their fears and their doubts about the unknown. They and they alone had to walk into the sea before the waters would part.

Each of us at some time in our lives—and for many of us, at many times in our lives—stands at the edge of the sea. Old monsters pursue us from behind; the deep swirling waters of the unknown loom ahead. We can be afraid, we can complain, we can hesitate, we can cry out against the injustice and the pain. Or we can walk into the waters, right up to our chin, and know that the sea will part and we can pass through. We will have entered the churning waters and emerged dry and safe.

Here is another invitation to *cheshbon hanefesh,* to soul-inventory, because Pesach calls us to confront our ghosts and to defeat them, to face our fears and to overcome them.

At our *seder,* we can add a new ritual for our own healing and growth, for our own inner serenity, for our own affirmation of our faith in God.

Just after the recitation of the ten plagues, recalling the moment when the Children of Israel came out of Egypt and came to stand at the sea, each *seder* participant can stand up and move to the next chair around the table.

Symbolically, of course, we are "crossing the sea" with our ancestors. But on a deeper, personal, spiritual level, we are symbolically crossing our own rough seas.

Since so many of us are creatures of habit when it comes to space—after all, most of us always sit in the same place at the kitchen or dining room table, the same seat in the classroom, the same row in synagogue—by the simple act of changing places at the *seder* table, we create just enough dissonance of order to vividly and dramatically declare that we can move from one place to another, from one psychological and spiritual space to another.

As we move places, as we "cross over" from one place, one state of being, to another, together everyone can recite this prayer:

> *O God, there are times when I come to the Red Sea in my life. Old doubts and fears pursue me; I am confronted by new and difficult challenges; the vast unknown looms before me. Sometimes I am afraid; sometimes I lose faith in my own abilities and my own strengths; sometimes I even lose faith in You. But in Your goodness, You have given me the courage to face every obstacle and the capacity not merely to endure but to prevail.*
>
> *Be with me, O God, as You were with Your children at the sea. Grant me a full measure of Your all-wise care and Your loving guidance so that I can emerge on the other side of my Red Seas healthy and whole, assured that a better world awaits. In love and gratitude, like my ancestors of old, I sing songs of praise to Your great and holy name. HalleluYah.*

By participating in this ritual of "crossing the sea," we declare to ourselves and our *seder* witnesses that we have the courage and the commitment to face our fears, to meet the challenges in our lives, and to jump into the unknown with the confidence of faith. We are reminded that there is sanctuary and comfort, transformation and healing, on the Other Side. We are assured that God will guide us and protect us, leading us toward the promised land of our own lives.

This new ritual may seem quite strange to us at first. But it was probably just as strange when long ago somebody suggested that a mix of chopped apples, nuts and dates, cinnamon, and wine would represent mortar and that we would ingest this substance to remind us of the bricks our ancestors made in slavery.

New and very different rituals always take time to capture the imagination.

Finally, here is a new ritual with cosmic significance that has already been added to many *seder* celebrations.

At the *seder,* we drink four cups of wine, corresponding to the four promises of deliverance that God made and recorded in the Torah. It is a very old and beautiful custom that when we recite the ten plagues, we pour out of a bit of wine from one of those cups as each plague is mentioned. A full cup is a symbol of complete joy, but our joy cannot be complete knowing that others suffered and died for our freedom.

The fifth cup of wine on the *seder* table belongs to the prophet Elijah. At a most dramatic moment in the *seder* service, Elijah is symbolically invited to join us and to sip from his cup of wine. When we open the door to welcome Elijah, magic happens, for in that instant the theme of the *seder* switches from the remembrance of historical redemption to the promise of ultimate redemption. For, as we know, according to tradition it is Elijah who will herald and announce the coming of *masheach,* the messianic time of the perfection of our world.

Yet we know that God will not just deliver the messiah to our midst. We have to do our part to prepare our world, to bring it toward balance and healing, harmony and tranquillity, justice and peace. We are equal partners with God in the sacred task of bringing *masheach.*

Joining with Elijah, we can now add a new ritual to the *seder.* Instead of just watching Elijah drink from his cup of wine, we can each pour a bit of wine from our own cups into Elijah's cup. When we poured off the wine of the plagues, we acknowledged our sorrow. When we pour in our wine and mingle it in Elijah's big cup, we affirm our proactive role as partners in bringing ultimate redemption to our world.

Like Elijah, we are the dreamers of humankind. "Every Jewish child is full of dreams. We receive them and pass them on, and they are always the same: an ancient kingdom restored, the messianic victory of humanity."

The sweet song of greeting to Elijah can echo in our beings for a long, long time, and its message can inspire us long after the holiday of Pesach is gone for another year. "Speedily and in our day, come to us, Elijah, come to us with *masheach.*"

Yom HaShoah

IN THE SHADOW OF AUSCHWITZ, IN THE WAKE of the horrific genocide in which six million of our Jewish brothers and sisters were slaughtered, we have added a new commemoration to our calendar: Yom HaShoah, the Holocaust Remembrance Day.

Not that we ever forget, not that it takes a specially designated day to help us remember, but Yom HaShoah serves to focus our energy and unite us in our grief. It is the day when the entire Jewish body, joined by men and women of goodness and decency of all nations and faiths, lets out the scream of anguish and pain over the limbs that have been cut off from us.

The tear-filled memorial services are right and proper. They pay most deserved tribute to those whose lives ended in a puff of smoke from a crematorium chimney; they give us place to weep bitterly over our unbearable loss; and they provide the moment for the survivors left to tell the tale.

≈❖≈

Yet for all its necessary and worthy place in Jewish life, Yom HaShoah's original purposes are no longer enough. Two new and vitally important spiritual legacies must be derived from the Holocaust experience and from the memories that it evokes.

What is it that connects contemporary Jews to Judaism? When asked what elements most contribute to their personal attachment to Judaism, most Jews report that on a scale of one to ten (with ten highest), their beliefs, ritual practices, ethical values, ethnicity, commitment to community, and connection to Israel all rank somewhere between four and eight. Yet most Jews also report that their feelings about the Holocaust and anti-Semitism rank a nine or ten on their scale of attachment. External threats seem to engender more Jewish sentiment and involvement than internal elements.

In the years since the Holocaust, we Jews have mourned deeply, and at the same time we have remained vigilant against any danger or threat to our well-being. But we have been less passionate about celebrating all that is great and wondrous about Judaism—the very reasons for our being. We have learned well to say *kaddish,* but we are not as fervent about saying the *hallel* psalms of praise. We have collected untold sums of money to fight discrimination and to build museums of memory. But we have collected far less money to build Jewish schools and to shape the next generation of Jewish hearts and souls. If an enemy were to post a sign on a synagogue that says, "Closed because we hate the Jews," every Jewish organization and almost every Jew would immediately rise up in righteous indignation and protest. If a rabbi were to post a sign on the same synagogue that said, "Closed for lack of interest," most Jews would nod sadly and yawn in indifference.

For the Holocaust to have real and ultimate meaning, for the six million not to have died in vain, we cannot give Hitler a posthumous victory. We have to live deeply and truly authentic Jewish lives. We have to bring Judaism back from the old, worn-out irrelevancies that have turned off and turned away so many. We have to recapture Judaism's deepest spiritual meaning and its eminent cosmic value. We have to find within Judaism its most heart-filling, soul-satisfying, and life-enriching beliefs and practices. We have to renew Judaism not just for ourselves and our own souls, but as the continuing and enduring spiritual legacy for generations yet unborn.

There is little sense in mourning for Jews and a Judaism that is gone unless it inspires and moves us to create the Judaism that will be. Yom HaShoah must be more than a lament, it must be an exhortation to revive and renew Judaism so that it becomes a vitalizing, invigorating, spiritual force at the core of each and every Jewish being.

One more thing must Yom HaShoah do.

Elie Wiesel, the chronicler of the Holocaust and the conscience of this generation, has taught us that while there is no answer to Auschwitz—no way to understand the genocidal mind of the madman—there is a response. That response is "Never Again!" Never again can we, the citizens of the world, men and women of peace and goodwill, permit such horror and atrocity.

Sadly, we have failed to heed Wiesel's admonition. In the half-century since the ghettos and the gas chambers, the litany of genocide has continued almost unabated. From Pakistan to Cambodia to Afghanistan to the Arab lands to Northern Ireland to Bosnia, humanity's inhumanity, and its lust for ethnic and racial superiority, has been one of the most driving and dominant forces on the planet.

Now, modern technology puts the killing into our living rooms instantaneously, and we go on eating dinner as if the horrid, unconscionable—almost unspeakable—reality is just another of television's fantasies. So Elie Wiesel also teaches that "to live through dramatic events is not enough. One has to share them and transform them into acts of conscience."

We have to work tirelessly and passionately to assure that "Never Again!" is not just a clever political phrase but an absolute reality for our world.

How can we do that? There is so much hate, so much horror, so much pain and suffering. How will we, the few and not particularly politically powerful, bring an end to the gross inhumanity that threatens to destroy all that is precious?

In the summer of 1987, hundreds of thousands of men and women all over the world joined in a one-day convocation that they called the Harmonic Convergence. They held hands, sang songs and played musical instruments, prayed, invoked peaceful thoughts, and spoke of world peace and harmony. They joined their energy together to move the world closer toward decency and goodness.

Most of us laughed. Intellectuals and the rational thinkers scoffed. The media could hardly contain their scorn. The convergers were called naive and silly; they were dismissed as "New Age freaks."

Yet within months of the Harmonic Convergence, strange and wonderful things began happening across the world. The Berlin Wall came down; communism fell in the Soviet Union and the satellite countries; blacks and whites began riding the bus together in South Africa; the shootings and bombings stopped in Northern Ireland; and ancient enemies in the Mideast sat down at the negotiating table.

Mere coincidence?

Perhaps.

But perhaps the combined prayers and spiritual energy of hundreds of thousands of diverse and otherwise disconnected citizens of the world had a positive cosmic effect on the energy of the world. Prayer works. Sending focused energy into the universe works. Combined spiritual and energetic forces can alter momentary reality.

That is why the Talmud teaches, as we know, that if every Jew observes Shabbas twice in a row, *masheach* will come (BT Shabbat 118b). Not that *masheach* particularly cares about religious ritual observance, but if the energy of harmony, tranquillity, and peace that Shabbas evokes can be sustained from one week to the next, then all of earth will be enveloped in *masheachvelt,* the atmosphere, the world, of the messiah.

So what if we were to gather hundreds of thousands, even millions, of men and women from all over the world once a year on Yom HaShoah? We could join together to sing and to pray for an end to war, an end to genocide. We could send thoughts of goodwill and peace out to the universe.

What would happen?

First, of course, if more and more people began to participate in our Yom HaShoah Convergence for World Peace, there would be fewer and fewer people available to fight wars. But, more significantly, we would bring a new gestalt, a new worldview, a new energy to our planet. Instead of so much self-interest, there would be more universal concern. Instead of shouts of war, there would be songs of peace. Instead of hateful energy, there would be loving energy flowing among people, among countries.

Would it make a difference?

How could it not?

How could people and nations not be touched and affected by the new, positive, life-affirming, shared energy that would envelop the earth? How could a new world order not be born?

Are these but the "over-the-edge" musings of a spiritualist gone too far, the foolish dreams of a naive and unapologetic optimist?

Perhaps.

But perhaps as God reveals more and more of the secrets of existence and as human consciousness continues to evolve, we may come to understand more and more of our spiritual power, of our energetic ability to affect and move the universe.

Surely, we can do no harm. Possibly—most probably, I confidently contend—we can do great good. Our hatreds and our guns have brought only the darkness of suffering and despair to our world. Let's try letting our spirits bring the light of new hope. Let's turn the memories of the Holocaust into acts of conscience that will open the world to love and peace.

Shavuot

THE TORAH PRESCRIBES A CAREFUL COUNTING of forty-nine days between Pesach and Shavuot. This period, known as Sefirat HaOmer—the counting of the *omer,* a measure of grain with which to enumerate the days—leads to the observance of Shavuot, an agricultural festival marking the spring wheat harvest and also the picking of the first fruits.

The postexilic Jews quickly tired of another holiday that was closely linked to living on the land from which they had been banished. So to keep Shavuot from being ignored, the sages infused it with new meaning. Doing some "creative mathematics" with Torah time, the sages declared that it was exactly forty-nine days from the time the Hebrew slaves went free from Egypt until they stood at Sinai to receive God's law. Shavuot, the sages insisted, is not only another agricultural festival, but it also commemorates the anniversary of the giving of the Torah.

With this new meaning, Shavuot became an all-important holiday, for it celebrates the theophoric moment of receiving of Torah and the centrality of Torah in Jewish life.

Even the Sefirat HaOmer took on new importance. No longer is it just a period of counting to assure the right moment for harvest; it is also a time of loving courtship between God and the Jewish people. The exodus from Egypt was the betrothal; Sinai will be the wedding, with the mountain as the *chuppah* and the Ten Commandments as the wedding gift. The Sefirat HaOmer is the seven-week engagement, when love grows and the eternal covenant is made.

With this new mystical interpretation of the counting of the *omer* and the new cosmic meaning to Shavuot, some have suggested that the forty-nine days of the Sefirat HaOmer be a time for deep inner introspection. After all, if we are about to symbolically "marry" God, we want to come to our groom with as much self-realization as possible and with a fully open heart.

To guide us in this inner work, we can meditate on the *sefirot,* the emanations between God and us. As we learned in chapter 6, each *sefirah* represents a quality of being and personality, so during the *sefirah,* we can meditate on each *sefirah,* and each *sefirah* in combination with the others (no coincidence here in the similarity of names for the numbering of the days and the numbering of the steps to God and the overlapping of time and function), to help build up in ourselves the inner qualities that each *sefirah* represents.

Shavuot itself can bring us further on our mystical journey. One of the most beloved traditions of Shavuot is staying up all night studying and learning text, because the night of the giving of Torah is dedicated to continual learning of Torah. This custom is called Tikkun Layel Shavuot, usually translated as "the prepared (texts) of the night of Shavuot."

But we know that the word *tikkun* has another, deeper meaning. In both personal and cosmic terms, *tikkun* is "healing," the balancing, repairing, transforming, and perfecting of ourselves and our world. The mystical meaning of Tikkun Layel Shavuot is the "healing on the night of Shavuot," specifically healing for the exile of the *Shechinah,* the sheltering, nurturing presence of God that accompanied the Jews when they were exiled from the Holy Land. A people in exile can never be completely whole, so the personal and collective yearning of the Jewish people is for the *tikkun,* the healing that will take place—and, in our generation has already begun—when we, along with *Shechinah,* are restored to our land and our psyches and souls are made whole again.

The purpose and the goal of the Tikkun Layel Shavuot can be to use text, prayer, meditation, visualization, songs, and chants to heal our relationship with God and to bring our souls in from exile.

Shavuot also calls us to confirm our relationship with Torah.

From the moment Moses received Torah at Sinai, its words and ideas, its injunctions and mandates, have formed, shaped, and rhythmed Jews and Judaism.

Yet, truth be told, as Judaism enters its third era, the place and power of Torah have been greatly diminished. Few contemporary Jews outside the Land of Israel, where Hebrew is the *mama loshen,* the native language, can read Torah in its original language, and few take the time to read it in the vernacular. The two places where Torah is regularly read and studied—the synagogue and the Jewish class room—are largely empty of Jews coming to hear and learn its words.

Even when Jews come to a synagogue or prayer place where the Torah is read in its regular cycle, the process is largely futile. Long sections of nonunderstood Hebrew are chanted, and rather than being educated or inspired, most worshipers are simply bored.

Throughout the Jewish world, dozens of suggestions have been made for renewing Torah learning, for getting Torah back into the hands, minds, and hearts of the Jews.

Torah learning is now being taken out of the synagogue and the classroom by Torah teachers who come directly into homes, offices, and clubs—anywhere Jews are willing to gather and learn.

If learning cannot be done in person, the newest technologies are being employed to bring the message of Torah. One year I mailed out a weekly Torah lesson, called "Torah Talk," to members and friends of my then congregation. In easily understood, easily digestible one- or two-page lessons, Torah was brought directly into Jewish hands. Newer technologies have gone even further. Teachers and organizations of every place on the Jewish spectrum are faxing Torah lessons directly from their fax machine to yours. Torah lessons are available by calling 900 numbers and listening to the recorded message. A wide variety of Torah lessons and discussions are now available on-line on the Internet.

But we need even more. We need to revamp and rejuvenate the weekly Torah reading in its traditional synagogue or prayer group setting so that more Jews might come more often to hear, study, and be inspired by Torah words.

The Torah reading cycle that we now employ, with its lengthy weekly readings, has not always been the way we have heard Torah. Originally, the entire Torah was read only once every seven years (Deuteronomy 31:10–12). Later, Torah was read on a triennial cycle— the entire Torah from beginning to end over a three-year period. Only much later was the Torah divided into the verses, chapters, and portions that we read today and the one-year reading cycle established.

God did not give instructions at Sinai for dividing up, reading, and learning Torah. Those decisions were made by Torah scholars in certain times and places. Now the new time has come for contemporary Torah scholars to devise a new Torah reading plan.

Let's change the Torah reading.

Instead of a lengthy reading that takes up to forty-five minutes and is not understood by many, how about making the Torah reading only one or five or eight or fifteen verses?

Let's choose verses that are powerful, poignant, and spiritually uplifting. Let's choose verses where Torah truly teaches us and inspires us, forcefully and immediately.

Are ten or fifteen verses not enough? Then let's read Torah more than once during the service—still in small, easily digestible doses. Perhaps we can learn from the Catholic mass—patterned on the Jewish worship but with innovative changes—which has three separate scriptural readings, all with a limited number of verses.

Does making selections and limiting the amount we read during our prayer service mean that we should discard or disregard parts of Torah? Of course not. Every word of Torah is holy; every word, every story, every law, every concept has something to teach us.

So what happens to the rest of the Torah, the stories and the laws, the injunctions and the statutes, that might not make it into our new Torah reading cycle?

They can be taught in revitalized Jewish classrooms and innovative Jewish educational settings, where they can be studied in depth, where they can be scrutinized and debated, where seeking and probing minds can learn their valuable lessons. Jewish learning will come alive again when it echoes with the original word of God.

Where and when we read our Torah verses can also help determine Torah's impact.

When does a family, a tribe, a clan, a community tell its tales and pass its stories from one generation to the next? At night when it is dark, when the children are sleepy, when there is magic in the air.

Let's tell our tales—the stories we call Bible stories, the tales and the legends of our people—at night when tales are told. Let's tell Bible stories on Friday night, when the mystical Shabbas first envelops us.

And when do people, when does a community learn ethical values, hear inspiring words, seek spiritual uplift? In the fresh, crisp morning when bodies are refreshed, heads are clear, minds are open.

Let's hear our words of Torah wisdom and inspiration on Shabbas morning. Let those words inspire and enflame our spirits to become better human beings, to better understand God's word and will, to help us enter into God's presence.

Then let's begin to understand Torah to mean Torah in its broadest sense, including the other books of the Bible, the great Jewish literature of the ages, the inspirational Jewish literature of contemporary times.

Currently, every Shabbas and holiday morning, a selection from the biblical prophets is recited following the Torah reading. Called the *haftarah,* this passage was chosen not so much for its inherent beauty or wisdom but because it is thematically connected to the Torah portion of the week. It is supposed to amplify, enhance, and deepen our Torah lesson of the day. In the contemporary service, it is another long chunk of chanted Hebrew that is understood by few, and it is the bane of every Bar Mitzvah boy and Bat Mitzvah girl's existence.

Let's change the *haftarah* reading.

What if we were to eliminate the *haftarah* as it is now recited and replace it with a different kind of *haftarah* based on a model that was used some two thousand years ago? Then, the *haftarah* was recited not immediately following the Torah reading but at the very end of the service, as a final inspirational message before leaving the sanctuary of the sanctuary. While it is most likely that only selections from the Prophets were used, we could expand the repertoire of choice to include the vast expanse of Jewish inspirational literature.

There is a wealth of profound and inspirational Jewish teachings that we never hear. How many Jews know more psalms than the few that are part of the liturgy? Except for the famous "Woman of Valor," which is recited as a blessing from husband to wife on Erev Shabbas and is heard at funeral services, how much of the wisdom of Proverbs do we know? Have we ever heard the fervor of the mystics or the soul-cries of the Hebrew poets or the fanciful stories of the Yiddishists or the musings of the modern thinkers?

Let's use the most sublime, the most beautiful, the most poignant, the most inspirational, the most spiritually uplifting Jewish literature as our *haftarah* portions. And let's ask our fellow worshipers to share with us passages and stories that they have found particularly meaningful.

In our *minyan,* which meets in our members' homes, we ask the host family to select and read a *haftarah* passage for the day. Over the years, we have been treated to beautiful and powerful renditions of truly inspiring words.

One Shabbas morning, at *haftarah* time, the host brought out a copy of *Pirkae Avot,* the Ethics of the Fathers. I assumed that he was going to read one or more of the proverblike statements of wisdom. But instead he said, "I would like to share with you the inscription in this book. It says, 'To Bob, from Dad, originally from Zayde. Because you have now asked the questions that I once did.'"

The young host continued, "As many of you know, my wife is a recent convert to Judaism. When I first got married, it wasn't important to me that I marry a Jewish woman. But as Judaism somehow became more important to me, it became important to her, so she converted, and now we are bringing up our two sons as young Jews. They go to the Jewish day school, and we belong to this *minyan*.

"Many of you know that I was away from Judaism for a long time, but I always kept this one book with me, because it was a link to my father and to my grandfather and to their faith. I guess I knew all along that I would be back one day, but I could not imagine when that would ever be. I want to thank each and every one of you for coming to our home today, to make it a sacred place, a Jewish place. And I want to especially thank the older members here for keeping Judaism alive and strong, especially during all those years when I was away, so that when I was ready to come back, it was still here for me."

Tears flowed down his cheeks and ours. That one *haftarah* was at least as powerful, at least as meaningful and inspirational, at least as holy as all the lengthy chants from the prophetic books—all too often parroted from a tape by an indifferent Bar or Bat Mitzvah youngster—that I have ever heard.

It is time to stop using a Torah and *haftarah* reading structure that clearly does not work for most people and that consigns Torah words to being chanted in almost empty rooms.

If we have the courage to set aside the old and outmoded and embrace that which moves our spirits and brings us closer toward God, then our Torah and *haftarah* readings can offer us new wisdom, great insight, deep emotion, and high spiritual inspiration. They can be clear expression and evidence of God's continuing revelation.

Let's use Shavuot, the anniversary of receiving the gift of Torah, as our impetus and inspiration to recapture the grandeur of Torah in a form that is appealing enough to be gladly accepted and warmly embraced. For Torah to immerse us in its great and wise teachings, for Torah to touch us in our hearts and our souls, for Torah to inspire us to higher and greater living, we need to be exposed to Torah, we need to hear and learn Torah in creative new ways.

The sages taught, "Do not look at the container, rather look at what is in the container" (Avot 4:27). It is time to change the Torah reading's container so that we all can go inside to learn Torah's life-affirming, life-enhancing words of wisdom and beauty.

Two new rituals can help us know Torah—personally, intimately, dramatically.

On Shavuot, many prayer groups unroll the entire Torah, "revealing"—as in the moment of revelation—the entirety of God's will. The rabbi or prayer leader takes the worshipers on a journey through Torah, pointing out and reading the highlights of the human and the Jewish experience and the core commands of law and love: the creation, the flood, the covenant with Abraham, the burning bush, the confrontation with Pharaoh, the exodus, the song at sea, the coming to Sinai, the moment of theophany, the Ten Commandments, the trek through the desert, the blueprint for human conduct, the rebellions and the reconciliations, the declaration (and mantra) of faith, the priestly blessing, the charge of leadership, the death of Moses, the people poised to enter the Promised Land. With the Torah Scroll unrolled and the whole message of the Torah unfurled, the scope and grandeur of Torah become vivid, powerful, and deeply moving.

To give worshipers a sense of real involvement with Torah, a sense of real engagement with Torah, in many groups the worshipers—especially the children—are literally wrapped in the Torah. They stand encircled by the unrolled Torah Scroll, literally surrounded and enveloped by the word of God. It is a moment of high drama that evokes a deep and passionate connection to God and to the Jewish people.

Some prayer groups use this new ritual of the "Torah wrap" at other times during the liturgical year. For more than twenty years, I have put the children in the kindergarten class of the religious school and the children in the first grades of the day and Hebrew schools in the middle of the unrolled Torah on the day that they are "consecrated" to their Hebrew studies. Sometimes this takes place on Chanukah—the festival of dedication—and sometimes it takes place on a day designated just for this purpose. These young children stand encircled in the word of their God and are blessed at the beginning of their journey in Jewish learning. This grand ceremony deeply impresses these little ones with the sacred purpose and the great joy of their quest.

We also unrolled the Torah when my *minyan* acquired and dedicated a new Torah Scroll. The humility, gratitude, and palpable joy of the community was deepened and greatly enhanced by the vivid visual reminder of what Torah is and what Torah says.

Another new ritual literally places the Torah in the hands of each and every Jew. When it is time to read from the Torah Scroll, it is the custom in most every synagogue and prayer group for the prayer leader to take the Torah from the Holy Ark, hold it, and carry it throughout the prayer place. Most worshipers reach out and touch and kiss the Torah as a sign of respect, honor, and devotion.

An even greater way for each worshiper to express love for Torah is personally to hold the Torah Scroll. So in my *minyan* and in a number of other prayer groups, instead of the Scroll being carried by the leader, the Scroll is passed from person to person. We sing HalleluYah, and the people take the Torah, one from the other, and hold it in awe, in reverence, and in love. They cuddle it and sway with it; they caress and kiss it; they whisper tender words and weep gentle tears. And the Torah Scroll hears their words and catches their tears.

An elderly woman who was visiting our *minyan* said, "I am seventy-three years old. This is the first time in my life that I have ever touched the Torah. In my days, girls weren't allowed to come near the Torah, you know. And I haven't felt this way since I held my newborn daughter in my arms fifty-one years ago." And she wept. And we all wept with her. Torah has that power.

When it is literally put into the hands of every Jew, Torah has the inherent energy and the innate beauty and grace to touch us at the deepest core of our beings. The simple ritual of passing Torah from hand to hand helps us to transcend and to come into God's holy presence.

We come to Torah renewal with humility but with confidence and joy, for no less than to our ancestors, God comes to us with the Divine word. As Rabbi Eugene Mihaly taught,

Sinai is ever-present; not only a past event.
Wherever people gather to seek God's presence,
To renew the covenant, to discover God's will,
Whenever we listen and hear, receive and transmit,
We stand at Sinai.

Tisha B'Av and Yom HaAtzmaut

ON TISHA B'AV WE REMEMBER AND MOURN THE destruction of the Holy Temples in Jerusalem, first by the Babylonians in 586 B.C.E., and again by the Romans in 70 C.E., and we lament the exile that made us wanderers from land to land.

For almost 1,900 years Tisha B'Av, which falls in the summer months of July or August—complete with its rituals of mourning, its day-long fast, and its haunting chant of the biblical book of Lamentations—was etched into the Jewish consciousness as the sad but necessary commemoration of our national tribulation.

But in 1948 the Third Jewish Commonwealth, the modern State of Israel, was born. Mourning turned into dancing. Yom HaAtzmaut, Israeli Independence Day—the fifth day of the Hebrew month of Iyar, which in that year corresponded to the 14th of May—took its place on our Jewish calendar as a day of national pride and celebration.

To be sure, there can never be complete joy, for every Yom HaAtzmaut commemoration is preceded by Yom HaZikaron, the Memorial Day for all the soldiers who have fallen in battle creating and defending the land. No home in Israel is untouched, because from every home a son, a husband, a brother, a sister, a cousin, a childhood playmate, a neighbor, a beloved friend has died. The price of freedom and independence has been great, so there is no celebrating without remembering.

Also, for the first nineteen years of modern Israel's existence, the celebration was muted because Israel was like a body without her heart. In the wake of the 1948 War of Independence, Jordan occupied the Old City of Jerusalem—the site of the Holy Temples, the Mount of Olives and the sacred Jewish cemeteries, the ancient Jewish city, the Hebrew University, Hadassah Hospital—and resolutely refused to permit Jews to visit our most holy and precious places. For nineteen years, we wistfully looked through barbed wire and around armed soldiers, hoping that one day we would be able to claim what was rightfully ours.

That day came in 1967 when, with the lightning speed of the Six Day War, Israel took back the Old City. All of Jerusalem was reunited; Jerusalem was whole and complete, the eternal capital of the Jewish people back in Jewish hands.

Since 1948, and, surely since 1967, many wonder why Tisha B'Av should still be observed as a day of mourning. There is almost complete agreement that it should remain a day of remembering the destruction and the exile and all the other persecutions Jews have suffered throughout the centuries. But why continue mourning over exile when the exiled have been returned? Why continue mourning over destruction when the destroyed has been resurrected?

An equally compelling question goes far beyond the one day of Tisha B'Av to every day of the year and to the prayers said three times a day, every day.

During all the centuries of exile, Israel and Jerusalem were never for a moment out of the Jewish consciousness. Three times a day pious Jews prayed, "Cause a new light to shine upon Zion. . . ." "Gather us in peace from the four corners of the earth. . . ." "Sound the great *shofar* proclaiming our freedom; raise the banner to assemble our exiles, and gather us together. . . ." "Return us in mercy to Your city of Jerusalem, and rebuild it in our day. . . ." "May our eyes witness Your return to Zion. . . ." "Next year in Jerusalem. Next year in Jerusalem. Next year in Jerusalem."

Heartfelt prayers. Worthy prayers. Necessary prayers for a people long dispersed, a people that kept its land at the center of its consciousness, a people that never gave up the hope for return, a people that had abiding faith that one day they would be restored to their rightful place, the Promised Land of Israel.

But why are we still saying these same prayers today?

Half a century after the return, after the establishment of the state, after Jewish freedom and independence in the Jewish land, why are we still, three times daily, saying prayers for restoration?

Except for a few Jews who still refuse to recognize the modern State of Israel, claiming that only the messiah can bring true restoration of the Jewish homeland to the Jewish people, most Jews—from every place on the religious and political spectrum—recognize and celebrate the reality of Israel.

Certainly we would like it to be free from strife and contention; certainly we would like it to be the "light unto the nations" that the prophet envisioned; certainly we would like it to be the messianic center of peace in the world.

But just as certainly, we are thrilled and grateful to be part of the first generation in 1,900 years that has witnessed the return to Zion.

So why haven't our prayers recognized the new reality?

Why should we still pray to God to return us to Zion? God has. Why should we still pray to God to gather the exiles from the four corners of the earth? God has. Why should we still pray to God to sound the *shofar* of our freedom? God has. Why should we still pray to God to restore us to Jerusalem? God has.

Instead of just mouthing these old words though habit or because they are printed on the prayerbook page (Change the old, outmoded prayerbook? What a revolutionary thought!), let's recognize that our prayers have been answered!

Now let's pray: "Thank You, God. Thank You for answering our prayers. Thank You for bringing us back to the Land of Israel, the land You promised to our ancestors. Thank You for making us part of the generation that has witnessed the return. Thank You for gathering the exiles from the four corners of the earth and for bringing them to Zion. Thank You for the beauty and the glory of the holy city of Jerusalem, where we can walk among the golden stones and breathe the air of eternity. Thank You for making the journey to Israel only an El Al flight away. Thank You for turning our yearning into reality. Thank You for Israel reborn."

This is the perfect example of how tradition must change to meet reality—how, in the words of Rav Kook, "The old must be made new, and the new must be made sacred."

Surely on Yom HaAtzmaut and, perhaps, on Tisha B'Av as well, let's now say *hallel;* and every day, let's say, "Thank You, God, for Israel restored, for Jerusalem reunited, for our prayers answered in our time. Thank You, God, for doing miracles for us as You did for our ancestors in days of yore."

The Torah bids us "rejoice in your festivals" (Deuteronomy 16:14).

How much deeper and more satisfying our rejoicing can be when we combine the richness of our traditions with new and renewed rituals and practices that enflame our spirits and animate our souls.

"How happy we will be! How good will be our portion, how pleasant our lot, how beautiful our heritage!"

II

Animal, Vegetable, Mineral

THE MIDRASH ASKS, "WHY DID GOD REVEAL Himself to Moses in a bush of thorns? In order to make manifest that there is no place where God's radiance is not; it may even be found in a thicket of thorns" (Shemot Rabbah 2:9). To this teaching the Koznitzer Maggid added, "As the atmosphere encircles the earth, so God envelops the world. There is no place where God's majesty is not."

It makes sense. If God created the world and everything in it, then everything—everything—has within it a spark of the Divine. The soul of human beings, that which gives us breath and life, is a spark of God's light. Every living thing—cows and butterflies, grass and trees, rattlesnakes and thorn bushes—is given life through a spark of the Divine. A piece of bread, an apple, and a radish all have God within. Even those objects we call "inanimate"—a mountain, a piece of glass, a rock, a chair, a grain of sand—are all animated by God's light and filled with God's energy. Scientists may call it the phenomenon of faster or slower moving atoms. We call it God.

Every day we Jews affirm our core belief that God is one, and because God created us we are one with God. Since God created everything, then, like us, every particle of creation is one with God. We are not separate from the cows or the thorn bush, the radish or the rock. We are all one; we all hold a scintilla of God's energy within; we are all one with God.

Sometimes we forget. Sometimes we become enamored with and blinded by our own place or our own power. We forget that we are inextricably linked in collective oneness with the whole of God's creation, and we begin to treat the skies and the seas, the animals, vegetables, and minerals as if they were totally disembodied, totally disconnected from us. We begin to think of them as inorganic, inanimate objects that we can manipulate at our will and use for our own purposes. We forget that they are filled with the same life force as we—that their spirit, like ours, is the spirit of God.

So Judaism gives us constant reminders and many ways to acknowledge and celebrate our interdependence with the earth, our connection with the elements of the earth, our mutuality with the produce of the earth.

Every morning, as the "uniform" worn during our prayers, traditional Jews put on a *tallit*.

Worn by men throughout the centuries and by many women in recent decades, the *tallit* is the garment we use to aid us in fulfilling the commandment to "put fringes on the corners of our garments . . . look at them, and remember all of God's commands, and do them" (Numbers 37:38–39).

The *tallit* is the vehicle for fulfilling the command of the fringes, for the fringes attached to its four corners serve as the constant visual reminder to do not just this one, but all of God's commandments; to comport and rhythm our lives according to God's ethical and ritual injunctions.

But the shawllike garment has also taken on its own identity and its own inherent importance.

This prayer shawl is most often woven of fine wool, the coat of the sheep; sometimes it is made of rich silk, the cocoon of the silkworm.

(Although synthetic materials are, ultimately, the work of God and the produce of the earth, too, we focus on the *tallit* made of natural fiber rather than the increasingly popular polyester.)

In this covering, the gift of our friend the sheep or the caterpillar, we wrap ourselves in the produce of the earth. Like our Native American brothers and sisters whose deep connection to the land leads them to don colorful woolen cloaks when they invoke their deities, we come before God wearing a holy garment made from the bounty of God's creation. We are symbolically whole and one with our God and our universe.

The very blessing we recite while donning the *tallit* does not praise God for commanding us to put it on or to wear it but *l'hitatef,* to "enwrap ourselves" in the fringes, in the *tallit.* At the morning service—when we have just left the shelter and security of a warm bed, where we were wrapped up in cozy and protective blankets and covers—wrapping in the *tallit* makes the transition from night to day a little less harsh, a little more gentle. We spend a few more minutes wrapped in warmth and safety as we ready ourselves for the vagaries of the everyday.

When we wrap ourselves in the *tallit,* we wrap up not just for physical warmth, but for spiritual closeness. We encircle and enwrap ourselves in a womblike cocoon with God. We "cuddle" with God under a holy blanket. As morning unfolds for us, we can still whisper the endearments of the night; we can still speak tender words of affection and commitment. We can shed the tears of yearning or fulfillment; we can mouth the secrets that we want only God to hear. Wrapped in the dark folds of the *tallit,* we can listen for God's still small voice, and we can hear God's sweetest and most holy words.

Wrapped in this garment of the fibers of the earth, our souls can soar to the highest places. The cloth of the *tallit* connects us with the oneness of God's creation; using it wraps us up with God. It is an all-enveloping, all-encompassing garment of deepest intimacy and of greatest love.

Joining the *tallit* as the uniform of Jewish prayer at the morning service is *tephillin,* phylacteries.

Worn by men throughout the centuries and by some women in re-cent decades, *tephillin* are small leather boxes, filled with scripture written on parchment, that are wrapped on the arm and set on the forehead between the eyes.

They are used to fulfill the biblical command that "these words which I command you this day [to "love the Lord your God with all your heart, all your soul, and all your might"] shall be upon your heart . . . and you shall bind them as a sign upon your hand and let them serve as a symbol (or frontlets) between your eyes" (Deuteronomy 6:6, 5, 6, 8).

In order to fulfill this injunction, our ancestors used the produce of the earth. Using a quill, the feather of a bird, they wrote with the ink of a gall nut on parchment, the skin of an animal, usually a sheep. They placed the parchments, which were tied shut with the hair of a calf, into leather boxes, the hide of a cow. The boxes were hand-sewn closed with thread made from the sinew or vein of an animal, a sheep or a cow. Attached to the boxes were leather straps, which is the way the boxes were bound to arm and head.

The *tephillin* that we use today are made in exactly the same way; no printing presses, synthetic substances, or modern machinery have replaced the ancient materials and techniques.

Of what purpose are the *tephillin*?

They serve as a physical sign of the spiritual relationship of faith and love between God and us. When we wrap *tephillin*, it is as if we are wearing a ring—or a necklace, bracelet, or pin—that is the pledge-gift of commitment and devotion between lovers. Mere words can rarely describe the feelings, the intensity, the intimacy, of real love, but the ring—or the *tephillin*—serves as the token and the symbol.

That is why *tephillin* are not worn on Shabbas. There is no greater sign of God's love for us than the gift of the holy Shabbas. Another sign, even a sign as meaningful and precious as *tephillin*, is not needed on Shabbas. The day itself is the manifestation of unspeakably deep love and devotion.

Six days a week, we wrap the *tephillin* on our left arm, placing the box right next to our heart, symbolically showing that we accept the injunction to love God "with all your heart." The strap binding the *tephillin* is wrapped seven times down the arm—reflecting the seven days of creation—symbolically showing that we accept the injunction to love God "with all your might."

As we wrap the strap around our hand, forming the Hebrew letter ש *shin,* standing for *Shaddai,* one of the biblical names of God, we recite words from the prophet Hosea: "I will betroth you forever. I will betroth you with righteousness and justice, with goodness and mercy. I will betroth you with faithfulness. And you shall know God" (Hosea 2:21–22). What a gorgeous and majestic declaration of love!

We place the second *tephillin* box in the center of our forehead, right between our eyes—in the place of our third eye—symbolically showing that we accept the injunction to love God "with all your soul."

Our mystics taught that a person who wears *tephillin* is "enveloped by the supernal mind, and the Divine presence does not depart from him" (Tikunay Zohar 69:159a). To this, Rabbi Nachman of Bratslav added that the *tephillin* are "the innermost light and glory of Israel."

Tephillin are the most potent and powerful and magical of signs. For, wrapped in these quaint parchment-filled boxes made of the holy elements of the earth's bounty, we literally bind ourselves to God. With *tephillin,* we enter into the most intimate and deepest of all loving relationships, and we reflect the radiant light of God's infinite glory.

There are two products of the earth that were used by our ancestors in ancient times to enhance their spiritual experience but that have been rejected and discarded in modern times. Many consider them to be associated with Eastern religions and practices; some consider them "New Age-y" and foolish; some even regard their use as bordering on idolatrous and blasphemous. But they are deeply and authentically Jewish.

The use of incense is mentioned more than one hundred times in the Bible. The Torah (Exodus 30:34) teaches that incense was made of four ingredients; the Talmud (BT Keritot 6a) contends that it consisted of eleven different spices. Either way, incense was an integral part of the sacrificial worship at the sanctuary in the desert and in the Holy Temples in Jerusalem.

Our biblical ancestors felt that one of the best ways to approach and please God was through animal sacrifice that resulted in *ray-ach ne-choach,* a "pleasing odor," a "sweet smell" wafting up to the Lord. They reasoned that the smell of the sweet incense that they added to the odor of the burning flesh would be doubly pleasing to God.

Maimonides contended (Moreh 3:43) that rather than being an additive, the sweet-smelling incense was really used to cover up what could have been the oppressive stench of the daily slaughter of dozens of animals.

Either way, incense was an important part of the rituals of ancient Jewish worship. With its sweet and pleasing odor, it was one more way to try to influence God for good. The Kabbalists even contended that by identifying with the rising smoke, we can visualize ourselves rising up through the *sefirot,* coming into closer and closer relationship with God.

As with the use of musical instruments, the use of incense as part of Jewish worship ended with the destruction of the Temple and the exile.

Except for those who still long for the Temple to be rebuilt and for animal sacrifice to be reinstituted, incense can be used as part of contemporary worship. This is another case of finding Jewish spiritual renewal by going back to our earliest practices.

Modern science also gives us good reason to use sweet fragrances in our spiritual practices. It teaches that the olfactory sense is our most primitive, primal sense and so has the power to connect us to our primordial roots and to trigger and awaken our earliest memories. In that "old" space, healing can take place, particularly healing of the emotional and the spiritual bodies, because in being carried back to the source we are given the opportunity to revisit, confront, work out, and heal any unfinished business, trauma, or pain. That is why the ancient but newly rediscovered practice of aromatherapy has become so popular in modern healing circles.

As well, particular smells can be powerful reminders of our origin and our beginnings; they take us back to the "Other Side," back to the times before we came to this earthly plane, back to God who made us.

With fragrances carrying this kind of power, why would we not want to make full use of them in our spiritual pursuits?

We are already used to using sweet-smelling spices as part of the *havdalah* ritual. Reluctant to bid farewell to the holy Shabbas, we smell the spices to keep the sweet fragrance of Shabbas in our beings for just a little while longer.

Incense, the compound of the vegetation of our earth, can be used to invoke and engage the earth's energies in our prayers in three very powerful ways: It can be used to bring sweet smells into our prayer place. It can be used, as it was in ancient times, to send "smoke signal" messages to God. Its smoke can be used, as the mystics suggested, as a visual aid to help us see our way up the *sefirot* on our journey to God.

The burning of incense is not just for adherents of Eastern religions or New Age practitioners. It is for Jews who wish to recapture an ancient and authentic Jewish ritual; who wish, as did our ancestors to enhance our spiritual practice and to deepen our *kavanah,* our spiritual intent, by making an offering of pleasing odor to God.

❦

The gems and jewels of the earth were so important to our ancestors that the breastplate worn by the High Priest as an integral part of his vestments contained at least twelve precious stones.

According to the Torah (Exodus 28:13ff.) the breastplate, made of pure gold, was hung around the High Priest's neck with chains of pure gold. Set into the breastplate were four rows of gems, with three gems in each row. These twelve jewels represent the twelve tribes of Israel.

The High Priest's breastplate was not just a decorative vestment but a holy object intended to draw the earth's energy and God's spirit into the priest and into his sacred tasks.

Like any other—every other—produce of the earth, jewels and gems contain vibrational energy. Not inanimate objects, precious stones contain the spirit of God. Each stone is different—different shape, different hardness, different color, different facets—and each stone carries in it its own particular identity, purpose, and intent.

In making and wearing the breastplate, the High Priest was well aware of its energetic powers and its function of drawing God's spirit into the midst of the people. For it was understood that these precious stones are amplifiers, because they resonate with and increase the earth energy that they hold. When we are in the presence of earth gems—and, even more, when we touch and hold them—their earth energy is amplified in us, and, in turn, our own spiritual energy is greatly increased.

The High Priest was instructed to set specific gems in a particular order into the breastplate because each gem serves a specific purpose; that is, it draws a specific kind of energy. The particular configuration of gems in horizontal and vertical rows combines to synthesize the individual gem energies into a greater, more powerful unifying energy.

The breastplate also contained two other jewels. (Some argue that these two were two of the twelve, but the majority of scholars agree that these were two jewels in addition to the twelve.) These stones were called the *urim* and the *tumim,* which most translate to mean "the lights and the perfections." According to the Torah, "They shall be upon Aaron's heart, when he goes in before the Lord, and Aaron shall bear the judgment of the children of Israel upon his heart continually" (Exodus 28:30).

While the purpose of the *urim* and *tumim* is never directly stated, it is clear that these stones were some sort of oracle. When there was a question, Aaron was to consult the oracle in order to ascertain God's will. He was to receive God's "light" and "perfection" on the question at hand. Some humorously suggest that the *urim* and *tumim* were like "heavenly dice." When the High Priest needed an answer, he would "throw the dice" and wait for the answer to appear.

To the modern, rational mind, these explanations may seem far-fetched at best. But in the world of God's spirit, they make absolute sense. The stones of God's earth contain the spirit, the energy, of God. When God wanted to make the Divine will clear—when God wanted to enlighten the mind and spirit of human beings—the *urim* and *tumim* would "light up" or "glow" with God's will. They served as the "stop" and "go" signs for God's revelations to the High Priest.

In modern times, with our advanced scientific knowledge, we willingly accept the fact that certain of earth's gems have phosphorescent properties that cause them to glow in the dark. Shall we simply call this a "natural phenomenon," attributing it to the "accidents" of mineral content, or shall we call this the work of God, who endowed each and every particle of earth with certain unique qualities and energetic forms, some of which, in ancient times, permitted the will of God to be known through glowing stones called *urim* and *tumim?*

❧❖❧

Can the minerals that are the beauty of the earth's bounty help enhance our worship today?

Some dismiss the use of crystals and other earth stones as New Age drivel; others contend that it flirts with witchcraft and borders on blasphemy. But many understand that by tapping into the same source of earth energy as did our ancestors, we can more fully tune into the earth's vibrational energy, enhance our own energetic connection to God, and be more fully attuned to God's energetic spirit.

When our *minyan* acquired its own *Sefer Torah,* Torah Scroll, we wanted the cover of the *Sefer* to be more than decorative. We wanted it to draw in spiritual energy and, through that energy, to deepen and intensify the words, the lessons, the spirit of Torah.

As a model, we looked to the breastplate of the High Priest, with its gems and jewels filled with earth's energy and God's spirit.

In our study, and relying on spiritual guidance that we received, we concluded that many of the gems on the breastplate still contain the same high level of vibrational energy that they did in ancient times. But, because of the many shifts in the earth during these past three millennia, some of the gems have lost their power and other gems have risen up to take their place. We also realized that some of the original settings and configurations have lost their potency and that other more powerful placements and combinations can be made today.

But the principle remained. As we designed our *Sefer Torah* cover, we were committed to placing the most powerful precious gems and jewels currently known into the most potent settings and combinations in order to draw the greatest spiritual energy to our precious Torah Scroll.

We chose the gems and put them into a setting of the symbol of infinity—interlinked and inseparable.

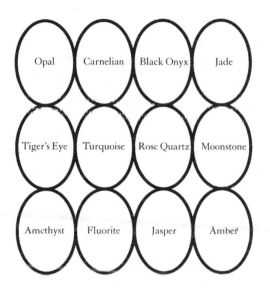

In the first row is opal, which is used to awaken both mystical and psychic qualities and to awaken the higher powers of intuition. Carnelian is used to produce connectedness with the spiritual world. Black onyx symbolizes benevolence and goodwill, encourages brotherhood and sisterhood among all, and is used to create the centering and alignment of each person with the higher powers so that we can each feel a connection with the whole of the universe. Jade brings accord and harmony to the environment, transmutes negativity, instills resourcefulness, and is used to facilitate peace within our physical, emotional, and intellectual bodies. These four stones combined in this configuration represent awakening, and they align with the physical (body).

In the second row is tiger's eye, which enhances clarity and opens us to recognize and love the pure and beautiful, encouraging a passion for life. Turquoise grounds us during spiritual work, attunes us with the spirit world, and brings wisdom and understanding. Rose quartz is the stone of gentle love; it brings peacefulness and harmony to relationships. Moonstone brings reflection, introspection, and balance. These four stones combined in this configuration represent peace and harmony, and they align with the mental (mind).

In the third row is amethyst, which harmonizes the intellectual, emotional, and physical bodies and provides a clear bridge between the earth plane and the higher planes. Fluorite is the stone of renewal and discernment, bringing the energy of rationality to the realm of intuition. Jasper is the nurturing stone that reminds us we are here on this earth plane not just for our own pleasure, but to bring sustenance and joy to others. Amber is used to connect the conscious limited self to the universal energy of unconditional love. These four stones combined in this configuration represent transformation, and they align with the spiritual (spirit).

When viewed in their vertical setting, these precious gems create four columns.

The stones of the first column—opal, tiger's eye, and amethyst—combined in this configuration represent creating and the element water. The stones of the second column—carnelian, turquoise, and fluorite—represent sustaining and the element fire. The stones of the third column—black onyx, rose quartz, and jasper—represent loving and the element air. The stones of the fourth column—jade, moonstone, and amber—represent connecting and the element earth.

All twelve stones combined in this configuration facilitate the cocreation of God's Kingdom.

Because of its jeweled cover—with the vibrational and spiritual energies of each of the gems in its particular configuration—our Torah learning can be so much higher, our understanding and discernment so much greater, and our connection to the energies of the earth and to God's spirit so much deeper.

To enhance being with Torah even further, we made a *yad,* a Torah pointer. The body of the *yad* is beautifully etched silver, and it has precious stones at the top and bottom and encrusted in the middle.

The bottom of the *yad,* the pointer itself, is clear quartz crystal, which provides for clarity of thinking as well as connecting the physical and the mental dimensions. It can amplify communication with spiritual masters, guides, and healers in other dimensions, and it is used to transform thoughts into sound. The very top of the *yad* is a knob of rose quartz, the stone of peacefulness and calm and gentle love, which is used for the spiritual attunement to the energy of love.

In the middle of the *yad* are two stones. Golden topaz has facets that provide alternating positive and negative currents, which act as a conductor of messages. By placing this stone in a silver wand, an additional conductor is activated; it is like a "battery" stone that stores information and thoughts, enhances faith, and supports our journey toward enlightenment. Lapus lazuli gives us access to the realm of the mysteries of the sacred texts and enhances our wisdom in order to understand the information we receive. It is a stone of complete awareness, representing not only intellectual expanse but also initiation into wisdom in the mystical realm.

This *yad* is the ideal conductor of God's word from the realm of God to the written text and to our minds, hearts, and spirits.

The stones that are in our *minyan's Sefer Torah* cover and *yad* are perfect examples of how the precious gems and jewels of our earth can magnify and intensify the spiritual journey toward God.

The use of precious jewels to enhance the spiritual quest does not belong to antiquity alone, and surely these and so many other gems cannot be casually dismissed as superstitious trinkets or as the play toys of the religious fringe. For, then and now, stones and minerals—the produce of the earth—have inherent spiritual qualities that can help bring greater understanding and clarity, greater attunement and enlightenment.

The psalmist teaches, "The earth and all its fullness is the Lord's" (Psalms 24:1). Everything—the whole of creation—is filled with God's being.

Everything—animal, vegetable, and mineral—is made of the same God-stuff. We and every particle of creation are one with God.

"And the earth God has given over to humankind" (Psalms 115:16). We are the inheritors, the beneficiaries, the betakers, of all that God has placed on this earth, in this universe.

So we strive to be both ever-cognizant partners with all matter of the earth and ever-faithful stewards of the gifts of God's bounty. For we know with the wisdom of the ages that "a generation comes and a generation goes, but the earth abides forever" (Ecclesiastes 1:4).

12

Growing Up Jewish

Reb Shlomo asked: why was a kohen, a member of the priestly tribe, considered *tamey,* ritually impure, and prohibited from officiating at the sacrificial rites at the Holy Temple when he had come in contact with a dead body?

Our rebbe taught that to come before God, to bring the worshipful offerings of the people, the *kohen* had to be filled with joy and gladness; he had to embrace his holy task with the fullness of his being. But when confronted with death, especially the death of a close loved one —a parent, a sibling, a spouse, a child—the *kohen* was not filled with joy but with grief, was not happy and lighthearted but distraught and angry.

Until his grief diminished, until his anger abated, the *kohen* could not come before God with joy or serve God with a full heart.

Then our rebbe asked: Why has so much of Jewish learning in postwar America been so dull and boring? Why, instead of being filled with the light of Torah, have our Hebrew schools been such dark and foreboding places? Why have we failed to convey the greatness of Judaism to two full generations of Jews, and why have we failed to "turn on" millions of Jews to the joys of Judaism?

Our rebbe's pained answer to his own anguished question is illuminated in the sweet but troubled poetry of Danny Siegel.

She used to teach us Aleph-Bays
in between her stories of the Nazis
. . . .
the rabbi was from Poland
and she was a Czech . . .
bringing us to Torah
by way of Terezin and Auschwitz. . . .
Whenever
we raised doubts about ourselves
   or said
   "Torah is boring,
   Enough is enough!"—
We'd remember her
   under the floor
   in the Goy's hidingplace
with the boots
   thundering louder than the storm
      at Sinai
   overhead.

So many of the teachers and the rabbis and the *melamdim* who stood in the classrooms of the urban and newly built suburban Hebrew schools in postwar America were like the *kohanim* of old. They had confronted death face-to-face. The stench of the ovens was still in their nostrils; the screams of agony still rang in their ears; the faces of the tormented and the murdered still floated before their eyes. And they were filled with bitterness and grief; they were filled with rage and anger.

And everything they taught was filtered through the horror of their experience, the nagging doubts in their minds, the searing questions in their souls, the painful aches in their hearts.

How could they teach us the joy of life when they were embittered by the universe? How could they teach us the joys of Judaism when their own wives and husbands and parents and children had been killed just for being Jewish? How could they teach us to come before God when they wondered where God was hiding? How could they teach us to sing praises to God when they were so angry with God?

It wasn't their fault. They did not know any better, for they were still in shock; they were still in deep mourning. They gave us the best they knew, the best they could. But it wasn't enough.

Two—now almost three—generations of Jews have grown up being taught by teachers whose words are haunted by the monsters and the dark shadows of Auschwitz. Is it any wonder that we never learned to clap our hands in joyous prayer, to laugh over a portion of text, to whisper sweet declarations of love to God?

This is why our elementary education has seemed so hollow and empty, and this is why our Bar and Bat Mitzvahs became self-perpetuating caricatures of themselves.

By age thirteen, our youngsters—we—had learned to survive Hebrew school, but we learned little of the richness and the majesty of Jewish teachings and Jewish lifestyle. At our Bar and Bat Mitzvahs, we parroted the *haftarah* tape—a record in the old days—that the cantor had made, and we gave speeches explaining a text we barely understood and making promises we never intended to keep.

This is why our Bar and Bat Mitzvah parties became such lavish —and empty—affairs. We and our families were supposed to be marking an ancient coming-of-age ritual in modern garb and celebrating newly matured attachments and commitments. But, in our heart of hearts, we knew that little personal growth work and less soul work had been done and that little dedication to history, heritage, or destiny had taken place. The ceremony was all form and little substance.

So we tried to fill our emptiness and cover our deep disappointment by partying to excess, renting out the Orange Bowl, chartering the QEII, or taking an African safari. While our elaborate celebrations became the fodder for comedians' self-incriminating jokes, spiritual vacuity gnawed at us.

Our Jewish souls were still sad. Our Jewish hearts made up self-righteous excuses and then hardened to protect ourselves from the bewilderment and emptiness that we could not admit and the hurt we inured ourselves from feeling.

This is why so many of our youngsters dropped out of Jewish learning after Bar and Bat Mitzvah. How could Hebrew high school, with its rote learning shrouded in sadness, possibly compare to the glitz and glitter and the perceived rewards beckoning from the secular world? So while we went on to achieve the highest levels of secular education, we remained Jewishly illiterate—the sum total of our formal Jewish learning not even the equivalent of one year of public school.

Yet, then and now, when faced with difficult philosophical questions that challenge heart and mind, we would like to have Jewish answers. When seeking meaning and purpose that define the soul, we would like to have Jewish touchstones.

⚜

There is always time—for ourselves and for our children—to recapture Jewish learning, to reinfuse it with joy, and to let our hearts and souls be filled with the wondrous, awe-inspiring teachings of our tradition.

For ourselves: Jewish learning can begin and continue anywhere, anytime. All it takes is desire and commitment. We've already discussed how easy it is to begin learning Hebrew and to reaffirm Torah learning. Now let's go the next step. Begin by reading one Jewish book, subscribing to one Jewish periodical, going to hear one Jewish speaker, enrolling in one Jewish course, listening to one Jewish audiotape, watching one Jewish videotape, joining in one Jewish discussion group on the Internet. From synagogue adult education programs to community-wide lectures to institutions of higher Jewish learning; from lunch-hour office classes to living room study groups to long-distance external degree programs, Jewish education is available in myriad settings and myriad levels. If we are serious about Jewish learning, we can do serious Jewish learning. For the learned Jew, it takes seven and a half years to study the entire Talmud—*daf yomi,* one page a day. Just think how much new learning we all can acquire in the next seven and a half years—one page at a time.

For our children: first, a word to those who establish and maintain our Jewish schools. It is hard, it is sometimes impossible, especially in smaller communities away from the large urban centers of Jewish life, to find qualified teachers for our schools. But we cannot settle for anyone but the very best. We now know the results of fifty years of scared, sad, angry Jewish teachers.

As a new generation of Jewish teachers slowly begins to develop, a generation brought up out of the ashes into the light of a new Jewish dawn, we are beginning to see the results of repopulating our classrooms with teachers who are in love with Judaism, who exude Jewish joy. We must find or train teachers who are knowledgeable, committed, observing Jews, who are models of Jewish life, who live what they teach, who love being Jewish. When there is Jewish excitement, Jewish energy, Jewish rejoicing in the classroom, our very bright, intuitive, insightful children will know how wonderful it is to be Jewish and will begin to reflect their teachers' knowledge, commitments, and joy.

One of the most difficult problems facing the Jewish Renewal Movement is and will be how to teach, how to convey a spiritually based Judaism to our children. How do we balance our desire and need to be steeped in traditional learning and practice with the sense that traditional Jewish learning and practice are often not God centered, rarely spiritual? Yet how do we help our children create and build a personal, intimate relationship with God without coming from an authentically Jewish context? How do we "reform" and "renew" without knowing the original that needs to be "reformed" and "renewed"? Yet how do we continue teaching and practicing the original if it no longer speaks to our hearts and spirits? How do we reach back into the rich spiritual traditions of the Jewish spiritualists and mystics and bring their teachings into our new age if we are not familiar with their original teachings?

As with the shifting of any paradigm, the didactic tension between the old and the new will be felt for a long time. The questions will continue to be asked; the issues will be the source of constant reflection and struggle. The process will be slow, and the transition will often be painful and sometimes maddening. But the wrestling is worth every bit of our energy. For what is at stake is the way we bring our children to their God and to their tradition, to their heritage and to their destiny.

For now, we have two words for the teachers of our children.

First word: *God.* Let everything you teach be infused with the presence of God. Put God at the very core of everything Jewish, of everything human. Let your main task be to help our children create their own personal, intimate relationship with God. Teach your children to seek God, to know God, to love God. Remember the opening words of our morning prayers, "The beginning of wisdom is the awe of God." And remember the words of Abraham Joshua Heschel: "God is of no importance unless God is of supreme importance."

Second word: *text.* We have tried it all. Every year or two, one or another educator, educational institution, textbook company, or foundation has come up with the "new, creative, innovative approach that will revolutionize Jewish education." First it was new texts. Then it was the way the schedule was arranged. Then it was the way teacher skills were used. Then it was camp weekends. Then it was experiential learning. Then it was family education. Then it was video games and computers. But, inevitably, today's innovation became yesterday's fad. And despite all the *challah*-baking, *havdalah*-candle-making workshops, despite the yummy texts and the clever computer programs, little Jewish learning has really taken place.

We need a paradigm shift in Jewish learning—a shift backward to our beginnings so that we can move forward to our possibilities. This is a perfect example of how Jewish *renewal* does not necessarily mean "new and radically different" but rather can mean "a recapturing of the old that has been lost." For we need to return to text. In our modern Hebrew and day schools—just as in the yeshivas of old—let's teach text: *Chumash* with Rashi, *Nach, Mishnah, Gemara.* We will have our own nonfundamentalist reading, understanding, and interpretation, but let's teach text because text is at the core of the Jewish experience.

Boring?

Not if text is cradled in the hands of a gifted teacher.

For in text is the record of our people's attempt to encounter God. In text is "the way in" to understanding the path to God. In text is

God's blueprint to a life of decency and goodness. In text are all the great questions, some of the answers, and the struggle to find the rest. In text is the continuing dialogue with God.

When our schools and their teachings begin to inspire and enflame young Jewish souls with the joys of being Jewish, then our Bar and Bat Mitzvah ceremonies can once again take on the life-enhancing importance that they were originally intended to have.

No discussion of renewing the Bar and Bat Mitzvah experience is going to be easy, for this ritual, more than any other Jewish ritual, is so caught up in the intricacies of human relationships and human emotion.

Listen to this familiar exchange.

MOTHER: *"Go study your* haftarah.*"*

THIRTEEN-YEAR-OLD: *"Ma, leave me alone!"*

MOTHER *(firmly): "Your Bar Mitzvah is only three months away, and you're not even finished with your* haftarah *yet. And you still have parts of the service to learn and your speech to write. Go to your room and study your* haftarah.*"*

THIRTEEN-YEAR-OLD *(adamantly): "I'll do it when I feel like it."*

FATHER *(calling out from the den, loudly): "Listen to your mother. Go study your* haftarah *now."*

THIRTEEN-YEAR-OLD *(angrily): "Don't you guys listen to me? I told you. I'll do it when I feel like it."*

MOTHER *(equally angrily and somewhat frantically): "Go to your room now, and study that* haftarah. *What's wrong with you? Don't you know that your grandmother and your aunts and uncles and all your cousins are coming all the way from New York? My God, I've already given the caterer the deposit. What are you going to do? Stand up there and look like an idiot? Do you want to embarrass yourself front of all your friends, your family, in front of the rabbi and the whole congregation? Now! Get up to your room and study your* haftarah."

THIRTEEN-YEAR-OLD *(furiously spitting out one word at a time):* "*You guys never trust me. I told you that I'll do it, and I'll do it. Just leave me the hell alone. Jeez, you always treat me just like a baby. Leave me the hell alone.*"

FATHER *(calling out from the den loudly):* "*Watch your language, young man. And don't talk to your mother that way. This is still my house, and we'll have a little respect around here.*"

A door slams, and an eerie but all-too-familiar-these-days silence settles over the whole house.

The writer James Michener has described the age of thirteen as "that agonizing age when the passage of a bird's feather across the hand can cut like a sharpened knife." Age thirteen is that fragile place, the delicate bridge suspended between the last vestiges of childhood and the tentative beginnings of adulthood. Age thirteen is defined by physical growth, raging hormones, emotional turmoil, and sexual awakening. Age thirteen is that momentous time when young people —and their parents—begin to grow up and grow out and grow beyond; to hang on and let go all at the same time; to explore and test and fail and try again; to reforge and reshape the relationships of a lifetime; to carve out new identities and assume new roles.

The argument between parent and child about studying for Bar or Bat Mitzvah is not about chanting a *haftarah* or writing a speech. It is about autonomy and independence, self-esteem and self-reliance, identity and maturity. It is about children growing up and breaking away and parents understanding and accepting the wisdom of the late psychologist Haim Ginott, who taught that "our need is to be needed, and their need is to not need us."

Yet few parents or children understand that their emotional wrestling is over much more than the subject of the moment. Without realizing what is really behind their struggles, parents and children often hold the Bar or Bat Mitzvah responsible for their conflict, and Judaism gets blamed for all their woes—and later discarded for the pain it allegedly caused.

Many suggest that the solution is to raise the age of Bar/Bat Mitzvah to sixteen.

Educationally, we will be much more confident that Bar/Bat Mitzvah means the accumulation and demonstration of real Jewish learning. No longer will the simple lessons acquired during the years of "pediatric Judaism" be the basis of Jewish knowledge. We will affirm the assertion of the great psychologist Jean Piaget, the expert on cognitive development, who taught that children are not capable of intellectual conceptual learning until well into adolescence. With the teenage years—years of growing emotional maturity and intellectual curiosity—dedicated to Jewish study, we can say to our young people that we are holding your Bar/Bat Mitzvah when it makes most sense—when you have had years of serious Jewish learning and training; when you are intellectually capable of comprehending the scope of history, the nuances of theology; when you have had the time and the space and the perspective to form your own personal relationship with God; when you are mature enough to form an identity and make serious, lifelong commitments; when you are working on forging your own life's philosophy; when you are mature enough to move into adulthood intellectually, emotionally, spiritually; when you know what it means to be a responsible, contributing part of a community; when you are ready for privilege tempered with responsibility.

If moving Bar/Bat Mitzvah to sixteen makes sense educationally, it makes even more sense developmentally.

It used to be that age thirteen was the cusp of the age of emancipation, the time when children left their parents' home to make their own livings, to get married, to start their own families. Then Bar/Bat Mitzvah was the awesome time of transition from childhood to adulthood, when fathers would teach their sons what it means to be a man and mothers would teach their daughters what it means to be a woman; how to be a husband, a wife; how to create a home. Parents would give over the hidden stories and the unwritten rules of the tribe; they would share the secret words and forms and rituals; they would set up rites of initiation. That's what a coming-of-age is; that's what a Bar/Bat Mitzvah is —the intimate teaching of wrapping in *tallis* and *tephillin;* the coming to the *minyan* and being counted as one of the community; the recitation of the holy incantations and formulas for having an *aliyah*. Bar Mitzvah, Bat Mitzvah, is father giving to son, mother giving to daughter, the mysteries of Jewish adulthood.

But now emotional maturity, financial independence, emancipation, and marriage—coming-of-age markers—have been postponed. Children rarely leave home until age eighteen, when they go into the armed forces or go to college, and many are still financially dependent on their parents, who pay the college bills.

In contemporary society, the first real manifestations of growing up are at age sixteen. That is when the state says that children are old enough to have the responsibility and the freedom of a driver's license and when many young women still have a sweet sixteen party or a coming out, an early prelude to being eligible for marriage.

Receiving a driver's license at age sixteen has become such a powerful symbol of coming-of-age that some have suggested that there should be a special public rite of passage—a new Jewish ceremony complete with prayers and blessings—to mark this occasion in the life of a young person and his or her parents. There are those who humorously suggest calling this new ritual a "Car Mitzvah," for we cannot ignore the significance of this watershed age and the reality that for most of our Jewish youngsters getting a license and the car keys are much more important than getting called to the Torah for an *aliyah*.

Having Bar or Bat Mitzvah at age sixteen can be the impetus for parents and children to do the real work of growing into maturity. The months and days leading to Bar and Bat Mitzvah can be used for the deepest and most intimate sharing of experience, of values, of love. We do not have to go off to the woods to beat drums in order to teach our sons to become men; we do not have to sit in sweat lodges in order to teach our daughters to become women. We just need to realize that it is a holy task that still must be performed. And then we just need to give our children our time, our energy, our spirit, the commitments of our hearts, and the depths of our souls and to share with them the intimate conversations and the meaningful whispers that convey wisdom and experience from one generation to another.

Eventually, our Bar and Bat Mitzvah ceremonies can begin to reflect the personal and spiritual growth that we and our children are experiencing. In renewal, our Bar and Bat Mitzvah ceremonies can become what they were originally intended to be—the public declaration of coming-of-age, of personal responsibility, of joining and committing to the community, of taking rightful and joyful place in the ongoing process of life. In the deepest sense, at our Bar and Bat Mitzvah ceremonies our young people will embrace their history and their heritage and will accept the invitation to their destiny—as men, as women, as Jews.

It will be hard to move away from such a deeply ingrained and time-honored custom of holding Bar or Bat Mitzvah at age thirteen. It will take a generation for the transition to take place while, out of tradition, convenience, or inertia, many continue to insist on the old custom. And perhaps we will have to create some new ritual for age thirteen, to keep the community involved in the process of helping children and their parents through the hormonal-driven turmoil of reaching puberty, coming into adolescence, and taking the first tentative steps toward emotional maturity and emancipation.

But if the Jewish community unites over this issue, then there will be no choice. After all, there is no choice now. Want to be Bar/Bat Mitzvah? You cannot do it at eleven; you have to wait until you are thirteen. The new reality will eventually set in. Want to be Bar/Bat Mitzvah? It will be when you are sixteen.

Jewish spiritual renewal is about taking the risks to make the changes that respond to evolving need.

≈✥≈

No matter how much we renew our B'nai Mitzvah rituals, no matter how much we reform our schools and reconnect with our teachers, there is only one real way—no surprise—for children to learn about Judaism and to fall in love with its teachings and traditions.

We, their parents, must teach our children well.

"Come, my child, come. Put this toothbrush in your hand. Squirt just a little bit of toothpaste onto the bristles. That's it. Gently. Now, put the toothpaste in your mouth just like this. That's it.

Now, brush. Up and down, up and down. Brush. Very good, my child, very good."

"Why, Mommy? Why?"

"Because, my child, when you brush every day—two, three, four times every day—then your teeth will stay healthy and strong. Your smile will be white and bright. See my teeth. See how strong and white they are. If you brush every day, just like I showed you, you'll have strong teeth, just like Mommy's, when you grow up."

"Come, my child, come. I want to read you this story. Here, look at the pretty pictures in this book. Come, let me teach you your ABCs so you can read. Very good, my child, very good. You are reading so well. Now let's go down to the library so that you can get your very own library card and read any book that you want."

"Why, Daddy? Why?"

"Because, my child, in books are knowledge, new learning, new experiences. In books are ideas that will excite you and challenge you. See how I read; see how I learn. When I read books, the world opens up to me. And when you read, the world will be yours, too."

"Come, my child, come. Let's sing a song. Let's listen to this beautiful music. Let's look at this pretty painting on the wall. Let's go to the symphony, to the art gallery, to the theater, to the museum. That's it. See, listen, learn."

"Why, Mommy? Why, Daddy? Why?"

"Because, my child, in music, in art, in drama is beauty, is worth, is meaning. In the arts is your soul. See how much Mommy and Daddy love to listen to music; see how excited we are at the museum; see what beauty there is on the walls of our home. When you know music and art and drama and dance, just like we do, your life will be so happy, so full, so good. The beauty of the world will be yours to behold and cherish."

"Come, my child, come. Let me show you. This is a baseball. See how you hold it; see how you throw it. And this is a soccer ball. See

how you kick it. And this is the basketball hoop that hangs on our garage. See how you shoot the ball into the hoop. And this is the field where we go to watch our team. And this is the field where you can play, where you can throw and hit and run and kick."

"Why, Daddy? Why, Mommy? Why?"

"Because, my child, sports will teach you how to be strong, how to be agile, how to be quick. You'll learn individual skills and the greater good of the group. You'll learn grace, both in losing and in winning. See how much I like to root for my team. See how good I feel when I play in a tough game. You'll love it, too."

"Come, my child, come. Put your fingers on the piano keyboard, just like this. Put your fingers on the computer keyboard, just like this. Tie your ballet shoes, just like this. Put the tent stakes in the ground, just like this. Cast the fishing line, just like this. Hold your fork, just like this. Pet the doggy, just like this."

"Why, Daddy? Why, Mommy? Why?"

"Because, my child, you need to learn the skills and the talents that will help you succeed in life. You need to be well rounded and to have a good background. Just watch us, and Mommy and Daddy will show you the way. We'll show you what to do, so that you can grow up and be just like us."

"Come, my child, come. Let me drive you to Hebrew school."

"Why, Daddy? Why?"

"So that, my child, you can learn the language and the literature and the laws of your people."

"Daddy, can you help me with my Hebrew homework?"

Now, here come the choices.

Choice #1:

"I'd love to, my child, but it has been so long since I've read any Hebrew—probably since my Bar Mitzvah. Ask Mommy. Maybe she'll be able to help you."

"Why, Daddy? Why?"

Or, Choice #2:

"Sure, honey. To tell you the truth, I may be a little rusty, because it's been a long time since I've read a Hebrew schoolbook, so

I hope I remember. But, if not, I'll start going to that adult Hebrew class at the synagogue so I'll be ready to help you as soon as I can, because Mommy and I can hardly wait until you know Hebrew. You'll be able to read God's word. You'll be able to say all the prayers, and to talk to your cousins who live in Jerusalem. You'll love knowing Hebrew, my child. It's such a beautiful language."

"Mommy, this is Friday night. In Hebrew school, my teacher said that on Friday night we are supposed to light candles and say special prayers over wine and bread and eat a special meal at home. Can we light Shabbas candles, Mommy?"

Choice #1:

"Well, my child, we would like to. But tonight we are going out to dinner. And next Friday night we have tickets for the theater, and the Friday after that is the office party, and the Friday night after that we are going to the symphony. But maybe in a month or six weeks, we'll be able to light candles on a Friday night. Okay?"

"Why, Mommy? Why?"

Or, Choice #2:

"Of course, my child. Let me teach you the blessing we say when we light the candles. Here, taste a drop of this sweet wine, sweet because Shabbas is so sweet. Now let's dance around the table to welcome our beloved Sabbath. Taste this, my child, eat this delicious food, our best meal of the week, in honor of the holy Sabbath. Now, sweetest child, come sit in my lap while we sing Shabbas songs. That's right—sing; clap your hands; make beautiful Shabbas music. There's no day that is more wonderful than Shabbas; it's the queen of days. It's God's gift to us, and we are so lucky to be able to celebrate it together. Shabbat shalom, my child. A gutten Shabbas."

"Come, my child, come. It's time to go to services at the synagogue."

"Why, Mommy? Why, Daddy? Why?"

"Because, my child, Shabbas is the most important of all days.

You need to learn the prayers and listen to the melodies and know the traditions of your people. All your friends from Hebrew school will be there and your teacher and the rabbi and the cantor. You'll like it."

"Will you come with me, Mommy? Will you sit in services with me, Daddy?"

Choice #1:

"We would like to, my child. But we're going to play tennis. And afterward we are going to the supermarket and the mall. You know how hard we work all week, and Saturday is our only day to relax and play and do all the shopping. You understand, don't you? But don't worry. We'll be back in time to pick you up right after services."

"Why, Daddy? Why Mommy? Why? Why?"

Or, Choice #2:

"Of course, our child. Where else would we be? It's Shabbas, so we all go to shul *together. It's so wonderful to be in this beautiful place; it's so special, so holy. We pray to God, we see all our friends, we sing Shabbas songs. Here, stand next to me. That's it, real close. Doesn't it feel wonderful when I wrap you up in my* tallis? *Here, take the corner of the* tallis *and touch it to the Torah. That's it. Kiss the Torah. You kiss the Torah, and we kiss you, our sweetest, sweetest child."*

The choices are yours.

Everything—everything that matters, everything that you cherish, everything that is holy, everything that was and that will be—depends on the choices you make.

For the results of your choices will shape precious souls and will echo through eternity.

Teach them.

"Teach them the good way they are to walk. . . ."

Teach them.

Teach them, diligently.

Teach your children well.

Part Three

Connecting with the Universe

W hen God created the universe, God placed within it
everything that was and that would ever be.

All of the elements of God's eternal plan that stretched
from Eden back to Eden—from the paradise of the beginning,
through all the growth and discovery, through all the pain and
the triumph, back to the Eden of masheach—were laid out
by Divine design. Like a ladder with its feet rooted firmly in
the ground and its steps reaching upward toward the infinite
expanse of sky, the history of the universe and of human exis
tence stood ready to be climbed, and all the ingredients that
God had placed there stood waiting to be discovered.

The saga of the human sojourn is the story of climbing
the ladder step by step; of uncovering the component parts
one by one; of growing in knowledge, wisdom, and experience; of balancing and repairing the ills that beset us; of expanding consciousness, understanding, and enlightenment;
of moving closer and closer toward the top of the ladder—
back to Eden where it all began.

Jewish tradition calls the top of the ladder y'mot
hamasheach, the days of the messiah, the time when we will

have moved our world back to perfection—to the peace, tranquillity, harmony, and love that infused the world at its very beginnings. Using an old image from a childhood game, we call that time "Sky Blue," the time when our whole world will be wrapped in a sparkling clear blue sky with a stunning rainbow of rich and glittering color stretching from end to end.

Sky Blue, y'mot hamasheach, will not just happen. It will come only through our actions, when we have climbed the ladder high enough to discover and pluck out all the ingredients for perfection that God placed there.

Fortunately for us—perhaps because of us—we live in an extraordinary time when human consciousness is expanding in almost never-before-seen quantum leaps. More and more of God's light is filtering into our plane of being, and more and more of the hidden is being revealed to us. The universe is offering up so many of its long-held secrets; the pathway for the journey is unfolding right before us.

So much that until recently was derided as the product of mere speculation and fanciful imagination is now being confirmed as real and true. So much that was rejected through the demand for rational explanation and scientific data is now being proven and affirmed as coming from the unfolding world of the spirit.

As more and more channels open, we reach backward into our past and stretch forward into our future at the very same instant. For the journey to and from God is without time or space.

As more and more is revealed and becomes known, we are challenged and blessed to be the transformers, bringing our world to new dimension, bringing ourselves and our God to a new plane of existence.

We are, in the image of the popular television show, "going where no man, no woman, has ever gone before." We hope and expect that "the force—the spirit of God—will be with us."

13

Meet Your Angels

I F W E W E R E P E R M I T T E D A G L I M P S E I N T O T H E
highest heavens, what would we see?

The Talmud (BT Hagigah 12b) offers us a dazzling inventory: "In
the highest heavens are found: righteousness and justice; the treasury
of life and peace and blessings; the souls of the righteous dead; the
souls of those who are yet to be born; the dew with which God will revive the dead; the holy beasts and the ministering angels."

In the early 1990s, angels became "big." Bookstore shelves
were filled with books about them. Two major newsmagazines published cover stories about them. A popular summer movie was a com-
edy about angels coming to the aid of a floundering baseball team. And
angel stores sprouted up all around the country carrying a wide array
of angel paraphernalia, including pins and tie tacks of wings and halos.

Despite the Talmudic notion that God's ministering angels reside
in the highest heavens along with the most precious objects of all creation, most contemporary Jews, products of highly rational education

and training, believe that little if anything about angels is Jewish. Angels, if they are not considered as a mere figment of imagination, are regarded as the invention of other faiths or communities and have taken on strong Christian connotations.

But in reality—noted in this Talmudic passage and seen over and over again in Jewish literature and stories—angels are very, very Jewish and a very, very important part of Jewish life. (For a full description of Jewish angelology, see the illuminating book *A Gathering of Angels: Angels in Jewish Life and Literature,* by Rabbi Morris B. Margolies.)

According to Jewish thought, an angel—*malach* in Hebrew—is a minister, a deputy, or messenger of God. Some angels bring God's will to us in word or vision. Some angels are assigned specific tasks in helping to oversee the functions of the world, for different angels are in charge of watching over wind, rain, snow, hail, thunder, lightning, earthquakes, hurricanes, comets and constellations, and many more of the functions of the universe.

Yet for all their majesty, we are taught that angels are to be considered as nothing more than God's assistants. The Talmud teaches that God insists, "If a man is in distress, let him not call on Micha'el or Gabriel [well-known and powerful archangels] but let him call directly on Me, and I will hearken to him" (JT Berachot 13a).

The prayer that we recite as we take the Torah from the Holy Ark confirms our understanding of the relationship between God and the angels. "We are the servants of the Holy One, blessed by God. . . . Not in men do we put our trust, nor upon any angel do we rely, but upon God in heaven who is the God of truth. . . . In God do we trust."

There are many legends and stories of God's interaction with the angels during the time of the creation of the world. One legend has the angels arguing with God over the creation of human beings. "Don't do it," say the angels. "All they [men and women] will ever do is cause You heartache" (adaptation of Genesis Rabbah, Bereshit 8:5). Another has the angels insisting that God's place is in the heavenly realm. "Why will You abandon the creatures above, and descend to those below? It is Your glory that You should be in the heavens." But God is not to be dissuaded. "See how greatly I love the creatures below that I shall descend and dwell beneath the goats' hair" (Tanchuma Buber, Terumah 47b).

The angels are so beloved by God that despite their objection to the creation of humankind, they served as the model for man and woman on earth. "The angels are created in the image and the likeness of God, but they do not multiply and increase. The animals multiply and increase, but they are not created in the image and likeness of God. So God said, 'I will create man in the image and likeness of the angels, but he shall multiply and increase like the animals. . . . So, I will create him with something of the nature of both. . . '" (Genesis Rabbah, Bereshit 8:11). Of the dust of the earth we are created, but we are just "a little lower than the angels" (Psalms 8:6).

Almost every book of the Bible contains references to angels, and some of our most well known Bible stories are about angels.

It was angelic travelers who informed Abraham and Sarah that they would have a son in their old age (Genesis 18:10). It was an angel who assured Hagar that her son would live and be the progenitor of a great nation (Genesis 21:18). It was an angel who stayed Abraham's hand from sacrificing his beloved son (Genesis 22:11–12). It was angels who strode up and down the ladder of Jacob's dream assuring him that God would be with him wherever his journeys took him (Genesis 28:12ff.). It was an angel—or perhaps God or perhaps the depths of his own psyche—with whom Jacob wrestled on his journey home, forging his own identity, becoming Israel the father of a people (Genesis 32:29). It was an angel who appeared to Moses out of the bush that burned but was not consumed, who introduced Moses to God (Exodus 3:2).

In each case, the angel comes with God's message: "You will be saved"; "You are not alone"; "You have met your test"; "You have a sacred task."

There are some angels with special name designations and special tasks. Cherubim are winged creatures with the faces of children who are protectors of sacred places. According to the biblical text, they stood at the entrance of the Garden of Eden after Adam and Eve had been expelled (Genesis 3:24). Artistic depictions of them guarded the holy Ark of the Covenant in the desert. There two cherubim, overlaid with gold, faced each other on the Ark's cover (Exodus 25:18–20), and their images were embroidered on the curtains of the tabernacle (Exodus 26:1). When God appeared to Moses in the tabernacle, it was from between the two cherubim (Numbers 7:89). When the Holy Temple was built in Jerusalem, figures of cherubim were placed high over the Ark (1 Kings 6:27–28). Legend has it that when the people were faithful to God and obeyed the commandments, the cherubim faced each other, but when the people forsook the commandments and turned away from God, then the cherubim over the Ark turned their backs on one another. In all of these cases, the cherubim seem to be angelic deputies or assistants representing God's presence and protection.

Throughout the Bible and rabbinic literature, a number of other name designations—such as *seraphim* and *ophanim*—are given to the protecting angels. The most well known of these are the *chayyot haḳodesh,* the holy creatures, who, in the theophoric visions of the prophet Ezekiel, are the guardians of God's heavenly throne.

These angelic names may be familiar because they are still recited in a number of the prayers of the traditional Jewish liturgy.

Not all the angels are doers of good. The most famous negative angel, known as Satan—the name simply means "adversary"—came to a meeting between the Divine beings and God and challenged God to a test over the man Job (Job 1:6ff). Satan tried to make Job's life so difficult and miserable that Job would renounce God.

Unlike later Christian theology, where Satan becomes the devil, an independent, highly negative life force bringing evil into the world, the Jewish concept of Satan remains as the adversary, the tempter, the challenge to unequivocal belief in God. In a prayer in the evening service in the traditional Jewish liturgy, the Hebrew word *sa-tan* means "adversary" or "temptation" and is part of a litany of negative forces or influences that we ask God to remove. "Remove from us every enemy, pestilence, sword, famine and sorrow, and take away *sa-tan,* the adversary or temptation, from in front of us and behind us."

Some of the angels never appear on earth but always inhabit the heavenly realm. There they assist God in a variety of tasks.

They join with God in intervening in the affairs of humankind, and they sometimes argue with God when they do not agree with the Divine decision.

God decreed that Moses was to die before he entered into the Promised Land. Angered and saddened, Moses argued with God over his fate and tried to bargain for a reversal of decision. The angels came to the defense of Moses. The ministering angels said to God, " 'Why did Adam die?' God said, 'Because he disobeyed My command.' So the angels said, 'But did not Moses obey Your commands?' God replied, 'It is My decree, which falls upon all humankind, for it says, "This is the law, that a man dies" ' " (Sifre Deuteronomy Ha'azinu 339). The angels caught God in a logical contradiction, but, even so, God would not be moved. Moses died without entering the Promised Land.

There were times when the angels joined with God in deep sadness over the folly of the people. When God destroyed the Holy Temple, the angels wept with God and arranged the traditional rituals of mourning for the heavenly inhabitants who came to console God (Lamentations Rabbah, Introduction 24).

Some of the angels assist God with everyday tasks, but in the heavenly realm even an everyday task is far from the ordinary.

"The angel who is appointed to prayer [that is the one who first receives all the prayers that are recited by the Jewish people] waits until all the Jews in the last synagogue have finished their (morning) prayers, and weaves them into a crown, which he places on God's head" (Midrash Tehillim 88:4).

There are times, however, that despite their high station and their sacred tasks, the angels display petulance and even jealousy.

When God was about to give Moses the holy commandments, the angels objected. The angels said, " 'What does a son of a woman [a human being] have to do among us?' God said, 'He has come to receive the Law.' The angels said, 'The beautiful Torah which You have hidden away since creation, You propose to give it to a creature of flesh and blood?' " God called on Moses to answer the objections of the angels. Moses argued that the law really applied to human beings, who need direction and guidance to face the challenges that living on earth poses. Human beings, he contended, need God's law much more than the angels, who live in God's paradise. The angels understood and accepted what Moses said, and "then they praised God, and became friends with Moses" (BT Shabbat 88b–89a).

More than anything, the angels are God's happy companions and advocates. They love their job; they love their God. The vision of the prophet Isaiah is of angels—in this case *seraphim*—standing in attendance of God and guarding the heavenly throne. In their joy, they call out to one another, *"Kadosh, kadosh, kadosh*—Holy, holy, holy is the Lord of Hosts. The whole world is filled with God's glory." In doing so, they create the love vibration that emanates from God's heavenly throne and fills the universe.

This phrase is so familiar to us because it forms the core of the *kedushah,* the prayer sanctifying God's name that is said as part of the communal *amidah* in morning and afternoon worship services. The well-known custom is that as we recite the words *kadosh, kadosh, kadosh,* we rise up on our toes three times, symbolically lifting ourselves up to the level of the angels, whom we are imitating by calling out the same words of praise about God.

Some of the heavenly angels come to earth, where we often encounter them.

Each week, as Shabbas begins on Friday evening, we sing the popular hymn, *"Shalom Aleichem,"* which means "Peace be unto you." To whom are we saying *shalom aleichem,* to whom are we wishing peace? Not to one another. The song says, *"Shalom aleichem malachei hasharet, malachei elyon."* "Peace to you—ministering angels, the angels of the Most High." The song is a greeting to the angels who come each and every week to spend Shabbas with us.

There is a legend that says that there are really two Shabbas angels—one a good angel and one an angel of evil. They both accompany a man home from *shul* on Friday night. If the man comes home to a table set for Shabbas dinner, with the candles lit and the *kiddush* cup brimming with wine, the good angel says, "May it be like this next Shabbas." And the angel of evil is forced to say "Amen." But if the table is not set, the candles are not lit, there is no wine in the *kiddush* cup, then the angel of evil says, "May it be like this next Shabbas." And the good angel is reluctantly and sadly forced to say, "Amen" (adaptation of BT Shabbat 119b).

Probably the most famous angel of all, the angel who brings the grimmest of news, is the *malach hamavet,* the angel of death. It is said that the *malach hamavet* is covered with eyes so that he should not miss even one person. Custom is that when a person is ill, his or her name is changed so that the *malach hamavet* might get confused and not be able to find him or her. But no matter how we try, no matter how much we try to avoid it, the *malach hamavet* is the last angel we will see in this lifetime, for the fate of every human being is to face the *malach hamavet* and be scooped up back to the heavenly realm.

The stories of the Yiddish writers, especially those of Shalom Aleichem, Y. L. Peretz, and the Nobel Prize winner, Isaac Bashevis Singer, are full of the imagined exploits of angels. Many of these tales revolve around the work of prosecuting and defending angels who represent our interests as we come before God's throne of judgment seeking to enter the heavenly realm and win eternal reward. The earthly decree of the *malach hamavet* is mitigated by the angels on high who usher us into everlasting bliss.

There are four angels whose identity, place, and power set them apart from the rest. These are the four primary archangels who bring some of God's attributes to earth.

Micha'el performs the unique miracles of God. Gavriel, who is the only one of these archangels with feminine attributes, is the emissary of God's strength. Uriel brings God's light. And Rafael brings God's healing. These are the angels we can call on by name to intercede for us with God, to ask God to provide us with the Godly traits and characteristics that each archangel represents.

As part of the traditional Jewish bedtime prayer recited by children—and by adults who never give up the habit—the angelic presence of these four archangels is invoked. They, along with *Shechinah,* the nurturing, feminine aspect of God, are asked to provide protection and safety during the dark hours of night, during the long hours of sleep. For some say that while we sleep, our soul leaves our body and goes up to the heavens. With the archangels watching over us and guarding us from every direction, we are safe until our soul reunites with our body when we wake.

The angel prayer is one of the sweetest and most tender of all Jewish prayers.

B'sheim HaShem   בשם השם
Elohay Yisrael   אלהי ישראל

Y'meeni Micha'el	ימיני מיכאל
U'me'smoli Gavri'al	ומשמאלי גבריאל
U'milfanai Uri'al	ומלפני אוראל
U'mayacharai R'fa'el	ומאחרי רפאל
V'al roshi, v'al roshi,	ועל ראשי ועל ראשי
Sh'chinat El.	שכינת אל

In the name of the Lord, the God of Israel,
May Michael be at my right;
Gabriel at my left;
Uriel, before me;
Rafael, behind me;
And above me, the Divine Presence of God.

Reb Shlomo Carlebach's sweet, sweet melody to this prayer makes it a lullaby that we can sing to our precious children each and every night. What better way to put our children to sleep than with this angelic prayer of protection, sung as the most gentle of all songs?

But the angel prayer is not for children alone. It is a most beautiful way for each and every one of us to end the day, to drift off to sleep in the presence, under the wings, of God's ministering angels.

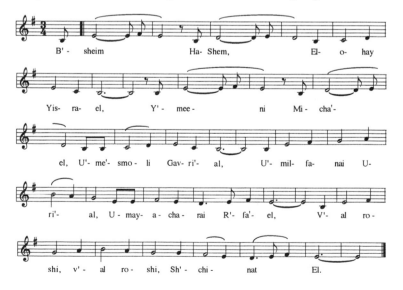

What does all this angel-talk really mean to us?

Does it mean that we have guardian angels who will save us from all harm, even if we walk straight into traffic? No.

Does it mean that we have miraculous powers at our disposal? No.

The presence of angels in our lives means that we have spiritual guides—or spiritual guidance—available to us continually.

It means that there is a messenger of God always present, always ready to hear from us, and always ready to speak to us.

It means that God is always near—just an angel away.

Can we meet our angels? Can we come to know these spiritual guides?

Angels are always within the circle of our consciousness; they are always "fluttering" around us.

So to meet them, we just have to ask.

In prayer, in deep meditation, we can ask to meet the angels in our world. We have to focus, we have to concentrate, we have to be willing to let them reveal themselves in their own manner, but if we ask, they will come.

In visualization, we can see them. In meditation, we can hear them.

When we ask, they will offer us guidance, they will offer us direction, they will offer us good counsel.

When we ask, they will help us understand some of the mysteries and some of the secrets of the universe, for being in their presence expands our consciousness and enlarges our vision.

When we ask, they will take us up to higher dimensions and lead us closer to God.

When we listen carefully, they will be true messengers of God, bringing us God's word and will.

Angels love us deeply and are most pleased when we call upon them. They are waiting to be found and are waiting to happily serve us, just as they joyously serve God.

And what of angels who "walk the earth"?

Connecting with the Universe

We all know of stories of very special men and women, people who in quiet, self-effacing, but very determined ways make extraordinary contributions to the world. They are usually not well known or famous; their words and deeds get little publicity or public recognition. But their actions have a tremendous impact and make an incredible difference in the lives of others.

They are selfless and giving; they are self-sacrificing and generous of spirit. They are humble and unassuming.

They are often called "God's angels."

Jewish tradition says that at any given moment there are thirty-six of these uncommon human beings alive on earth. They are called the *lamed-vovniks,* from the Hebrew letters ל *lamed,* which has the numerical value of thirty, and ו *vov,* which has the numerical value of six.

The *lamed-vovniks* are of both genders, of all races and ethnicities, of all faiths and religions, and they live at every social and economic level. Their identities are never revealed; it is said they do not even know who they are. But, it is said, they form the very foundation of the world, the pillars on which the whole world stands. The entire universe exists and survives because of their decency and dignity, their modesty and humility, their extraordinary goodness, kindness, and compassion, and their altruistic and noble service to their fellow human beings.

When one of the *lamed-vovniks* dies, the world teeters on the brink of impending disaster until God designates the replacement.

The *lamed-vovniks* sustain the world not only through their own unselfish acts, but also because they serve God as God's own personal, internal check and balance.

Legend says that after God destroyed the world in the flood, there was remorse in the heavens. The evil people with their wicked ways surely deserved to die, but what about the innocent children, the infants who were not corrupt, whose visages still shone with the light of God?

God knew that there would be more times of anger, that Divine mercy would be sorely tested by the follies of humankind. Yet the innocents could not again die for the transgressions of their elders. They would have to be saved. But the little ones would not be able to speak up for themselves; they would have no advocate in God's courts. And in time of anger, God might forget and again destroy the children.

So God placed the *lamed-vovniks* on earth. They have voice; their deeds speak their praise. They are God's safety net. For the sake of the *lamed-vovniks,* God can never destroy the world, and the innocent children will never again be wiped away.

Not only does the moral condition of the world depend upon the *lamed-vovniks,* but also the world itself continues to exist in them, because of them, and through them.

There are other angelic beings who inhabit our earth. They are the teachers, the sages, the masters, the gurus, the rebbes, who open our hearts and open our eyes. They are the spiritual guides in human form who bring God's word into this world. They are the earth-beings who inspire us to seek and climb the heights of our human potential, to strive toward earthly perfection.

Our greatest teachers are human beings who both think and feel, who combine the world of the mind with the world of the heart and spirit.

Our greatest teachers are human beings who are able to go beyond their own egos, who let go of self. In this way, they become pure channels of God. In this way they can "crawl inside" their disciples to teach from out of the disciples' needs instead of their own.

The Talmud instructs, "Get yourself a teacher" (Avot 1:6).

To this simple injunction, we add: get yourself a rebbe who is a true servant of the Lord, who will gently guide your mind and passionately inspire your heart. Get yourself a rebbe who is worthy of the trust of your spirit, who will take you under earthly angelic wings, and who, in love, will lead you toward God.

One of the most beloved characters of all Jewish history is Eliyahu HaNavi, the prophet Elijah.

He was a fiery prophet—angry at inequity and impatient when justice waited to be served. He was a loyal servant and a fierce champion of God.

If his spirit and his prophecies were not enough to distinguish him, he is unique among all people who have ever walked this earth. For with the exception of Enoch—and according to rabbinic literature, Elijah and Enoch are one and the same—Elijah the prophet is the only man ever to ascend to the heavens without passing through the normal process of earthly death: "A fiery chariot suddenly appeared . . . and Elijah was taken up to heaven in a whirlwind" (2 Kings 2:11).

What shall we say of a man who lived but who did not die?

Is he a mortal man? Is he an immortal Divine being? Is he an angel, a messenger of God?

Elijah is all of these things—and more.

For Elijah has become the stuff of the most precious Jewish dreams.

According to Jewish tradition, at the end of days, it is Elijah who will herald the coming of *masheach,* the messianic era of worldly harmony and peace.

So it is Elijah who attends every *bris,* every ritual circumcision —sitting in *kesey Eliyahu,* the specially designated chair of Elijah—to hint that perhaps this newly born child is *masheach* himself or, at very least, that the Jews are still fulfilling the *mitzvot* that make us worthy of the coming of *masheach.*

It is Elijah who attends every *seder,* drinking from the fifth cup of wine, magically turning the moment from celebration of historical redemption to the promise of ultimate redemption.

It is Elijah who is so wise and learned that when *masheach* comes, Elijah will answer all the still-unresolved and still-disputed questions of Jewish law that await end-of-days wisdom.

It is Elijah who appears in dreams and visions to scholars and to simpletons, to rich people and to paupers, giving instruction by revealing the mysteries of Torah.

It is Elijah who turns up anywhere at any time, disguised as a king or as a beggar, as a woodchopper or as a traveler, to offer comfort and aid to those who need Divine intervention.

It is Elijah who continually summons us up from our lethargy and keeps the vision of *masheachvelt* always before our eyes.

Stories abound of Elijah's mystical powers and deep, deep lessons.

This one will stand for them all, for it opens our hearts, the way Elijah always does.

Elijah arrived at a wedding feast dressed in the clothes of a beggar. When the father of the bride saw this poor, bedraggled man, he ordered him to leave.

A little while later, a very handsome man, dressed in a fine suit of clothes and carrying a gold-handled cane, arrived at the same feast. Although no one knew his name, he was warmly greeted and invited to partake of the food and drink. He was even invited to sit at the table of honor with the bride and groom.

As the meal was served, the guest took each course and shoved it into his pockets—the fish, the meat, the potatoes, and the vegetables. When he finished stuffing his pockets, he poured wine all over his suit.

The other guests at the wedding were dumbstruck. They stood watching this strange display but did not know what to say. Finally, the father of the bride asked for an explanation.

The guest explained: "When I came to your feast dressed as a beggar, you threw me out. But when I came dressed in fine clothes, even though I was a total stranger, you welcomed me and gave me honor. As a person, I was no different, but you did not know that because you welcomed my suit of clothes, not me. So I gave the wedding feast to the clothes that you so respected and honored."

With that, Elijah disappeared. But the gold-handled cane remained.

Yes, Eliyahu, we understand the message you bring us from on high. We understand your warnings about our foibles and our failings. We understand your angelic interventions to lift up our spirits to make us worthy of *masheach. Zachur latov,* and we remember you for good.

The very last words of biblical prophecy are the enduring charge to Elijah and to us: "Behold, I will send Elijah the prophet to you before the great and awesome day of the Lord. And he will turn the hearts of the children to the parents, and the hearts of the parents to the children" (Malachi 3:23–24).

❦

For all his already-achieved greatness, Elijah the prophet, Elijah who went up in the whirlwind, Elijah the angelic messenger of

God has one great and grand role still left to play. As the forerunner of the messiah, he will usher in the new age for our world, the age of harmony and peace, faith and love.

To invoke Elijah's presence, to hasten the coming of *masheach,* we can sing Elijah's familiar and beautiful song not only at its traditional time as Shabbas ends, but as part of our daily meditations and prayers.

Come to us, Elijah. Come to us now. We need you now more than ever before.

E- li- ya- hu ha- na- vi, E- li- ya- hu ha- tish- bi,

E- li- ya- hu, E- li- ya- hu, E- li- ya- hu ha- gil- a- di.

Bim- hei- ra v'- ya- mei- nu, ya- vo e- lei- nu,

im Ma- she- ach ben Da- vid, im Ma- she- ach ben Da- vid.

The Talmud (BT Sanhedrin 98a) says that Rabbi Joshua ben Levi found Elijah sitting disguised as a beggar at the gates of Rome. He asked, "When will you come to proclaim the messiah?" And Elijah replied, "Today, if only you will hear his voice."

Every angel, every messenger of God—from the most humble to the most high, to *masheach*—is waiting for its voice to be heard.

If we are quiet enough, if we listen well enough, we may just hear our angels' "wings" flapping.

If we open our hearts enough, we will meet our angels.

If we open our hearts enough, we will meet our God.

14

It's Right Under
Your Nose

Do you know that little indentation on your upper lip, right under your nose?

What is it, and why is it there? It seems to serve no discernible purpose; there is no medical need for it; and surely it plays no part in facial glamour.

If we thought about it for a moment or two, we might conclude that it is there, either by design or evolution, to make it easier for air to pass out of the nostrils, sort of a built-in corridor for exhaled air to make it "over the hump" of the upper lip.

Actually, most of us never think about it. It is just there—part of our anatomy that came as "original factory-installed equipment" but that has no role or function as part of daily existence. We do not even know what to call it. It does have a scientific name; it's called the philtrum. But if we ever refer to it at all, we just call it "that little indentation right under my nose."

However, Jewish tradition knows what the philtrum is and what an important place it has in our lives.

According to *midrashic* legend, every soul created by God has all knowledge of the universe, especially the knowledge of good and evil. Yet when a soul comes to earth and is placed in a physical body, it cannot bring with it the totality of knowledge. In a human form, the soul must accept the limitations placed upon it by the boundaries of human existence.

So, according to the legend, just before a soul, now placed into the body of a baby in the womb, emerges into human life, an angel, whose name is Lailah, taps the baby on the upper lip—creating the little indentation we call the philtrum—and in doing so takes away the entirety of knowledge.

The new baby can now come into this earthly plane and live and grow in this world with all its earthly limitations and possibilities. The philtrum serves as a lifetime reminder of what was once known, what must be learned, and what will one day be known again.

❧❖❧

A fanciful legend, right? Yes, if we view the universe and our existence on a completely intellectual, rational basis where everything begins and ends with us. A fanciful legend, unless we accept the notion that there is something much greater beyond earthly existence as we know it. A fanciful legend, unless we accept the notion that the greatness and grandeur of God fill the entire universe, not just the tiny part we can each see, hear, smell, touch, and experience. A fanciful legend, unless now and then we catch glimpses of the deepest memories of what we once knew and see momentary flashes of what we can know— and be—again. A fanciful legend, unless we believe in the eternity of the soul and its continuing and evolving place in God's eternal plan.

A story that has been told so often that if it is not true, it has achieved the status of an urban legend:

Recently, a baby was born. When the parents brought him home from the hospital, the baby's older brother, a child of four, kept asking, "Can I be alone with my brother? When can the baby and I be alone?"

The parents, not understanding why their older son wanted to be alone with the baby, and concerned about jealousy and sibling rivalry, kept putting off the request saying, "It's good for *all* of us to be together." But the four-year-old was insistent, so the parents finally told him that he could go into the baby's room, and if he wanted privacy he could close the door behind himself.

Curious and worried, the parents turned on the intercom so they could hear what transpired. As soon as the door was shut, the four-year-old went up to the crib, looked right down at his newly born brother, and said, "Quick, baby, tell me what I am supposed to remember. I'm forgetting already."

If the story is apocryphal, no matter, for *this* story really happened:

A young couple, parents of a three-year-old boy, told me that at his preschool, their son had made very good friends with a little fellow named Philip. The parents were surprised, because they thought that there were a number of other children whom their son might have chosen as best friend, but their Jared was particularly drawn to Philip and spent most of his time with him.

I had a hunch (or a "hit" of intuition or knowing). I asked Jared, "Have you ever known Philip from before?"

"Sure," he replied matter-of-factly.

"Where, when?" I asked.

Jared looked at me as if I were rather stupid to be asking such a simple question. He pointed his finger upward and nonchalantly said, "When we were with God."

Ask some two-, three-, or four-year-olds the right questions, and they may be able to tell you about their infancy, their birth, perhaps about being in the womb or even recollections of the world beyond.

But by the time a child reaches five or so, the angel's tap has taken permanent hold, and all that was once known is forgotten.

Later, as adults, we will have those flashes of deep memory.

Some call it intuition; some call it déjà vu; some call it extrasensory perception; some call it past-life memory. The Kabbalists and the mystics call it *gilgool hanefesh,* the "transmigrating" or "rolling of the soul." It is what is commonly known as reincarnation.

At the deepest place of our memory, we know that it all goes back to that magical moment of creation when God said, "Let there be light"

(Genesis 1:3). At that very instant, God created every soul that would ever be. Only later in the process would two of those souls be put into human form, in the earthly vessels we call bodies, when God said, "Let us make man in our image. . . . Male and female created He them" (Genesis 1:26, 28).

God created only a finite number of souls to inhabit the entire universe. These souls continually move between the heavenly realm and the earthly plane—sometimes in soul energy, sometimes in human body. They "transmigrate" or "roll" between one plane of existence and the other.

While there has never been one unilateral, definitive Jewish theology about the age-old question "What happens to me after I die?," and while much of Jewish thought, particularly in the 250 years since the Enlightenment, is very rational about matters of life and death, this world, and worlds to come, *gilgool hanefesh,* reincarnation, is one of Judaism's most powerful answers to the eternal question. (For a full and detailed explanation of the Jewish theologies of life and death, see "An Essay on Life and Death" in my *Living Judaism: The Complete Guide to Jewish Belief, Tradition, and Practice.*)

Gilgool hanefesh is traced by some back to the Bible, is hinted at in rabbinic literature, and is clearly articulated in the mystical tradition of the Kabbalists.

We are taught that when God created the world, God created every soul that was ever to come into body on this earthly plane.

Each soul has not only an everlasting but also an independent existence.

The eternal soul dwells in the heavenly realm and is endowed by God with ultimate and universal knowledge.

Now and then souls make agreements—called contracts—to come into body on this earthly plane in order to fulfill a specific mission or to work out a particular life issue (what the Hindus call karma). As we have already seen, when a soul is in human form, it gives up universal knowledge.

When a soul's sojourn in a particular earthly body is complete—sometimes the contracts take a long time to fulfill; sometimes they are fulfilled in weeks, months, or a few years—the soul leaves the earthly plane and "passes away" or "passes over" back into the spiritual plane. There it rests and is cleansed of imperfections that may have attached during the earthbound journey. It incorporates the karmic lessons that were learned—usually seven in each earth life—and adds the earthly experience to soul memory. It reenergizes and prepares for another earth journey, or it moves on to other Divine tasks, such as becoming a spirit guide.

At any given time, some souls are in earth body; some are in the heavenly realm.

One legend contends that there was one time when every soul that was in body and every other soul that had ever been or would ever be in body came together in one massive gathering. That was at Sinai, when God gave the commandments enjoining all of us to lives of holiness. Those commands were given, according to the Torah, "with those who are standing here with us today before the Lord our God, and with those who are not with us here this day" (Deuteronomy 29:14). Rational thinkers explain that this text simply refers to those who will be born in future generations. The mystics know that it means the holy convocation when all souls—those in body and those not—came to the once-in-time majestic theophany.

Gilgool hanefesh means that the soul is never abandoned but is beloved and cared for by God in all of its forms. It means that each soul retains complete memory of all that has happened to it and to every other soul with which it ever came in contact on both the earth and the heavenly planes. It means that each soul joins in the conscious decision-making process of what role it will play and what task it will have at any given moment.

When a soul returns to earth in a new *gilgool,* it may come in either a male or female body, regardless of what gender body it had in any previous lifetimes. For the soul chooses to come in the gender that will best help it achieve the purpose and spiritual work that it has come to do.

Souls often return to earth to continue the work of a previous lifetime.

Some souls return to earth to make up for the transgressions or mistakes of a previous lifetime—to fix the karma. In a most puzzling verse in Torah, we are taught, "For I the Lord your God am an impassioned

God, visiting the guilt of parents upon the children, upon the third and fourth generations of those that reject Me, but showing kindness to the thousandth generation of those that love Me and keep My commandment" (Exodus 20:5–6 and, similarly, Numbers 14:18 and Deuteronomy 5:9).

What a harsh and seemingly unfair fate! Why should unborn children be punished for the transgressions of their parents, grandparents, or great-grandparents? Though it would be unjust, we can understand how a young man might be regarded if he introduced himself by saying, "Hello, I'm Jack the Ripper, Jr." While he may be the finest and most cultured of all men, his father's reputation would taint him, and, in the image of the Torah, the sins of the father would be visited upon the child.

But the mystics explain the verse very differently. What is really being taught, they say, is that every third or fourth human generation, our soul returns to earth in a human body in order to do the work of *t'shuvah* and *tikkun,* of repentance and healing—to fix the karma—for the mistakes we made in that previous lifetime. In the image of the old joke, we keep coming back until we get it right, until we resolve the unresolved and fix the unfixed. Only in that way is the eternal soul ready to move on to its next mission, its next lessons.

Some souls return to earth to add to the work and the progress of the world, to help it move forward toward balance and perfection. These are usually souls that have worked through much of their karma and have agreed to serve for the greater good. While these souls will still have personal issues to work on while in body, their soul evolution permits them to volunteer for a mission of high purpose.

All souls come to earth in body by choice, in order to continue learning and evolving and in order to continue working through karma. Souls that choose not to return for another lifetime on earth continue their evolution in the higher dimensions. Some of the most highly evolved souls—those that have reached the "soul hall of fame"— eventually become spirit guides for those in body, sending messages of assistance and enlightenment from the Other Side.

Souls that have been together in one lifetime often return together in one or more future lifetimes, playing out their relationships, correcting and healing past wrongdoing, enhancing past opportunities, learning, and growing.

When people who have never met before feel an immediate affinity and intimacy, when lovers who have been searching all their lives finally find their "soul mate," it is no accident. Souls that have been together in previous lifetimes often transmigrate together, and their *gilgool* reunites them in a new earthbound lifetime.

Souls often come to learn one particular lesson or to assist other souls in learning a specific lesson. That is why it is said that children choose the parents and the families they will be born into. As the souls interact in human form on this earthly plane, they bring up and trigger karmic issues for one another. They use this lifetime to confront, work through, and teach one another what must be learned for soul evolution.

The English poet William Wordsworth captured the essence of the transmigrating soul and its infinite worth in each place and in each *gilgool:*

> *Our birth is but a sleep and a forgetting;*
> *The soul that rises with us, our life's Star,*
> *Hath elsewhere its setting,*
> *And cometh from afar;*
> *Not in entire forgetfulness,*
> *And not in utter nakedness,*
> *But trailing clouds of glory do we come*
> *From God who is our home.*

The *brit milah,* the ritual circumcision of an eight-day-old Jewish boy (commonly known as the *bris),* has always been a most hallowed ritual because it marks the renewal of the covenant with God in each new generation. But it has an even greater holy purpose.

Lailah, the angel who touched the baby's upper lip in the womb, has prepared the soul for its earthly sojourn.

Now the *bris* is the transcendent moment when the newborn child is passed from the hand of God to the hands of the earthly parents. It is an awesome moment of cosmic significance. It is a sacred moment of shared responsibility, privilege, and joy.

The prayers and blessings we recite at the *bris* of our sons and at the covenant ceremony for our daughters can be renewed to reflect not only the traditional tribal and covenantal commitments, but also the celebration of the soul-journey that is taking place.

In further recognition of the cosmic import of the soul coming to this earth plane, we can revive and renew a *bris* ritual that is now practiced in only the most traditionally observant families.

The night before the *bris* is known as *layel shimurim,* "the night of watching." It is customary for the father, other members of the family, and close friends to stay up all night in a vigil, watching over the baby to ward off anything that might interfere with the *bris.* This tradition has roots going all the way back to ancient paganism, when the baby was to be guarded from any evil spirits that might want to take his life before he underwent the initiation ceremonies of his tribe. His night-time watchers protected him from any external threat or harm. The Jewish version of this rite features all-night study and learning—faithful commitment to the covenant that the baby is about to enter.

Even though they are probably already exhausted from childbirth and from caring for the newborn infant, in Jewish renewal young parents are invited to stay up with their baby all night before the *bris* or covenant ceremony. It can be a time of deep love, and, even more important, it can be a time when parents think about, talk about, meditate, and pray over the tremendous spiritual responsibility they are about to affirm. Being the caretakers of one of the precious souls of the universe is no easy job; it is the highest and holiest of all earthly tasks. By staying up all night with their baby, the parents can begin to form the spiritual bond with the soul that is about to come from God's hands to theirs.

With the psalmist of old, the parents can know that "the cries of infants attest to God's power" (after Psalms 8:3). They can know that they are partners with God in renewing this eternal soul in this *gilgool.* And they can know, in the words of the Yiddish proverb, that "each child carries his or her own unique blessing into the world."

Gilgool hanefesh means that life can be celebrated, for it is the obvious answer to the age-old question, "Who am I and what is my life?" Affirming the concept of *gilgool hanefesh* affirms the eternity and the value of the soul and of life.

And *gilgool hanefesh* is the obvious answer to finding meaning and purpose in life.

We are on a mission.

We are here on this earthly plane for a particular reason—to fulfill a particular contract or to work out a specific piece of karma or to advance a particular truth or to do a specific task. All of this helps our own souls evolve, but, even more, it helps the earth evolve into higher and higher dimensions.

Reb Shlomo often told the story of Reb David Leikes, a devoted chasid of the Baal Shem Tov.

Reb David decided to spend Yom Kippur with his holy master. He started out in plenty of time to get to the Baal Shem before Yontif, but delay after delay kept him from his destination.

Finally, it was only an hour before Yom Kippur was to begin, but if he hurried, he would make it on time. To be sure that the horses would not falter on the way, he stopped for a precious moment to water them.

In that moment when the horses were drinking, some people from the little village approached him. "Please, good man," they said, "please help us. We are but nine Jews in this tiny village. We need one more person to make our *minyan* so that we can say our prayers on the holiest day of the year. Please. Please stay here and *daven* with us on Yom Kippur."

Reb David barely listened to their pleas. "What?" he asked incredulously. "Don't you know where I am going? I am traveling to be in the court of the holy master. I am going to *daven* Yom Kippur with the holy Baal Shem. I would like to help you, but how can I give up being with the holiest of all men on the holiest of all days?"

Chastened and saddened, the men stepped back, and Reb David grabbed his horses and rode away.

When he came to the holy Baal Shem's court, the master was wishing everybody a "good Yontif." When it came Reb David's turn, the

Baal Shem skipped over him. "It must be an oversight," thought Reb David. "The Baal Shem just didn't see me."

When Yom Kippur was over, once again, the holy Baal Shem greeted all who had come to *daven* in his court, but once again he skipped over Reb David.

By the time Succot came and went and he had been skipped over time and time again, Reb David knew that it was no oversight, no accident, that the Baal Shem had not greeted him. Ready to return home, but crestfallen that the holy master had failed to recognize his presence, he cried out, "Please, Rebbe, please, holy master. Tell me what I did so wrong that you should ignore me like this."

And the Baal Shem Tov looked deeply into Reb David's eyes and said, "Tell me, David. Tell me how many hundreds of years, how many *gilgoolim,* has your soul been waiting to *daven* Yom Kippur with those nine men? You came into this world only to pray with them."

As Reb Shlomo would say, "Gevalt!"

An entire *gilgool* for this one mission, an entire *gilgool* to *daven* Yom Kippur with nine men who needed a *minyan!*

Think about it for a moment.

Is there any greater task, any greater mission?

Perhaps.

Perhaps that which we deem so important is really important in the ultimate scheme. Perhaps my books will be read one hundred years from now, or perhaps they will turn to dust. Perhaps the monuments we build—out of whatever of life's materials—will endure, or perhaps they will crumble and fall.

But *davening* Yom Kippur with nine other men who need a *minyan?* Ah, that's a reason for being! That is a holy soul-moment worthy of eternity.

Gilgool hanefesh calls us to treat every moment as a life-mission. *Gilgool hanefesh* calls us to constant dialogue with ourselves and with our universe, to intimate moments of soul-talk that guide us toward continual soul-growth and soul-evolution, for that is what we have come here to do.

There are some for whom soul-talk seems meaningless, for they are happy to live life just as it is, unbothered by universal concerns.

There are others who are content to lead an uncomplicated, unexamined life. For others, soul-talk seems a luxury, for people who are hungry use their energy earning their bread, not in cosmic speculation.

We know, of course, that those who ignore soul-talk, those whose plight seems to be too miserable for soul-talk, are doing just as they must. For outward manifestation is no indication of inner soul work. The karma is being fixed, and the soul is evolving in perfect plan.

Yet, as human beings, whose earthly existence can lead to soul evolution, we want to be whole with our souls. We want the satisfaction that comes from stimulating work and gratifying play, from mutually interdependent relationships of caring and sharing, of loving and being loved. We want to know ourselves and be true to ourselves. We want to be inner directed, focused, centered; to be solid and certain at our core; to be ever evolving. We want to be in tune with our environment, in touch with our integrity, involved with our possibilities. We want to be connected and at one with the universe. We want serenity, contentment, and inner peace.

And we want to be holy in our souls. We want to know God and be like God. We want to reflect God's qualities of knowledge, of reason, and of memory, to have God's capacity for seeking justice and feeling compassion. We want to be partners with God in the ongoing evolution and perfection of our world.

To be whole and holy, we have to nurture our souls.

We have to care for our souls with things of beauty: art, music, the sight of a majestic mountain, a bubbling brook, a delicate butterfly.

We have to ennoble our souls by reading good words, hearing good talk, debating great ideas.

We have to enrich our souls with caring and love.

We have to journey with our souls toward life's deepest meaning and richest happiness.

As Jews, we have to touch within our souls that *pintele Yid,* that spark of Jewish identity—Judaism's intimate covenantal relationship with God; Judaism's values of human decency and dignity, kindness and righteousness; Judaism's lifestyle, which sanctifies the ordinary; Judaism's sense of belonging and bonding; Judaism's celebration and affirmation of life with certain knowledge and even deeper faith.

As Jews, as human beings, we must remember that everything we need for soul evolution is right within us, right within our souls, for in each and every one of us is the entirety of the human experience, the grandeur of human achievement, the vastness of human potential.

And in our souls is our soul giver, our soul partner—God.

And in our souls is our reason for being, our greatness, our eternity, for in the deepest part of our souls, we find the holiest and most precious of all of God's gifts in the universe—ourselves.

When we touch the deepest, most intimate, and most sacred places in our souls, we can enrich and ennoble our existence, and we can make this *gilgool* worthy and worthwhile.

And, finally, *gilgool hanefesh* is the answer to the mystery and the fear of the ultimate unknown, death, for it shows us that there is little distinction between what we know as life and what we call death. For life and death are part of the continual flow of the wholeness of the universe, and the veil between them is very, very thin. As the Kotzker Rebbe taught, "Fear not death. It is just a matter of going from one room to the other."

How can we—rational intellects that we have been trained to be—accept and affirm this highly spiritual notion of *gilgool hanefesh,* this completely unproven theory of reincarnation?

For some, belief in *gilgool hanefesh* demands the suspension of all rational thinking—a complete leap of faith. For others, it is the most logical, natural, and irrefutable explanation of the mysteries of the universe.

Are we to think that there is no more to this world than what we can see and hear and experience at this moment?

Because a radio is capable of receiving only AM frequencies, does that mean FM frequencies are not out there?

Because the camera lens can be opened only so wide, does that mean there is nothing outside its view?

Because we cannot hear the high-pitched sound of the dog whistle, does that mean the sound does not exist?

As the universe unfolds, as it divulges more and more of its secrets and reveals more and more of its mysteries, we begin to see and grasp things that were there all the time but that we had not yet developed the capacity to perceive.

Gilgool hanefesh has been part of God's eternal plan since the beginning of time. When our souls are on the Other Side, we understand it well, for it is a natural part of our soul's eternal existence and a certain component of our universal knowledge. But when we choose to come into body on this earthly plane and we are stripped of universal knowledge, it is hard to tap into or grasp the momentary flashes of deep memory.

But now, as human consciousness evolves, as more and more eternal truths are uncovered, and as we are given more and more glimpses of what we once knew, we are coming closer and closer to bringing universal knowledge to this earth plane.

We are transmigrating, we are "rolling through" continual evolution, and each *gilgool* of each soul brings us closer and closer to *y'mot hamasheach,* the days of Sky Blue, when peace and harmony will envelop the earth.

So we have to open our eyes wide and attune our ears sharply. We have to watch and listen carefully to our daydreams and our night visions. We have to hold on to the tiny glimpses we are given of what was, and to be open to the momentary flashes of what might be.

Our soul-journey of earthly existence is, at the same time, a soul-journey back to the source, back to ultimate origin, back to infinite knowledge, back to God.

The angel who feels bad for having taken away soul-knowledge becomes a lifetime companion and guide.

And God gently shows our souls the way back to what we once had and to what we will have again.

The philtrum—staring at us from the mirror each and every day—remains a sign of what we are missing and a beacon guiding us back to where this journey will carry us.

⚜

Reb David Leikes—the very Reb David whom the holy Baal Shem Tov chastised for not *davening* Yom Kippur with the nine who needed a *minyan*—must have been forgiven from On High. From his failure to fulfill the singular mission that his soul came here to do, there must have been great learning, great evolution, even while here on earth. For Reb David lived to be more than one hundred years old and was considered one of the great rabbinic authorities and judges of his generation.

Reb David's reprieve gives us all great hope, for we learn that, confronted with their transgressions, our souls can do *t'shuvah* and *tikkun,* repentance and healing—and be forgiven.

When Reb David was on his deathbed, a complicated case arose, and all the other rabbinic judges were hoping that Reb David's mind still might be clear enough to help them adjudicate the case and make their difficult decision. They came to his house and requested to see him. But Reb David's children insisted that their holy father not be bothered, that he be allowed to die in peace.

Suddenly the door to his bedroom opened, and the dying rabbi came into the room with his rabbinic colleagues. He said to his children, "The Talmud teaches that one who judges a case correctly becomes a partner with God. Please do not deprive me of this opportunity."

Reb David listened to the case in deep concentration, and he rendered his decision in a remarkable display of brilliant reasoning. Then, with the help of his children, he returned to his bed, and a moment later he died.

Rabbi Moshe Sopher taught, "Many people complain that they have nothing with which to live. Would it be more sensible for them to complain that they have nothing with which to die?"

Reb David's holy soul gave him that with which to live *and* that with which to die.

From him—from his soul-journey from rebuke to renown—we learn that our souls can and will evolve from *gilgool* to *gilgool* when we nurture them and honor them; when we affirm and celebrate the holy mission on which they lead us and guide us; when we learn from them the precious life lessons they continually have to teach.

In this *gilgool* and in every other, we can add our soul-voices to those who sing soul-hymns to God.

My soul desires the shelter of Your hand,
to know the secrets of Your mysteries.
May my prayer ever be sweet to You;
my soul longs and yearns for You.

I put my soul into God's hand,
both when I am awake and when I am asleep. . . .
God is with me;
I will not fear.

15

Of Exile and Return

A LONG, LONG TIME AGO, THERE WAS A PRINCESS who was like no other princess in the world, for she was not made of flesh and blood but was made entirely of light.

Her father, the king, lived in a heavenly palace, but the princess lived in the Holy Temple in the holy city of Jerusalem. The king missed his daughter, but he had sent her on a very special mission—to give blessings to the world.

Not many people could see the princess, for most of the time she was invisible. Every once in a while, a few people might see her in a vision or a dream. Sometimes she appeared as a royal princess; sometimes she looked like a beautiful bride; at other times she seemed to be a Divine spirit. The people were very happy to see the princess, for they knew that as long as she hovered over the Temple and the city, her father, the king, would protect her and all the people with her.

But one day, a great catastrophe occurred. The Holy Temple was destroyed, and the holy city lay in ruins. The princess wept and wept, for her heart was broken. She saw the people she loved being sent away from their land, off to exile. She said to herself, "I do not want my people to be sad and lonely. I will go with them to keep them company on their journey."

When the king heard that his daughter had left the holy city, he called every prince in the world to go out to find her. He said, "Whoever finds the princess will be her husband. But do not think that it will be easy to find her, for though she is always with her people, she is very well hidden."

Every prince in the world wanted to marry the beautiful princess of light, so they all began to search. They looked everywhere in the world—in big cities and in tiny villages, in forests and deserts—but no one could find her.

Finally, only one prince was left. He was a very smart prince, so he approached the search in a very wise manner. He thought to himself, "Where could it possibly be that the princess is with her people but is also very well hidden?"

To help answer this question, the prince came to a rabbi. "Please tell me," he asked the rabbi, "where is it that the princess could be where she is always with her people, yet very well hidden?"

The rabbi replied, "There is only one thing in the world that is always with the Jewish people, and that is the Torah."

The prince thought for a moment and then asked, "Oh, wise rabbi, will you please teach me Torah?"

It took many years of patient study before the prince learned Torah, but on the day he mastered it, the prince found the princess. For she was hiding in the words of Torah, and she understood all of Torah's many secrets.

Now that the prince knows where the princess is, he is determined to set her free. When he does, the whole world will celebrate the day of their wedding. In his gladness, her father the king will rebuild the Holy Temple in Jerusalem as a wedding gift to his daughter and her prince. And they will all live happily ever after.

For almost two thousand years, we Jews were a people in exile.

We wandered from place to place and from land to land. Our precious Torah was always with us, and we sensed that the princess of light, the *Shechinah,* accompanied us on our journey and cared for us under her sheltering wings. But we always longed to come home, to reclaim our land, to rebuild our Temple, to restore our sovereignty and self-respect.

Every day, three times a day, we fervently prayed for return.

As Yom Kippur concluded and the Pesach *seder* ended, we cried out, "Next Year! Next year! Next year, home."

The one remnant of the Holy Temple, the Western Wall, became known as the Wailing Wall, for it heard our mournful lament and was drenched with our tears of longing.

Even at our moments of greatest joy, we yearned for home. At our weddings we smashed a glass, a remembrance of the destruction and the exile.

And when we built our houses we left a corner of the ceiling unfinished, unplastered. Our dwelling place could never be complete because no matter how lovely, no matter how grand, it could never be a permanent home. Home is Jerusalem.

⚜

Physical exile is tragic enough.

But as the physical exile grew longer and longer, the pain and the anguish of separation and isolation began to seep into the Jewish consciousness, into the Jewish psyche.

Exile became not only a physical reality, but also a state of mind, a state of being.

Galus, exile, became our definition of ourselves—not only *where* we were, but *who* we were.

Our souls felt a rootlessness and an impermanence. Nothing was stable, definite, durable. We were always scattered and unsettled, displaced and dislocated. We were insecure and afraid. We were empty and bereft.

Year after year, century after century, our communal soul suffered and our individual souls took on the collective angst. No Jew ever felt whole or complete—or completely safe.

To combat our *galus* mentality, we turned to one another, to bolster and strengthen ourselves in ourselves. Everywhere we went, if permitted to do so, we built communal institutions—synagogues, schools, *mikvaot,* cemeteries—so that we could gather together and find comfort in one another. The needs of the community always took precedence over individual wants. Even in the times and places of greatest acceptance and creativity, our inner loyalty and our commitment to the common good often determined our survival.

Yet all too often we did not survive. *Galus* meant being fodder for the Crusades and the Inquisition and the pogroms and the ovens of Hitler's hell. *Galus* meant being the outcast, the betrayed, the hunted, the hated, the dead.

That is why all our prayers, all our learning, all our holidays, all our life-celebrations were tinged with sadness. How could there be complete joy when our souls were so battered and bruised?

That is why our eyes and our hearts rarely looked forward, except in the wildest of our speculative imaginings. The days of *mosheach* were a far-off dream, and we could not even begin to imagine that earthly salvation would ever come, that we could ever again be free and proud, that our souls could come in from exile. So we kept looking backward to Israel and Jerusalem, to those long-ago heady days of freedom and independence. Our ideal, that for which we strove, became not a vision of what we might become and be, but a misty, illusory notion of what once was.

No wonder so many Jews and so much of Judaism have been sad and languid for so long.

Worst of all, as the exile dragged on and on, our collective and individual souls became sick, more and more disillusioned and diseased. We lost hope, we lost spirit, we lost faith, and we became more and more separated from God. We wondered why God had turned His face from us, even as we turned our faces further and further from God.

That is why, despite the mostly foiled attempts of the Kabbalists and the Chasidim, most Jewish God-talk during the two millennia of exile was highly rational and intellectual. We could talk *about* God, but we had trouble talking *to* God. Our spirit—and thus our spiritual quest —was crushed. We reached the depth of all depths: our souls were in exile from God.

Finally, finally, after almost two thousand years, in this, our generation, the Miracle Maker wrought the miracle.

In 1948, the third Jewish commonwealth, the modern State of Israel, was born. The exile was over. We could go home.

But it was not to be an easy homecoming. Almost immediately those who wished our exile to continue rose up to oppose us, to beat us back, to close the gates almost before they could be opened.

With stunning certainty, we defeated them, for although their military might was far, far greater than ours, our will, our determination—our need—was far, far greater than theirs.

We were once again "a free people in our land, in the land of Zion, in Jerusalem." A new spirit—a spirit of possibility, of hope, of renewal —began to envelop the Jewish people. We began to take the first tentative, tender steps toward rebuilding our land and rebuilding our souls. Emboldened by the revival in Israel, the rest of world Jewry basked in new pride and began to build up new institutions and community structures.

For coupled with our return to our land was our newfound status in the lands of our diaspora. In the United States following World War II, we were accorded our rightful, earned place in American society, for, like our neighbors, we had fought and died in the foxholes of Europe and on the battleships of the Pacific. We still received the sympathy of the world for the continually unfolding horrors of the Holocaust and were given the world's goodwill at the establishment of the State of Israel. The old quota system disappeared, and Jewish youngsters were able to attend the finest universities in the country. Most of the old impediments broke down, and jobs and professions that were once off limits to Jews now vied to hire the best and the brightest Jewish minds. With the help of the G.I. Bill, Jews could participate in the great American dream—owning a house in the suburbs. Over the years our acceptance, our affluence, our influence grew.

Yet our euphoria was far from widespread. We were like a body without a heart, for we were still cut off from the holiest of our places in old Jerusalem. We were still beleaguered by enemies who wished to destroy us; we hardly knew how to govern ourselves or set our national agenda; and, particularly with the survivors still staggering out of Holocaust Europe, we could not quite rid ourselves of the sense of being the victim and the attitude of being in *galus*.

That was all to change in 1967. With lightning speed, the mighty Israeli army decimated the enemy armies attacking from three sides—all in six days. Body and heart became one, for the holy city of Jerusalem was reunited and whole. The image of the Jew as the eternal victim was wiped out by the brave and heroic fighting Israeli soldier. The burden and the pain of exile—the mind-set of *galus*—was over. Finally, finally, the Jews were home.

Slowly, over time, our collective and individual souls began to heal. We began to feel more comfortable and at home, more secure and settled. While we remained ever vigilant, we became less afraid. And our spirits began to revive. Tentatively, almost bashfully, we began to seek God and reconcile the long-felt rift.

Our celebrations have begun to take on a purer, deeper joy. Our prayers and our learning have begun to unfold in new enlightenment. Our rabbis and our teachers—the first of our spiritual guides in two thousand years to be born in postexilic freedom—have begun to reinvigorate our faith.

Out of the end of exile—the exile of body, the exile of spirit—Jewish Renewal is being born.

For the first time in centuries, the needs of the individual Jew have begun to be heard with as much urgency as the needs of the Jewish community.

It used to be that when a Jew was in personal pain—the pain of physical illness or spiritual distress—he or she or a family member would come to the rabbi and say, "Please say a *mi sheberach,* a prayer for healing, for me, for my loved one." The sages who composed this prayer well understood what modern scientific and spiritual explorers are just rediscovering—that in the complex nature of human beings, there is deep holistic connection between the mind and the body, between the physical and the spiritual worlds. That is why this old prayer asks God to "bring healing of soul and healing of body." But custom was to say the prayer in a public setting on behalf of another.

Most other Jewish prayers for healing also were recited in community as part of communal worship. They all used the traditional collective rubric of Jewish prayer, "Heal *us,* O God. . . ." Only the prayer of thanksgiving for recovery has a personal aspect, praising God "who has dealt graciously with *me."*

This was all a reflection of our exile from God. In the midst of community, it felt acceptable to ask that the needs of the members of the community be met. The private petition, although surely said by many, felt just too personal, just too intimate, to ask of a God from whom we felt such distance.

But now, as the mind-set of exile dissipates, as we slowly but assuredly reconcile with God, heal the hurts, and come closer to the Divine presence, we feel comfortable with personally asking for our individual needs to be recognized and met.

That is why a new attitude toward prayers for healing and a phenomenon of Jewish healing services are growing up all over the country. For, in our own confrontation with spiritual exile and physical illness, we have come to realize that a spontaneous, personal plea for healing—an unadorned, instinctive, involuntary supplication—is one of Judaism's oldest and most powerful soul-cries to God.

In one of the most moving passages of Torah, Miriam the prophetess, the sister of Moses, is stricken with leprosy. The text indicates that she is being punished for speaking against Moses, and it implies that she is jealous of him for having direct prophetic communication

with God. Perhaps, too, she was offended that she had no major leadership role or that she was not tapped for priesthood or that she was not
included in the council of seventy elders. Perhaps her illness stemmed
from her separation from God. Perhaps she was in pain at the sup-
pression of the last vestiges of goddess energy at the very time that the
notion of a powerful, authoritarian, masculine God was taking root.
Perhaps she was cleverly protecting her brother from the false-prophet
dissidents in the camp by refracting the attention from them onto herself. Whatever the reason, Miriam swiftly becomes very, very ill with
what was then considered a dread contagious disease.

Moses does not hesitate for a second; he is utterly unconcerned that
Miriam may have been agitating against him. All he knows is that his
sister is very sick. With poignant brevity and in beautiful poetry, he
cries out five simple, heart-rending words, אל נא רפא נא לה *El na, r'fa
na lah,* "O God, please heal her" (Numbers 12:13).

The prophet Elijah was a personal healer. The Bible tells that,
in the name of God, he multiplied the food supply of the widow of
Zarepthath so that she and her young son would not starve to death
during the drought (1 Kings 17:11ff.). When the child fell so ill that
"there was no breath left in him," Elijah cried out to God for healing,
"O Lord my God, let this child's life return to his body." The boy was
revived and lived (1 Kings 17:17, 21ff.).

The prophet Elisha, the disciple and successor of Elijah, also dis-
played healing powers. He, too, provided food when there was almost
none (2 Kings 4:38–44) and continually filled the empty oil jugs of a
widow so that she could pay her debts (2 Kings 4:1–7). And Elisha
brought healing and life to the seemingly dead son of the Shunamite
woman just as his master Elijah had brought life to the son of the
widow of Zarepthath (2 Kings 4:32–37).

In the days before he taught the principles of *chasidut,* the holy
Baal Shem Tov was a well known traveling healer. He was often called
"the miracle maker."

Like our prophets and our teachers, we can come to God with our
own deepest and most fervent expressions of need and hope for God's

protection and healing. We can find ways to renew old rituals and to devise new modes in order to invoke God's healing powers, to seek comfort when we are in pain and to bring hope to all who are ill.

Every evening, the traditional worship service includes a prayer called *Hashkivenu,* which asks God for protection from the many and varied travails and afflictions that may confront us. In striking imagery, the prayer asks God to "spread over us סכת שלומך *succat sh'lo-mecha,* Your tabernacle of peace." In reciting these words, we can visualize ourselves standing under God's *succah,* the delicate yet sturdy and invulnerable dwelling that God builds to house and protect us. "And I shall dwell in the house of the Eternal One all the days of my life" (Psalms 23:6).

We can also use another popular image for our visualization of God's protection, when we see ourselves תחת כנפי השכינה *tachat kanfei haShechinah,* "under the wings of the *Shechinah.*" What a wonderful place to be—protected under the sheltering, nurturing wings of God!

Finally, we can use the most powerful of all visualizations of God's protection when we see ourselves in the middle of the six-pointed Star of David, the Jewish star. Popular insignia of our people for millennia,

this star is an ancient symbol of great power. The two inverted triangles, with their sharp tips pointing in all directions, create in their center a safe haven from all harm. What better place to be than within the insignia of our people, protected by our God!

In many synagogues and prayer groups, the prayers for healing are recited no longer by the rabbi on behalf of those who are ill, but by the stricken themselves or by their close family members. In some places, all the worshipers chant over and over again the phrase from the *amidah:* סומך נופלים ורופא חולים *someich noflim v'rofey cholim,* invoking God who "lifts up those who are fallen and heals those who are sick." Between each chanting of the phrase, one by one the worshipers personally call out the names of those for whom they are praying and often speak about the person and the affliction.

In other places, worshipers pray for healing in the same powerful words that Moses used when praying for his sister. The prayer is made even more poignant when it is sung to the sweet melody of Hanna Tifereth Siegel. Chanted over and over again, it evokes both hope and promise. "Oh, God, please heal her and him."

El na r'   fa - na lah,   El   na   r'   fa - na lah,

El   na   r'   fa - na lah,   fu - ah sh'   ley   muh.

In some places, the ill are encircled by their friends and fellow pray-ers so that when the words of prayer are spoken and chanted, the energy flows directly to the one for whom the prayers are needed.

In a few places, there is direct hands-on healing. Sometimes, one person in the prayer community seems to have special healing powers, seems to receive healing energy directly from God. By placing hands on the ill, healing energy can flow from the Source right to the source of the ailment. Throughout our communities, a few very precious souls have been gifted by God not with their own power, but with being the messenger, the conveyer, of God's healing power. When they remain in awe of their gifts and use them in holy ways, they can be God's healing hands on earth.

In a few places, the spiritual work of doing *t'shuvah* and *tikkun* on Rosh HaShanah and Yom Kippur is enhanced by the spirit-body connection. On Yom Kippur afternoon, these unique prayer groups set out massage tables for Reiki healers to use their hands to bring healing and balancing energy to those seeking the reconciliation and healing that repentance can bring.

In every place where healing is desired, it is good to invoke the presence of the archangel Rafael, the angel in charge of God's healing. Rafael can be asked to heal any vibrational disturbances on the earthly plane that could be affecting individual health, and to bring God's healing powers into the energy field of the one who is ill.

It may seem as if Jewish healing practices are far out on the fringe of Jewish life, practiced mainly by those who identify with the so-called New Age. But the underlying motivation, the soul healing that is taking place as a result of the end of exile from God, combined with great communal and individual need and the powerful results that are evidenced, have brought Jewish healing practices into the mainstream of contemporary Jewish life.

Services of healing are being conducted in synagogues, including some of the venerable old synagogues, throughout the country. Gathering on Tuesday mornings, Thursday nights, Monday lunch hours—at any time and every time—people are coming together to pray for healing.

Prayers are being recited by those and for those with physical illness, especially those with long-term debilitating or degenerative disease and those diagnosed with terminal illness, those with emotional distress, those with addictions, and those who have been the victims of abuse or trauma. In recent years, particular attention has been focused on those who are HIV-positive or who suffer from AIDS. Anyone and everyone who is hurting and in pain—and their family members and friends who love them—attend these services. The members of the synagogue and community who attend and join in the prayers form a caring, loving support group.

Services of healing are being written that include prayers, readings, meditations, songs and chants, and blessings. To the basic rubric and liturgies of these services, time is being added for personal testimonies. The emerging "national anthem" for healing seems to be *Mi Shebeirach,* the popular chant of the "high priestess" of modern Jewish music, singer Debbie Friedman. Her song asks, "May the source of strength who blessed the ones before us help us find the courage to make our lives a blessing. . . . Bless those in need of healing with *r'fu-ah sh'lemah* [complete healing]—the renewal of body, the renewal of spirit, and let us say, Amen."

To support and facilitate Jewish healing work, the National Center for Jewish Healing has been established, with offices in New York and California. The center publishes materials; sponsors programs and conferences; offers advice and counsel to healing professionals; encourages the work of synagogues, community centers, and hospices; coordinates the work being done in communities throughout the country; and helps facilitate the efforts to address the spiritual needs of Jews living with illness and loss.

That such an organization exists—and that its work is being partially funded not only through individual contributions but also through corporate and foundation grants—attests to the importance and wide acceptance of its mission. The organized Jewish community is coming to recognize the great need for healing in all its many forms and the great power that the world of the spirit brings to the quest.

꙰

Western medicine, with its demand for hard scientific evidence garnered from rigorous research, is just coming to acknowledge what has been known anecdotally for a long time. There is a vital holistic connection between mind and body, between mental attitude and physical well-being.

Now Western medicine is being confronted with another truth: there is a vital holistic connection between *spirit* and body. Research data now proves what spiritualists have known all along: prayer works. Prayer works because God who made us listens and responds. Prayer works because it creates a vibrational energy that moves and changes the prevailing condition. Prayer works because it inspires the healers and the caretakers. Prayer works because it focuses and channels the attention and love of family, friends, and community. Prayer works because the believer believes that prayer works, and faith is a powerful healer.

Rabbi Nachman of Bratslav taught a great deal about healing, although he purposely hid many of his teachings because he thought that they were too advanced to be readily accepted in his day. For many, these teachings may still be too advanced for our day, when the prevailing notion is still that viruses and bacteria attack with arbitrary randomness. For the core of Reb Nachman's teaching is that illness is caused by separation and alienation from God and that healing comes through reconciliation with God. That certainly would explain why prayer works to heal.

And, more, it certainly explains why in our day we are able to focus on healing. As our psyches and our souls return from exile, as we reconcile with God and heal our separation from God, we do *t'shuvah,* we return to God—and God returns to us—and we do *tikkun,* healing with God. Then we are able to focus on our individual needs and to ask for healing for ourselves.

More and more, we are coming to recognize the efficacy and the reality of the old prayer, "Heal us, O God, and we will be healed."

⚜

There is an urgency to our prayers for healing, not only because we desperately desire personal wellness, but also because we are coming to realize that we cannot heal the world of its ills until we heal ourselves of our own ills.

For a long while now, Jews—particularly the Jewish community of the United States—have focused on *tikkun olam,* the balance, repair, and healing of the world. We have been deeply committed to acts of social justice, and in the tradition of the ancient prophets, we have been the champions of the downtrodden. We have worked diligently and well to feed the hungry, shelter the homeless, clothe the naked, educate the illiterate, free the captive, and give hope to the hopeless.

Even though our efforts have been largely successful, we have never felt the deep, deep inner joy that should come from all that we have given and done. For at our core, we are empty. We cannot truly heal another when we have been hurting so much, when our souls have been in exile, and we have been separated from our source, from our God. We have been like the man who went to his doctor to complain that he was sad and depressed. After a thorough physical and mental examination, the doctor said, "There is nothing wrong with you. I suggest that you go to the circus to see the great clown, Grumaldi. You will laugh and laugh, and you will be cured." The patient looked at the doctor and then lowered his head and wept. "But, doctor," he said, *"I* am Grumaldi."

In order to heal the world, we have to bring full healing to our own souls. Then out of personal *tikkun* will come *tikkun olam;* out of deep inner peace will come world peace.

War between nations comes when we human beings are separated from one another. We are separated from one another because we are separated from ourselves—from our own core, our own source. We are separated from ourselves because we are separated from our God.

When we heal with God, we heal ourselves, we heal with one another, we heal our nations and our world.

Only out of personal *tikkun* can universal *tikkun* come.

Just months before he was assassinated, the late Yitzchak Rabin, the prime minister of Israel, poignantly illustrated this concept when he came to Washington, D.C., to sign the peace treaty with Jordan. At the state dinner, he explained his motivation.

He said that when Israel declared independence, he was a young soldier fighting for his country's existence. During the Six Day War when Israel reunited Jerusalem, he was chief of staff of the army. During the Yom Kippur war, he was a member of the government. Each time he went to war, it was with a passionate fervor. He knew that the fate of his people, the existence of his country, the lives of his wife and children were all at stake. And he knew, he said, that right across the narrow border, King Hussein was going to war with the same passion and the same fervor for *his* country.

Now, Rabin said, it was almost fifty years later. War had accomplished nothing; it had only filled the cemeteries of both countries with the finest of their children. And then he said, in essence, "King Hussein and I are both old men now. He is ill, and I look into the eyes of my granddaughter"—the very granddaughter who was destined to give a deeply moving eulogy at his funeral—"and I know that we can no longer make war. Peace has come to our hearts, and so we have come here to make peace for our countries."

Out of their personal *tikkun,* their personal healing and reconciliation, Rabin and Hussein brought *tikkun* to their nations. Out of the peace that had come to their hearts and souls, they brought peace to their people.

When each and every man and woman on the face of this earth heals with God and returns to God, then we will heal within, and we will come to one another in love. Then all God's children will touch hands in peace, and peace will fill the earth as the waters fill the sea.

✵

Our long and painful exile—from our land, from ourselves, from our God—is over.

Physical and spiritual *galus* have come to an end.

Healing and reconciliation, return and renewal have begun.

Turn us unto You, O God, and we will return.
Renew our days as they were at the very beginning.

16

Becoming One

I GREW UP ON THE OLD SOUTH SIDE OF CHICAGO. It was a place made famous by the politics of Mayor Daley (vote early, vote often) and by the song "Bad, Bad Leroy Brown," and it was a nice place to be a kid.

My neighborhood was in the ever-changing but always middle-class inner city. In 1945 it was a Polish Catholic steelworkers' neighborhood; in 1960 it was a Jewish neighborhood; and by 1970 it was a black neighborhood.

In the late 1940s and early 1950s when I was growing up, all the kids played together in the parks and on the playgrounds. Then, for kindergarten, some went to the local public school, and some went to St. Mary Magdalene's, the local parish school.

By the time I was eight or nine years old, I was being beaten up on a fairly regular basis by my old friends, who had learned—from their priests and nuns—that I, Wayne Dosick, had personally killed their Lord.

They acted, of course I now know, from the deep-seated prejudice that is born out of ignorance and fear. But the physical blows that I received did not hurt nearly as much as the pain of bewilderment and rejection.

Yet the prejudice and fear of the time was not confined to preadolescent boys alone. Many of the Jewish grandparents of our generation—grandparents who in their own youth had fled from the czar and the oppressive governments of Eastern Europe—would spit three times on the sidewalk if forced to walk in front of a church. Long-held hatreds and blind intolerance were part of the sorry lessons of our childhood, too.

⚜

Now, some forty years later, I am a rabbi who is a professor at a Catholic university, teaching the only courses in Jewish studies in the Department of Religious and Theological Studies. I have dear and precious friends on the faculty; one of my closest friends in the world is a Jesuit priest. Not long ago, I stood in the pulpit of the Immaculata, next to a statue of Jesus, delivering the homily at our annual All Faiths Service.

We have come a long way.

The winds of change began with a twinkle-eyed pope.

When I was in high school, during one of those four-minute breaks between classes when we had to go from the first-floor gym to the fifth-floor study hall, a girl ran up to me in the halls. "Wayne, Wayne," she said, "I forgive you. I forgive you."

Now, there were a number of girls in that school who might have had reason to forgive me, but she was not one of them. "What is it, Bonnie?" I asked. "For what are you forgiving me?"

"I forgive you for killing Christ," she said.

"What are you talking about? I didn't kill anybody! That was two thousand years ago. I wasn't there. I didn't even know him."

"It doesn't matter," she said. "I just heard on the radio that the pope said that we could forgive the Jews for killing Christ."

That, of course, was Pope John XXIII, and it was in the midst of Vatican II. Even though young Bonnie did not get her terminology quite right, that Vatican Council signaled a remarkable moment in the almost two-thousand-year history of Jewish-Christian relations. No longer would the Jews be yoked with the charge of deicide. Two religions, the founding mother and the precious offspring, could begin to regard each other with newfound tolerance, honor, and respect.

And so, in these decades since Vatican II, a growing ecumenism has begun to envelop our world. We have begun to learn about each other's faiths and faith communities; we have learned to rejoice in our similarities and to respect our differences. We have begun to share in each other's celebrations and to participate in each other's ceremonies.

And during this time, with our newfound sensitivity, we have opened our arms wide to embrace our brothers and sisters of other religious faiths and communities—Muslims, whose beginnings are so rooted in the Judaic Christian experience; Buddhists and Hindus of the Eastern religions; and Native Americans, whose teachings and traditions are winning new appreciation. The whole world of the spirit has begun to open, and a new light of understanding and acceptance is beginning to infuse every corner of our existence.

After all, God did not invent separate religions; we did. God does not care what we call Him/Her/It. God does not want any of us competing for attention or claiming that ours is the one, the only, true path to the Divine. God does not favor one community, one faith, one language, one prayer over another. God just cares if we love one another.

This is why my university holds an All Faiths Service. During the first week of the fall semester, we follow a four-hundred-year-old Catholic university tradition by conducting the Mass of the Holy Spirit. And now, out of the vision and determination of the monsignor who is the university's Vice President for Mission and Ministry, the first week of the spring semester begins with this All Faiths Service. Religious leaders of every faith and tradition join together in the pulpit of the Immaculata. Wrapped in the garb of our offices and the dress of our heritage, reflecting the wide diversity of backgrounds, beliefs, and practices that grace our campus, we chant and speak the sacred Scripture and liturgies of our faiths.

At a recent service, the invocation was given by a black Baptist minister; the opening prayer was offered by a Baha'i; I chanted the Ten

Commandments in the original Hebrew; a Lutheran minister read from the New Testament; there was a Buddhist chant, followed by a Hindu peace chant; an imam chanted from the Koran; the homily was given by an evangelical Christian pastor; Native Americans danced; and the benediction was given by an Episcopal priest. At this service, we create sacred space and sanctify time. We create a new holiness that surrounds, envelops, and touches the heart and soul of each of the thousands of people who fill the church.

From learning about and sharing one another's traditions and ceremonies, we have begun to learn that there is an even deeper ecumenism growing than we ever knew, than we ever thought possible.

It begins when my colleague and friend, a former nun who is the former chair of our religious studies department, leads a prayer at our Yom Kippur service, for while we pray in many voices, we come to realize that it is only one voice. It continues when my dear friend Father O'Leary attends our Pesach *seder*. In our great-grandparents' generation, at Pesach-Easter time, priests were accusing rabbis of blood libel, while rabbis were hiding in fear from the wrath of the Church. Now we sit together, speaking of slavery that imprisons the body and of bigotry that blinds the eye. It continues when the professor who teaches the class on the life and thought of Jesus takes her students to a synagogue service, because she contends that the only way to understand Christianity is to understand its Jewish roots and to participate in its worship the way Jesus prayed. It continues when I read the Hebrew Scripture in its original at the funeral mass for Father O'Leary's beloved and much-lamented mother, a woman I cherished not only as a friend, but also as a woman of deep and abiding Christian faith.

What we are learning is that we are all on the same journey and that our destination is exactly the same—from God, to God. That is the earthly sojourn; that is our shared calling.

To be sure, we build different bridges to carry us on our way. Some bridges are wide; some are narrow. Some are made of strong, hearty material; some are of delicate fabric that bends in every wind. Some are decorated with the finest, most precious, most beautiful jewels; some are plain and simple. Some people sing on the journey, and some walk in silence. Some trek on with fortitude; some take tentative steps.

There is value and worth and beauty in each of the bridges. There is uniqueness and significance to our separate paths, to our own history and language and song and poetry and imagery and metaphor and collective unconscious memory. I do not want Father O'Leary to be Jewish, and he does not want me to be Catholic.

But despite our outward differences—the unique ways we each build our bridges—what we have found is this much deeper and much richer ecumenism.

We have found that our stories, our myths, our parables, our deepest longings and most fervent yearnings, our highest dreams, and our greatest aspirations are all the same.

We have found, despite our surface differences in form and our real differences in substance, that there is much more that unites us than divides us. We are, each and every one of us, children of the universe. We are, each and every one of us, children of God.

And like any parent, God loves all the children, despite our differences, with equal intensity and equal passion.

When we all open our hearts, we understand this old mystical Jewish legend that everyone knows, and that tells the tale.

In the beginning—before the beginning—God's light filled the entire universe.

When God decided to create the world, God had to withdraw some of His light from the universe so that there would be space for the land and the seas.

So God breathed in some of the Divine light so that there would be room for all the things He wanted to create.

But what was God to do with the light—the light of His being that had filled the whole universe—now that He had breathed it in?

God put the light into jars, heavenly vessels that would hold His radiance. And then, God began to create: the sky and the earth and the seas and everything in them.

Creation was shaping up just perfectly. God was having a wonderful time.

But in the heavens there was trouble.

God's light, which He had put into the vessels, could not be hidden away. For no vessel, not even a heavenly vessel, could contain the radiant light of God. The glory of God's splendor was accustomed to filling the universe, not to being hidden away in little jars.

So it wasn't long until, with a blazing flash, God's light burst out of the heavenly vessels.

The force of the mighty impact caused the jars to shatter into millions of little pieces.

And the light itself splintered into billions of little sparks.

The broken pieces of the vessels fell to the newly formed earth and became the ills and evils that beset the world, the little pieces of anguish and travail that one day will have to be collected, repaired, and made whole again.

And what happened to the billions of little shards of light?

The Bible tells us: *ner Adonai nishmat adam,* "the light of God is the soul of human beings" (Proverbs 20:27). Each one of those shards of light became the soul of a human being.

What transforms the lump of clay that is a human body into a living, breathing human being is the soul. And the human soul is a tiny piece of God, a tiny fragment of God's light, a spark of the Divine that burst forth from the heavenly vessels and showered the universe.

Every one of us is created not only in the image, but with the light of God.

How can we possibly let superficial differences in color or creed, origin or ethnicity, religion or faith delimit us? How can we possibly let self-imagined greatness or weakness define us? How can we possibly let any earthly differences separate us?

We are all human beings whose souls are pieces, sparks, of the light of God.

And we all have the same Divinely given task, the same sacred mission, for God did not put us here just to breathe, live out a measured number of days, and then die.

We are here to joyfully share the universe with God, to be His companions and helpmates, His resident caretakers and earthly stew-

ards. And we are each to be a partner with God in healing and transforming the universe, in picking up those little pieces of the broken
vessels, repairing them and making them and the world healthy and
whole.

We are the ones who, together, have to bring our world to harmony and tranquillity, perfection and peace.

For the world to come to perfection and peace, first, we individual
human beings must come to reconciliation and transformation. There
must be healing and peace in our hearts; our souls must be filled with
faith, filled with God's overflowing light and love.

And so, we have begun

Priests and ministers, rabbis and imams grasp hands in understanding and friendship.

Christian, Jews, and Muslims, Buddhists, Hindus, and Native
Americans return to their deepest sources—and find one another there.

The covenant of faith and love that God made with each and
every one of His children waits to be affirmed and renewed in this, our
generation.

⚜

While my story is, admittedly, very personal, it is being
replicated over and over and over again, in place after place. For
though interfaith relations have global, universal ramifications, they
begin—and end—in the intimacy of close personal relationships.

How can I disdain or even dismiss Catholicism when one of my
closest friends is a priest? How can I not be sensitive to Christian teachings when "my" priest is so committed to them? How can he, who
never even met a Jew until he was twenty-one years old, hang on to old
stereotypes or prejudices when he often sits at my dinner table?

If we want information, if we seek understanding, if we wonder
why we are still nurturing old hurts, if we grow wary or even indig-
nant over real or perceived differences, we have each other to ask, to
dialogue with, to debate. Now and then our friendship may be tested
or even strained over theology or practice or, more likely, ecclesiastical
politics—most usually not ours, but that of our larger groups—but it

will never be broken, because we have too much personal respect and affection at stake not to resolve our conflict.

Father O'Leary and I—my colleagues on the university faculty and in the community clergy and I—have learned that our spiritual journey toward universal at-one-ment begins with two people, two precious souls, at a time.

Understanding of religious differences, harmony between diverse faith communities will come when individuals come to know, understand, and accept each other.

So begin—as trite or as silly as this may sound—by taking a Hindu to lunch, by having dinner with a Buddhist, by going on a picnic with a Christian, by taking a long walk with a Muslim. Get to know and become friends with people of widely differing faiths and communities.

When we open our hearts to listen to their hearts, when we open our spirits to be filled with their spirit, then we come to know our brothers and sisters who are, like us, precious children of God. We come to understand and respect their beliefs, their practices, their worldview, their cosmic place. And they come to know us and to appreciate the core of our being.

As the old bumper sticker says, "Make peace, one person at a time."

＊＊＊

To hasten the coming of human harmony, we Jews can make one tiny but monumental contribution.

One of the most familiar prayers of our liturgy, a prayer that is recited at every Jewish worship service, is *Alenu*. Near the very end of the service, we stand and chant, *"Alenu l'shabe-ach la'Adon haḳol. . . ."* "We praise the Lord of all, we acclaim the Creator. . . ." Later in the prayer we say, "We bend the knee and worship before the King of Kings, the Holy One, praised be God." Matching our actions to our words, we bow in reverence and love before God.

It is a beautiful prayer, a prayer of high praise and deep humility, a prayer more than worthy of being the penultimate doxology of every worship service.

But, in between the original invocation, *"Alenu . . . "* and the adoration, "we bend the knee . . ." come words that are deeply troublesome to our moral sensibilities, to our sense of probity, goodness, and right.

These words praise God who "has not made us like the nations of the world, and has not made us like the other families of the earth. God has not made our destiny like theirs, or cast our lot with the multitudes."

In original intent, these words were probably meant to celebrate the Jewish notion of chosenness, that we Jews were singled out by God for covenantal relationship, for the heavy responsibility—not privilege, but responsibility—of receiving, learning, living, and teaching God's word and will.

But it is easy to understand why these words would offend and insult.

To people of other faiths, these words must seem the height of haughty arrogance. "Who do those Jews think they are? Do they think that they are better than we? How dare they dismiss us as the mere 'multitudes'? How dare they be happy that they are not like us?"

No wonder that during the Middle Ages, the ruling powers censored *Alenu* out of Jewish prayerbooks more than any other prayer. Government and church leaders tried to force us to stop saying words that were perceived as derogatory and disparaging toward them.

While, throughout history, there has been no lack of those who hated us and wished to destroy us, we must wonder if, perhaps, we did not bring just a bit of the ill will against ourselves with our self-righteous-sounding claim to superiority.

Today, there are some who wish to continue reciting these traditional words, understanding them in their contextual setting, and celebrating the responsibility of chosenness. But for others, the words turn to ashes on our lips. How can we come to mutual honor and respect, how can we come to newfound harmony with our brothers and sisters of other faiths and communities when, three times a day, we make us "us" and rest of humanity "the other"? It is hubris that we can no longer afford.

Over the years, from a wide variety of sources within the Jewish community, there have been many attempts to emend the words, to change them in order to give them some semblance of new meaning. But as valid as the attempts have been, none has ever been able remove the offense while retaining the original sense of the prayer.

It is time for radical surgery.

Let's simply eliminate the misunderstood and offending words from our prayer. We can continue to praise God without needing self-aggrandizement. We can continue praising God without affronting others.

Removing these hurtful and painful words from our collective vocabulary not only can renew the spirit of love between us and our brothers and sisters of all faiths but also will bring the light of healing to our own corporate psyche, which has, through the centuries, been damaged and darkened by this unholy anomaly.

Now, when we praise God, it can be with a full heart, knowing that all God's children can join with us in a shared chorus of reverence and adoration.

❦

The closing words of the same *Alenu* prayer give us the aspiration and the reward for becoming one with all the peoples of this earth.

We are challenged and charged to "perfect the world under the Kingdom of God," for, when that day comes, as the prophet of old foretold, "God will be recognized as King over all the earth," and every person on the face of this planet will join together to joyfully proclaim, "The Lord is God. God is One. And we are all God's children, hearing God's word, doing God's will, in faith and in love."

17

Ruach Hakodesh, The Holy Spirit

EVERYONE KNOWS THAT WHEN GOD SENT MOSES to bring the Children of Israel out of Egyptian slavery, Pharaoh was not very cooperative. Not only did he reject the request for freedom, but he increased the slaves' work and agony by taking away the straw with which they made bricks.

To offer the people assurance that their sad plight would soon be over, God had Moses convey a curious message. "I am Yahweh. I appeared to Abraham, Isaac, and Jacob as El Shaddai, but I did not make My name Yahweh known to them. I established My covenant with them to give them the land of Canaan. . . . I have heard the groaning of the Children of Israel . . . and I have remembered My covenant" (Exodus 6:2–4).

With these words, the Children of Israel are acknowledged as the rightful descendants of Abraham and are given the guarantee that the contract made with their forebear will be fulfilled with them. But almost lost in the satisfaction of knowing that freedom and independence were soon to be theirs is the announcement that God made at the beginning of the declaration.

"I am Yahweh," said God. "But even though this is My name, this was not the way I identified Myself to the ancestors. They did not know Me as Yahweh. They called Me by a different name. They called Me 'El Shaddai.'"

On the surface, this statement may not seem very important. It is as if I might say, "My name is Wayne. But the kids back in the old neighborhood didn't know my real name. They called me Bubba. But please call me Wayne."

But in reality, this is a major proclamation, a momentous juncture, a defining moment, a sea change, in the relationship between God and every being on earth.

For it is at this instant that God shifted Divine nature, identity, and role.

Earlier, when God appeared to Moses out of the burning bush and Moses was reluctant to accept God's assignment to go to Egypt to free the slaves, Moses asked, "When I come to the Children of Israel and say, 'The God of your fathers sent me to you, and they ask "What is His name?" what shall I say to them?' And God said to Moses, tell them '*Ehyeh Asher Ehyeh*'" (Exodus 3:13–14).

This cryptic phrase is most often translated "I am that I am" or "I will be what I will be," based in the Hebrew verb *to be,* indicating God's timelessness and eternity. This "Ehyeh," this "I Am" is God, the Creator God who made the world and everything in it.

But as Ehyeh manifests Godliness in the world, it is, at any given moment, with particular emphasis on certain Godly attributes.

When God calls Himself/Herself/Itself El Shaddai, it is because the feminine attributes of God are most predominant. The Hebrew word *shad* means "breast," and when God is called El Shaddai, it is because the sheltering, nurturing, motherly, feminine attributes of God are manifest.

It was this God who met Abraham and nurtured the fledgling Jewish people through the beginnings of the relationship with God.

But it was different attributes of God that were to be used to bring the Children of Israel out of slavery, lead them into the desert, take them to Sinai to give them the Law, and bring them into the Promised Land. For these tasks, the God of strong, powerful, masculine attributes was needed. When the masculine attributes of God are most predominant, God calls Himself/Herself/Itself Yahweh.

That is why God told Moses to, in essence, tell the Children of Israel, "I used to be called El Shaddai, but My real name is Yahweh. And tell them that it is Yahweh who is here to free them from slavery."

The shift between the feminine and the masculine attributes of God took place just when the childhood of the Children of Israel— which required the nurturing, motherly feminine God presence—was coming to an end, just when they needed the strong masculine God presence to help them face down their adversary, confront all the vicissitudes of the journey, and guide them through adolescence to adulthood, to peoplehood.

To imagine the shift in God energies, picture God anthropomorphically breathing. When we human beings breathe, each in-breath and each out-breath takes a second or two, and the tiny pause between in-breath and out-breath takes a millisecond. According to spiritual tradition, when God breathes, each in-breath and each out-breath takes more than 3,200 years, and the tiny pause between in-breath and out-breath takes three to five days.

When God is in breathing, the feminine attributes of God, the feminine God energy fills the earth. When God is out-breathing, the masculine attributes of God, the masculine God energy, fills the earth. The tiny pause between in-breath and out-breath creates a quiet stillness in the universe.

The last time the shift took place—when God moved from in-breath to out-breath—was at the time of the exodus from Egypt. That change shifted the God energy from female to male. That is why God told Moses that while She had appeared to Abraham as El Shaddai, as the feminine attribute of God, He would now be known as Yahweh, the masculine attribute of God. The goddess cult that was so well known in the ancient pagan world was coming to an end, and the male

God was now coming to the fore. According to spiritual tradition, the three- to five-day period that marked the brief pause between God's in-breath and God's out-breath was the time of the plague of darkness in Egypt, the quiet stillness that enveloped the land.

Now, approximately 3,200 years later, the shift will take place again. This time, God will go from out-breath to in-breath. The Yahweh masculine God energy will give way to the feminine God energy, which we now call *Shechinah*. Between out-breath and in-breath, there will be a three- to five-day period of stillness that envelops the earth.

It is no coincidence that over the last three decades more and more feminine energy has been coming into our world. It began with the so-called women's liberation movement and the feminist revolution of the late 1960s. It has been characterized by the birthing of *Ms.* magazine; growing equality for women in the workplace; the ordination of women clergy and full equality in religious and spiritual circles; egalitarianism in almost every phase of modern life; the great political power of NOW, the National Organization for Women. The female principle is coming to the fore and filling the world in anticipation and preparation for the shift to goddess energy, for the shift to *Shechinah* God.

The shift to predominant *Shechinah* energy will mean that feminine attributes, particularly creating, sheltering, nurturing, intuitive knowing, and unconditional love, will infuse the world.

This does not mean that the masculine Yahweh God energy will disappear entirely. During the last three millennia when the Yahweh energy predominated, the feminine *Shechinah* God energy remained as the shadow energy. With the coming shift, *Shechinah* will come to the fore, and Yahweh will become the shadow. The masculine God energy will probably play a greater shadow role than did the feminine God energy, for while the male principle is, by nature, exclusive, precluding the "other," the feminine principle is, by nature more open and inclusive. Just as the X chromosome contains the Y within it, *Shechinah* God energy will hold and honor the shadow Yahweh energy.

The new era will be primarily characterized and identified by the arrival and the recognition that within each one of us is *ruach Elohim*, the spirit of God, and *ruach hakodesh,* God's holy spirit. For even while the masculine Yahweh energy has been predominant during these last three millennia, those who have been our great leaders have been infused with *ruach Elohim,* the feminine God attributes of being able to gently and sensitively care for our people in the name of God.

But the spirit of God is not just for our leaders alone, it is for all of us. According to the Torah, when there was rebellion against Moses in the desert, Moses was told that two of the rebels, Eldad and Medad, were prophesying in the camp and that they should be stopped lest others think that they speak in the name of God. Moses replied, "Would that all God's people were prophets, that God would put God's spirit in all of them" (Numbers 11:29).

The *haftarah,* the prophetic selection that is assigned to the Torah portion that contains those words, reiterates this theme. "Not by might nor by power, but by My spirit says the Lord of hosts" (Zechariah 4:6).

What will be the reward when all God's people are filled with God's holy spirit? The prophet foretells, "In that day, says the Lord of hosts, you shall call every man and his neighbor under the vine and under the fig-tree" (Zechariah 3:10). It will be the time of harmony and peace.

Out of the advent of the feminine God energy will come the atmosphere that will set the tone and the possibility for transformation—for newfound tranquillity and harmony that will envelop the world, paving the way for *masheach,* the coming of the messianic era of goodness and kindness, love and peace among all people.

<hr>

It will take a while for the feminine God energy to come and to settle in. But the transition is coming, and it will mean a mighty transformation for earth and every one of earth's inhabitants. Our perspectives will change, our attitudes will change, the very dimensional world in which we live will change.

The power to meet the shift of God energy is deep within each one of us.

Remember the story of the holy Baal Shem Tov who danced and danced and danced with the Torah Scroll on Simchat Torah.

When he handed the Torah Scroll to another, he continued to dance and dance and dance.

One of his chasidim said to another, "Our master is no longer holding the Torah Scroll. Why does he continue to dance?"

And the disciple replied, "Our master has set aside the visible, physical dimension, but the spiritual dimensions he has taken into himself."

Soon we will set aside the physical dimension of the world as we have known it and encounter a new reality. If we take the spiritual dimensions of God—in all His and Her forms and attributes—deeply into us, we and our world will be renewed, enlightened, and truly blessed.

Then we will all join in praising God who watches over and protects us, who nurtures and cares for us, who guides us and loves us, by saying, "Magnified and sanctified be the name of God throughout the world."

18

Kumu! Kumu! Get Up! Get Up!

In the old yeshivas, every morning at dawn one of the rebbes would bang on each of the students' doors and call out, *"Kumu, kumu l'avodas haBoray."* "Get up! Get up to do the work of the Creator."

What a wonderful way to be awakened! There is a simple yet profound reason for getting out of a warm bed on a cold morning—to do God's work.

And what a wonderful cosmic wake-up call for all of us! Each day's plan is very simple, yet it is filled with everlasting significance: we are to get up to do God's work.

A popular contemporary technique being used for therapy and healing is called "affirmation." Modern medicine and psychology are beginning to understand what the sages taught long ago: "As we think, so we are."

There is no separation—there is a holistic connection—between our mind and our body. Our every thought affects our physical being.

If we give in to negativity and despair, that is the message our minds give our bodies. If we think positively and optimistically, our bodies hear that hope and expectation. Our thoughts can help bring either continuing illness and further pain or healing and rapid recovery.

The essence of this mind-body connection is captured by the old Yiddish expression *"red zech ein,"* "you talk yourself into it."

Many doctors, therapists, and New Age healers—and the hundreds of authors of the thousands of self-help books currently on the market—recommend the use of positive affirmations for both physical and emotional healing, recovery and growth. By telling yourself that you are (choose one or more, or any one of hundreds more) respected, honored, loved, successful, self-reliant, highly motivated, or pretty, you will give the continuing message to your soul and your cells, and "as you think, so you will be."

The healers suggest that you repeat your affirmation in a mantra-like fashion, over and over again, so that the positive message will always be heard and will sink in to your psyche. They even suggest placing little cards with your affirmation written on them on your bathroom mirror, the dashboard of your car, your desk, magnetized to your refrigerator—anywhere and everywhere that you will see them and be reminded of your quest.

Affirmations work because they positively affect mind and body, giving us hopeful, uplifting messages about our character and our conduct.

Affirmations can also be used to give ourselves direction and to confirm our path, to assert our commitments and intensify our passions. Affirmations can be the way we tell ourselves about what is really important to us, what our goals will be, how we will best fulfill our mission, and what will guide us to our destiny. Affirmations can affirm what will really, really "make us" as human beings and how our lives will be whole and holy.

Where better to turn for our deepest and most sacred life-affirmations than our Jewish tradition, and where better to begin than where the yeshiva students start each day?

As the day begins, and over and over again, many times each day, you can say to yourself,

Kumu! Kumu! l'avodas haBoray
Get up! Get up to do the work of the Creator!

In recognition of God who gave us life and who, every day, renews the work of creation, our affirmation can be,

Baruch She'amar, v'hayah haolam.
Blessed is the One who spoke, and the world came into being.

Your affirmation does not have to be complicated or complex. It can be just one letter.

Everyone knows the story of the little boy who came to synagogue on Rosh HaShanah. All the men and women were deeply involved in their prayers, in their soul-cries to God on this holy day. All of a sudden, the little boy began reciting the Hebrew alphabet: *aleph, bet, gimel.* . . . Louder and louder he shouted the letters, until his voice almost drowned out the prayers of all the worshipers. They tried to hush him up so that they could continue with their prayers, but he persisted on shouting out the letters at the top of his voice. Finally, the service came to a halt.

The rabbi called the young boy up to the pulpit and asked him, "Why are you disturbing the prayers, why are you shouting out the alphabet?" And the young boy replied, "Rebbe, these are my prayers. I know what a holy day this is, and I want to be able to talk to God. But I do not know how to read yet; I cannot say the words in the prayerbook.

But I do know the alphabet. So I am shouting out each of the letters to God, and I told God, 'Here are all the letters. You use them to make up the words.'"

And the rebbe knew that the simple prayer of the little boy on that day was as holy, and as acceptable to God, as all the prayers of the whole congregation of Israel.

The thirteenth-century Spanish Kabbalist Abraham Abulafia taught that each Hebrew letter has infinite worth, that it stretches from before the beginning of time until beyond forever. By meditating on each letter—by using each letter as a life-affirmation—Abulafia contended that we can expand our consciousness and our souls to see the deepest depths and the highest heights of the universe, that we can touch the untold secrets of existence and come closer and closer to God. In each Hebrew letter, and in all of them together, is the full essence of our being and our becoming.

You may want to use the entire Hebrew alphabet for affirmation, or you may choose one letter—the first letter of your Hebrew name; the first letter of a favorite verse from Bible or liturgy—and focus your affirmation on that one letter alone.

With infinite meaning, each letter can open entire worlds for you, or you may want to concentrate on the one encompassing meaning given here. Either way, by repeating your letter or letters over and over again each day, you affirm your relationship to God, the universe, everything that ever was, and everything that ever will be.

Aleph

In *aleph* there is awesome silence.

Bet

In *bet,* the very first sound, is *b'reshit,* the beginning of beginnings, the awesome moment of creation that came from out of the awesome silence.

Gimel

In *gimel* is *gilgool,* the continual rolling from lifetime to lifetime, until we reach *ge'ulah,* redemption of body and soul and all being.

Dalet

In *dalet* is the *delet,* the door that opens to infinite possibility.

Hay

In *hay, hayah,* the totality of the past, merges for the briefest of seconds with *hoveh,* the immediate moment, laying before us the limitless future. What was and what is offer us the vision of what will be.

Vav

In *vav*—straight and tall, powerful, penetrating, and po-tent—is the ultimate union, the conjunction and connection that brings us all together with one another and with God.

Zayin

In *zayin* is *zachor,* the memory of what has been, and *zohar,* the glorious splendor of the hidden secrets telling us what it all means.

Chet

In *chet* is the promise of *chein,* everlasting grace, *chesed,* everlasting love, and *chaim,* everlasting life.

Tet

In *tet* is *tov,* all the goodness of God, and all the greatness of God's world, for, like God, we can look and see and know that it is all "very, very good."

Yud

In *yud* are the two little dots that make the name of God, and *yichud,* both God's splendid aloneness and God's intimate merging with us.

Kaf

In *kaf* is *kavannah,* the deep spiritual intent that brings us close to God so that we can give God all *kavod,* all honor.

Connecting with the Universe

לamed

Lamed

In *lamed* is the *lev,* the sweet and caring heart, which links us one to the other and all of us to God, *l'olam va'ed,* forever and ever.

מMem

Mem

In *mem* are *mitzvot,* the commands reverberating throughout the ages, calling us to lives of decency, dignity, and abiding worth.

נNun

Nun

In *nun* is the *neshamah,* the holy soul, the spark of God's light, which makes us human and humane.

סSamech

Samech

In *samach* is *sod,* the deepest mysteries of the universe, waiting to be discovered, waiting to be revealed; waiting, waiting until the Sinai of our souls is ready.

עAyin

Ayin

In *ayin* is another awesome silence, the silence that permits us to focus on the continual revelation of the *ayin,* the eye—the all-seeing outer eye of awareness and consciousness; the inner eye of perception and discernment; the third eye of intuition, insight, and in-sight.

פPay

Pay

In *pay* is the *prozdor,* the gateway to the Other Side, the gateway to all knowledge, the gateway to *pardes,* Paradise, to the presence of God.

צTzadi

Tzadi

In *tzadi* is *tzedek,* our never-ending quest for justice, for righteousness, for sharing and caring, for doing what is right.

קKuf

Kuf

In *kuf* is *kedushah,* the holy being of God, the holy presence of God, calling us to holiness—to be Godlike, to make our every word and our every deed precious and sacred.

ר **Resh**
In *resh* is *ruach,* the breath of life, the spirit of God, the spirit-breath of every human being—all flowing together in a celebration of life.

ש **Shin**
In *shin* is *Shechinah,* God's nurturing and sheltering presence, enveloping each one of us in *shalom,* wholeness and peace, balance, and sweet harmony.

ת **Tav**
In *tav* is Torah, for "everything is in it"; it is our *t'shuvah,* our eternal returning to God, to our higher selves, and to our inner selves; it is our never-ending *tikkun,* our joyful promise to heal ourselves and our world.

In gratitude to God for the *aleph* to *tav* of our lives, the all-encompassing alphabet of our lives, the many blessings of our lives, our often-repeated affirmation can be,

Modeh Ani
I thank You, O God, and I am ever grateful to You.

In acknowledgment of God's ever-present and utterly unique place in our lives, our affirmation can be,

Adonai Uree V'yesh'ee
God is my light and my salvation.

Connecting with the Universe

In recognition of our ever-present and utterly unique place in God's world, our affirmation can be,

V'shavti b'veit Adonai l'orech yamim.
I shall dwell in God's house forever.

When the struggle seems overwhelming, when hope seems dashed, when tears will not stop flowing, when all seems lost, our affirmation can be,

Ka'veh el Adonai
Hope is in God.

In the face of the pain and disappointment, the anguish and grief that inevitably come to each life, our affirmation can be,

Anee ma'amin
I believe. With perfect faith, I believe.

In response to the great triumphs and joys we experience, the deep happiness and the immeasurable love that we feel, the wondrous miracles that surround us at every turn, our affirmation can be,

HalleluYah
Praise God!

With abiding trust in God, and with everlasting faith in God's perfect plan, our affirmation can be,

B'yado afkid ruchi
I put my soul into God's hand.

Always ready to hear God's word and to do God's will—in this *gilgool,* this incarnation, or another; on this side or the Other Side; in this life or in the world to come—our affirmation, like that of our ancestors of old, can be,

Hinaynee
Here I am! I am ready to do Your work.

And with the sanction of the Jewish ages; with the witness of every holy person who has ever lived and died for the sanctification of God's great and sacred name; with the agreement of the angels in God's heavens and of every human being who lives in our earthly world, we seal our every affirmation with the supreme and enduring affirmation, the affirmation that sets in place and confirms our most fervent avowals and our most cherished hopes and desires,

Amen V'Amen
And so it is!

Afterword

Zol Shein Kumen De'gulah, "The Days Are a-Comin'"

EVEN WITH ITS PROMISE OF PERSONAL SPIRITUAL growth and intimacy with the Divine, even with its excitement of communal renewal and revolutionary effect, we might be tempted to linger; we might be tempted to passively wait for Neshamah Judaism to unfold in its own good time.

But now, more than ever, we cannot ignore the powers, the mighty forces of the universe, that are calling us to God.

An old story from the kabbalah reminds us that, in the words of the Bible, "a thousand years are but one day in the sight of God" (Psalms 90:4).

The kabbalah teaches that if indeed a thousand years are but one day to God, then as we Jews live in our year 5757 (the Jewish year when this book is published), we are in the last quarter of human-kind's sixth millennium, and we are at four o'clock in the afternoon of God's sixth day.

And the kabbalah tells us that God's seventh day is Shabbas, the seventh day that is the *ultimate* Shabbas, the Shabbas when *masheach* comes, when the messianic time of goodwill and peace envelops the world.

By God's count, we are late on Friday afternoon, late in the day of Erev Shabbas, getting ready for our final preparations for the days of the messiah.

But according to Jewish tradition, for *masheach* to come, we have to be ready. We have to open and balance and transform ourselves as human beings so that we can work to open and balance and transform our world. Only then can we and our world stand on the brink of the time of tranquillity and peace.

A troubled soul, an empty soul, cannot move toward harmony and perfection, so in order to do our job in bringing *masheach,* we have to bring our souls to God—to be filled with faith, to be filled with God's overflowing light and love.

It would be easy to turn away from our task—to live life at its shallow, surface level instead of going deeply to the soul-level—by looking at our battered and bruised world and declaring that there is so much hatred, so much bigotry, so much warfare, so much darkness, that the light of the dawn of the new age will never come.

To be sure, there is still very much wrong with our world.

But events leading to transformation are moving at an incredibly swift pace, a pace worthy of the last-minute preparations of Erev Shabbas.

In the places on earth where there is utter, forlorn darkness, where it is so dark that, in the image of the *Midrash,* brothers cannot even see each other's faces, where there is no chance of light ever coming, the natural order has taken over and any hope for healing seems sadly but inevitably to be ending in destruction and death.

But in so many other places, the forces of light are moving powerfully and swiftly. Walls of separation are falling; oppressive governments are dissolving; old hatreds are healing; old enemies are finding common ground; old divisions are moving toward unity.

And now, in biblical terms, the forces of light and the forces of darkness arrayed to do battle, perhaps the last battle, sit together at the negotiating table in the Middle East.

The transformation and perfection of our world may still be a long way off, but everything is pointing in the right direction, and the preparations have begun.

To help us toward the soul-connection that will bring us and our world closer to transformation, the very planet on which we live is collaborating in our quest.

The planet earth is part of an astrological system that is intricately and precisely aligned.

In accordance with this structure, the planet earth goes through cycles of approximately two thousand years of alignment with other stars in the system.

Now, lest you are worried that we are treading in places where no Jew should go—into the realm of divination and idolatry, which is highly condemned by our ancient sages—know that our ancestors were great believers in the power of the stars and the planets, in what we today call astrology.

The incredibly beautiful massive mosaic floor of the sixth-century synagogue at Beit Alpha in Israel, uncovered by archaeologists in a *kibbutz* field, has a giant depiction of the twelve signs of the zodiac, complete with pictures and Hebrew names.

And one of the most well known Hebrew phrases—almost ubiquitous in modern Jewish life—is *mazel tov,* which we translate as "good luck" or "congratulations." But the word *mazel* really means "stars." The ancient wish for success was that "you should have good *stars.*"

About six thousand years ago, when the history of humankind began—that is, when humankind became aware of and able to record its own place in the universe—the earth was aligned with the constellation Taurus, the bull. And in that pagan world, it was the bull that was the symbol of power and, for many, the symbol of the Divine.

Two thousand years later, the earth moved into alignment with Aries, the sign of the ram. It was then that Judaism, with its ram of the sacrifice and the ram of the *shofar* so central to its symbology, took center stage in the world.

Two thousand years later, the time of the coming of Christianity, the earth moved into alignment with Pisces, the sign of the fish, the symbol of Christianity even until today.

Now, two thousand years later, the earth has moved once again.

In January 1996, a monumental event took place in the heavens. The earth moved into alignment with Aquarius.

It was, literally, the dawning of the Age of Aquarius.

Aquarius is the water bearer, the symbol of cleansing, of purification, of rebirth, of renewal.

It is, indeed, the "dawning of the Age of Aquarius," but not just as the sixties hippies or the contemporary New Agers would have it.

It is the age of Aquarius, the time for synthesis, for the purification and rebirth of our world; for the coming together and blending of all the diverse elements that have divided us for so long; for the dawning of the light that will wipe away the darkness that has plagued us.

And the way into the Age of Aquarius for us and for our world is through the rebirth of the world of the spirit; the renewal of the covenant of faith and love between God and us; the intimacy of soul-connection and soul-talk that we can share with God.

⁂

When the Romans conquered Jerusalem, Judaism could have come to an end. But Rabbi Yochanan ben Zakkai took us to Yavneh where Judaism was reclaimed, reconstituted, and renewed.

Once again, it is time for Yavneh.

Once again, the time has come for the renewal and the renaissance of Judaism.

Ben Zakkai's Yavneh is no more.

But it is a state of mind.

And we stand at Yavneh.

Our quest begins with our soul-journey toward God.

Judaism's new era, Neshamah Judaism, is our pathway and our channel.

And we are, in the words of Abraham Joshua Heschel, "God's stake in human history. We are the day and the dusk, the challenge and the test."

Masheach is coming.

The new age awaits.

And we are there.

Index

Permissions Acknowledgments

Deepest thanks and appreciation is expressed to these authors, composers, illustrators, and artists for permission to quote from and use copyrighted and original material:

Catherine D. Ahrens for original line drawings and illustrations.

Central Conference of American Rabbis for "On This Day" from *Gates of Prayer*, 1975.

Shendel Diamond for original Hebrew calligraphy.

Debbie Friedman and Drorah Setel for *"Mi Shebeirach"* copyright © 1988 Deborah Lynn Friedman (ASCAP) Sounds Write Productions, Inc. (ASCAP).

Rabbi Vicky Hollander for stanzas from "A Rosh Chodesh Ceremony," reprinted by permission of the author. Rabbi Hollander resides in Vancouver, B.C., where she weaves together spiritual guidance, ritual consultation, workshops, retreats, and continues her writing. Formerly a hospice bereavement coordinator, she trained as a marriage and family therapist and melds the spiritual, emotional, and therapeutic realms.

Dr. Eugene Mihaly for permission to reprint "Sinai Is Ever Present."

San Diego Jewish Times for selections and adaptations from Rabbi Wayne Dosick's regularly featured column, "Rabbinic Insights."

Hanna Tifereth Siegel for permission to reprint *"Eyl na refah na la."*

Tara Publications for *"Ruach Elokim"* and *"Esa Enai,"* reprinted from *The Shlomo Carlebach Anthology* (Tara Publications, Owings Mills, MD 21117).

Betsy Platkin Teutsch/Reconstructionist Press for *Shiviti* from *Kol Naneshamah Shabbat V'hagim.*

Town House Press, Inc., for permission to reprint poetry by Danny Siegel from *Unlocked Doors,* 1983.

Rabbi David Zeller for permission to reprint *"Rebono Shel Olam,"* which is one melodic line from a much longer song by Rabbi Levi of Berditchov. It was taught as a mantra for meditation by Rabbi Nachman of Bratslav and is known today through the teaching and singing tapes of Rabbi David Zeller. For tapes of R. Zeller, call Sounds True, 800–333–9185, or Network of Conscious Judaism, 707–552–2199.

Every effort has been made to identify copyright holders and obtain permission. Any omissions or errors will be most happily and gratefully corrected in the next edition of this work.